The CPHIMS Review Guide

Fourth Edition

The CPHIMS Review Guide

Fourth Edition

Preparing for Success in Healthcare Information and Management Systems

First Edition published 2008

4th Edition published 2021
by Routledge
600 Broken Sound Parkway #300, Boca Raton FL, 33487

and by Routledge
2 Park Square, Milton Park, Abingdon, Oxon, OX14 4RN

Routledge is an imprint of the Taylor & Francis Group, an informa business

© 2021 Taylor & Francis

Library of Congress Cataloging-in-Publication Data
A catalog record for this title has been requested

ISBN: 978-1-138-33743-5 (hbk)
ISBN: 978-1-138-32761-0 (pbk)
ISBN: 978-0-429-44239-1 (ebk)

DOI: 10.4324/9780429442391

Typeset in Garamond
by KnowledgeWorks Global Ltd.

Contents

**SECTION III   HEALTHCARE INFORMATION AND
SYSTEMS MANAGEMENT**

Preface

Your purchase of this book is one step in becoming a Certified Professional in Healthcare Information and Management Systems (CPHIMS^{SM}) and being recognized for your specialized knowledge and skills. For two decades, CPHIMS certification has been the preeminent certification in health information and technology and is administered globally to health IT professionals practicing in a variety of work settings.

The development and maintenance of the CPHIMS exam is the responsibility of the HIMSS Professional Certification Board, which is comprised of experts from around the world who possess subject matter expertise in the areas tested on the exam.

This preface provides an overview of the eligibility requirements, testing procedures and content of the CPHIMS Exam itself. Specific questions can also be addressed to certification@himss.org at any time.

The benefits of CPHIMS certification are broad and far-reaching. Certification is a process that is embraced in many industries, including health IT. CPHIMS is recognized as the "gold standard" in health IT because it is developed by HIMSS, has a global focus and is valued by clinicians and non-clinicians, management and staff positions and technical and nontechnical individuals.

Certification, specifically CPHIMS certification, provides a means by which employers can evaluate potential new hires, analyze job performance, assess employees, market IT services and motivate employees to enhance their skills and knowledge. Certification also provides employers with evidence that the certificate holders have demonstrated an established level of job-related knowledge, skills and abilities and are competent practitioners of health IT.

Eligibility Requirements

To be eligible for the CPHIMS Exam, candidates must fulfill one of the following requirements for education and work experience:

- Baccalaureate degree, or global equivalent, and five (5) years of associated information and management systems experience,* three of those years in a healthcare setting.†
- Graduate degree, or global equivalent, and three (3) years of associated information and management systems experience,* two of those years in a healthcare setting.†
- Have at least 10 years of information and management systems* experience, with eight of those years in a healthcare setting.†

Additional Resources

The HIMSS Professional Certification Board recommends that review for the CPHIMS Exam focuses on resources and programs that cover the tasks in the CPHIMS Outline of Examination Topics. It should not be inferred that questions on the CPHIMS Exam are selected from any single resource or set of resources, or that study from this or other resources listed, guarantees a passing score on the CPHIMS Exam.

- CPHIMS Candidate Handbook: A must for all CPHIMS Exam candidates, the candidate handbook provides information that is helpful when applying for and scheduling the CPHIMS Exam. The handbook includes the CPHIMS Outline of Examination Topics, directions on how to apply for the exam and schedule your exam appointment and what to expect on the day of the exam as well as following the exam. It is recommended that all CPHIMS candidates download a copy of the handbook from www.himss.org.
- CPHIMS Practice Exam: The practice exam simulates the CPHIMS Exam in content, cognitive level, difficulty and format. After taking the practice exam, you will receive valuable, practical feedback in detailed score reports.

---

* Information and management systems experience includes work in the following areas: systems analysis; design; selection, implementation, support, and maintenance; testing and evaluation; privacy and security; information systems; clinical informatics; management engineering.

† Healthcare settings include providers of health services or products to a healthcare facility (e.g., hospitals; healthcare consulting firms; vendors; federal, state or local government offices; academic institutions; payers; public health, etc.).

CPHIMS Exam Administration

The CPHIMS Exam is delivered by computer at testing centers throughout the world. After applying and paying the exam fee through www.himss.org, candidates who meet the eligibility requirements will receive further instructions from HIMSS on how to schedule their exam through a testing center. The CPHIMS Exam is administered by appointment only, either Monday through Saturday (except major holidays) at a testing center, or through a virtual proctoring mechanism. As a candidate, you may test where you wish and when you feel you are prepared to take the CPHIMS Exam.

Special group administrations of the CPHIMS Exam may be scheduled with HIMSS chapters, corporate members, organizational affiliate members, nonprofit partners, regional extension centers, or other groups through arrangement with HIMSS. For more information on hosting an administration for your group, contact certification@himss.org.

The CPHIMS Exam is also administered at national and international HIMSS events as well. Special application and scheduling procedures may be in place for these events, so check with the event website to find out how to apply and schedule in conjunction with these events.

JoAnn W. Klinedinst, MEd, CPHIMS,
PMP, DES, CPTD, LFHIMSS, FACHE
VP Professional Development, HIMSS

Acknowledgments

HIMSS wishes to express gratitude to the contributing authors of the fourth edition:

- Penny Black, MHA, CPHIMS
- Karen R. Clark, MBA, CPHIMS, FHIMSS
- Shari Donley, MBA, CPHIMS
- Brent Hicks, MS, BEd, CPHIMS, FHIMSS
- Stephanie Hoelscher, DNP, RN-BC, CPHIMS, CHISP, FHIMSS
- Stephanie Koch, CPHIMS
- Mary Ellen Skeens, PMP, ASQ CSSBB, CPHIMS, DSHS, FHIMSS
- Kalyani Yerra, MBA, MHA, PMP, FHIMSS, CPHIMS

Editor

Mara L. Daiker, MS, CPHIMS, RHIA, SHIMSS is the Director Professional Development for the Healthcare Information Management Systems Society (HIMSS), a global advisor and thought leader supporting the transformation of health through information and technology.

Ms. Daiker has served in various health information management and information technology roles and has almost 20 years combined HIMSS and industry experience. Ms. Daiker is a Registered Health Information Administrator (RHIA) and a Certified Professional in Healthcare Information and Management Systems (CPHIMS) with a bachelor's degree in Health Information Management from The College of St. Scholastica and a master's degree in Health Care Informatics from the University of Wisconsin-Milwaukee. She is an adjunct faculty member for Kent State University where she instructs coursework related to health records management. She is a senior member of HIMSS (SHIMSS) and an active member of the American Health Information Management Association (AHIMA) and its component state association, the Wisconsin Health Information Management Association (WHIMA).

Ms. Daiker lives in the Milwaukee Wl area with her husband and two children.

HEALTHCARE AND TECHNOLOGY ENVIRONMENTS

Chapter 1

Healthcare Environment

Learning Objectives

At the conclusion of this chapter, the reader will be able to

- Articulate characteristics and services of different types of healthcare organizations (e.g., hospitals, clinics, ambulatory centers, community health organizations, healthcare payers, regulators, research and academic)
- Articulate characteristics of interrelationships within and across healthcare organizations (e.g., health information exchange, public, private, continuity of care)
- Describe the roles and responsibilities of healthcare information and management system professionals within the organizational structures in which they work
- Recognize the impact of commonly accepted laws, regulations, accreditation and other state and local rules that govern critical healthcare information and systems management services, including privacy, safety and security (e.g., privacy regulations, pharmacy, environments of care, patient rights) on the healthcare industry
- Evaluate trends in healthcare technology and implement strategies to improve patient outcomes (e.g., telemedicine, patient portals, wearable devices, population health)

Introduction

In order to best understand the context of healthcare information and management systems, it is necessary to first understand the concept of health. The World Health Organization (WHO) asserts that "health is a state of complete physical, mental and social well-being and not merely the absence of disease or infirmity."[1] The WHO has not amended this definition since 1948.

Why is it important that we more fully understand this more holistic concept of health? If we do not present for care until we are in an advanced stage of disease or arrive with injuries from unsafe working or living practices, the cost of providing that care is likely to be high and the health outcomes often less than desired. The practice of healthcare, and thus the systems and management processes supporting it, is increasingly focused on those activities that have the greatest impact on the overall health of the community and patient populations. A state of health is not best achieved by limiting our engagement to patients' visits to the doctor's office and admissions to hospitals, but is increasingly extended to wellness encounters with nonphysician healthcare providers, virtual encounters through telehealth or mobile health technologies and safety and preventive care outreach programs. The increasing strain of healthcare costs on national economies is forcing us to continually reevaluate our healthcare delivery paradigm to optimize health outcomes at an affordable cost. This is the macroeconomic context in which health information professionals and technologists will be performing their art.

The healthcare environment is an exceptionally complex one in which multiple players compete for placement on center stage. The four pillars of quality, access, cost and value require dynamic trade-offs in which healthcare professionals are under constant pressure to deliver the highest quality of care to the greatest portion of their supported population within tight cost constraints, while having to demonstrate the value of health information technology (IT). Placed upon this already complex four-legged stool are demands from multiple stakeholders, including governments, consumer groups, professional associations, regulatory organizations, payers/insurers and suppliers.

The Organisation for Economic Cooperation and Development (OECD) provides a solid basis for comparing international approaches with organizing and resourcing national healthcare with several key indicators on health system performance across countries. Figure 1.1 illustrates the substantial variance in spending by country and the proportion of public to private contribution to overall national health expenditures.

These investments have seen great reductions in cardiovascular and infant mortality rates, but lifestyle and risk factors show that more than 18% of adults continue to smoke daily,[2] while almost one-third of children 5–9 years are overweight, with the rate of overweight children increasing from 20.5% to 31.4% from 1990 to 2016.[2]

Therefore, it is not hard to develop a sense of the complexities of the healthcare environment in which we toil. The breadth of stakeholders, the balance of public versus private funding and the active engagement to improve the health of populations, one individual at a time, produce a daunting task. This is the arena the health information professional and technologist enter to ensure that the best possible information management and systems support are

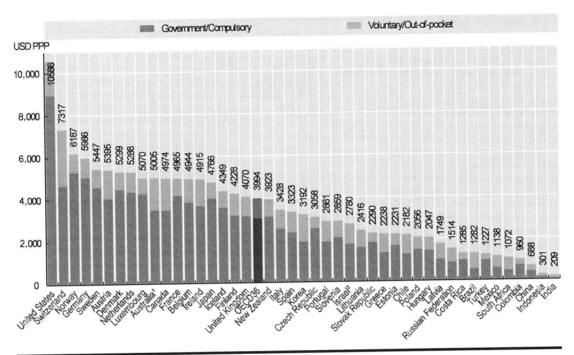

Figure 1.1   OECD health expenditure per capita, 2018. (From OECD, health expenditure per capita, in *health at a glance 2019: OECD indicators,* OECD publishing, Paris, https:// doi.org/10.1787/4dd50c09-en.2).

Note: Expenditure excludes investments, unless otherwise stated.

1. Australia expenditure estimates exclude all expenditure for residential aged care facilities in welfare (social) services.

available to improve the quality of life for the greatest number of our world's citizens.

Healthcare Organizations

The number and types of organizations involved in the provision of care, supporting the provision of care and paying for the care provided is large, complex and constantly evolving. The simplest way to categorize these is through the eyes of the patient. When speaking of accessing care, often a patient will say, "I went to see my doctor at her office" or "I was in the hospital last week to have my appendix out." So, in a broad sense, we have the constructs of hospital-based care—often referred to as inpatient care—and care from doctors' offices—referred to as outpatient or ambulatory care. Additionally, given the diverse types of diagnostic services and pharmaceuticals needed to support the healthcare process, providers of ancillary services are included as well. Lastly, regulators and payers of care are discussed. The interrelationships among these diverse players will be expanded upon in the next section. The following is an overview of many of these structures, which vary not only by country but also often by geographic location within countries.

Hospitals

While hospitals may be categorized in any number of ways, a single hospital may also be classified in more than one way. For example, a hospital may be a private, not-for-profit and specialty hospital, thus falling into three categories. Notable systems for classifying hospitals include classification by the following:

1. Ownership. Public (government-managed) versus private hospitals.
   a. In public hospitals, governments (at the national, provincial, state or other level) own and are responsible for the operations. The healthcare providers in such hospitals are generally private practitioners, although in some countries the providers may be government employees as well (e.g., in the National Health Service [NHS] of the United Kingdom or the U.S. Veterans Health Administration hospitals).
   b. In private hospitals, staffing arrangements span a broad spectrum of private practitioners or groups of healthcare providers. Private hospitals in some countries are further classified as for profit versus nonprofit.
      i. For-profit private hospitals, also referred to as investor-owned hospitals, often exist as part of a multihospital system with varying degrees of interrelationship among the system's hospitals. Examples of large, investor-owned hospital systems include the Hospital Corporation of America (http://hcahealthcare.com/) and BMI Healthcare in the United Kingdom (http://www.bmihealthcare.co.uk/).
      ii. Nonprofit private hospitals are not investor owned, but rather exist under laws at national and state levels allowing them to organize as nonprofit corporations, generally providing them the advantage of avoiding federal and property taxes. Canada's hospitals, although publicly financed, are almost exclusively private, nonprofit organizations,[3] albeit funded through the provincial/territorial governments. Just more than half of the hospitals in the United States operate as private, nonprofit organizations.[4]
2. Types of service provided. Hospitals are often classified by the types of service they provide. While the majority of hospitals will be general hospitals supporting the most common types of medical and surgical care requirements, hospitals specializing in more focused areas of care are becoming more prevalent. Such hospitals include psychiatric hospitals, which focus on mental healthcare; rehabilitation hospitals, which generally focus on restoring neurological and musculoskeletal functions following treatment in an acute care facility; and children's hospitals, which focus on the care and treatment of children.
3. Teaching status. In addition to providing inpatient clinical services, teaching hospitals train future physicians and other healthcare providers. Often associated with academic institutions, teaching hospitals may be further classified as academic medical centers or university hospitals. Many such

institutions also contribute substantially to medical research and publish much of the knowledge that advances the science of medicine.

4. Geographic location. Hospitals may be further classified as urban hospitals when located in large cities or as rural hospitals when substantially distant from major urban areas with greater resources. While such classifications appear mundane, the challenges of operating in urban and rural environments are different enough to require programs of specialization. Meeting government standards for classification as urban or rural may provide such hospitals access to special government funding programs.

Outpatient or Ambulatory Care—A Shift in the Care Setting

When a patient's care does not require the intensive management of a hospital setting that care is generally received in an outpatient or ambulatory care setting—most frequently in a doctor's office. Most primary care—the care practiced by primary care providers (PCPs) or general practitioners (GPs)—is provided in the ambulatory setting. Similarly, most PCP/GP referrals to clinical specialists for evaluation are completed in the ambulatory setting as well. The past decade has seen a dramatic shift from the acute care setting to less-expensive, more patient-friendly care settings. In the last few years, many less complicated surgical procedures that previously required an overnight hospital stay have been moved to the outpatient setting as well. Even major surgeries such as total joint replacement are now routinely performed in an ambulatory surgery center (ASC) with the patient going home the same day. Patients are demanding more flexible hours, and urgent care or injury clinics are opening up at a tremendous rate. Nontraditional care settings are springing up, with drugstores offering "minute clinics" and other walk-in options. Today's patient is accustomed to an always-on, always available experience and demands that from healthcare. There is a proliferation of direct appointment booking and "virtual" visits using video calling apps. These patients are no longer content to call a physician office and wait to be called back, or to wait weeks to see a specialist. Practices that are responsive to this new model will be the ones who thrive. There are multiple models of outpatient care, including single independent provider offices, larger multi-provider group practices in which a broader range of specialists may be available, and—while not a preferred approach from an expense perspective—hospital emergency departments.

Community Health Organizations

In the healthcare environment, a "community" generally refers to the specific geographic location in which healthcare is delivered. Thus, healthcare organizations serving the population of local areas tend to be broadly referred to as community health organizations. Community-centered hospitals and clinics in most nations provide most of the care available to their local populations. Some nations provide more formal designations of community healthcare organizations that impose both legally constrained definitions and operational characteristics. In Canada, a community health center (CHC) is a key provider of local health services and aspires to support access and comprehensive care, including health promotion and illness prevention, through a publicly administered process.[5] In the United States, CHCs are generally associated with medically underserved areas as defined by the Health Resources and Services Administration (HRSA). These health centers strive to provide comprehensive, culturally competent, quality primary healthcare services to medically underserved communities and vulnerable populations.[6] Small community hospitals located in rural areas of the United States may apply for designation as critical access hospitals (CAHs), allowing them to receive higher reimbursement rates.

Diagnostic and Pharmaceutical Services

The most effective healthcare treatment quite frequently requires the aid of diagnostic services and pharmaceutical treatments, commonly referred to as ancillary services. While larger hospitals will generally have these capabilities, smaller hospitals and outpatient care centers will usually rely on external providers of such services to support comprehensive care to their patients. Key services provided in this area include laboratory and anatomic/anatomical pathology services, diagnostic imaging/radiology services and pharmacies. Close associations with these service providers are formed with provider offices and hospitals to ensure effective and comprehensive healthcare delivery.

Healthcare Payers

From the perspective of the healthcare delivery organization, payments generally come from three types of entities: government-financed and managed programs, insurance programs administered by private entities and personal funds.

Government-financed and managed programs are generally funded through countries' general taxes. These programs may pay for the healthcare system directly, as does the single-payer system of the NHS of the United Kingdom, which finances hospitals and salaries of most NHS providers. Alternatively, government programs may provide funding for a national health insurance program, such as that in Canada, where the program is administered through provincial health plans. These plans fund hospitals through community trusts and pay providers through the government's insurance program. Multipayer systems, such as that of the United States, are more complex to administer. The U.S. system includes the federally managed program for Medicare, through which citizens 65 years of age and older have most of their healthcare needs provided for; the shared-cost federal/state program Medicaid, which supports care for low-income families; another federal/state program called the Children's Health Insurance Program (CHIP), which provides care to children of uninsured families that do not qualify for Medicaid; and several others for smaller groups of special populations. These three programs provide coverage for roughly one-third[7] of the U.S. population.

Insurance programs administered by private entities are generally funded by employers, citizens themselves or by a combination of both. Germany mandates shared health insurance contributions from employers and employees, but these funds are administered by about 1100 private, nonprofit sickness funds that cover more than 90% of the population by making payments to hospitals and providers. In the United States, roughly 55% of citizens have employer-based insurance and an additional 11% purchase insurance directly.[8] Even in many countries that have universal healthcare programs, people who can afford to purchase private health insurance are usually allowed to do so. The purchase of private health insurance generally allows the purchaser to receive services that may not be covered under a national benefit structure and may also improve access to care. When healthcare organizations treat patients insured through a private entity, they bill the private health insurance entity rather than a government organization.

Healthcare services are often personally funded by individuals who have government or employer-supported health plans, as well as by the uninsured. While patient co-payments were not required by many universal coverage programs in years past, an increasing number of countries are adding this requirement to offset growing healthcare costs. In the United States, co-payments are required under most healthcare programs, whether government or privately managed. Persons with higher incomes may choose to avoid the constraints of insurance programs and, as they can tolerate the financial risk, are cash payers. Lastly, and perhaps most perversely, those who fail to qualify for government-supported programs such as Medicaid in the United States but still cannot afford to purchase health insurance find themselves at the mercy of a healthcare system that charges premium, nonnegotiated rates to those least able to afford such costs. A 2019 study on bankruptcies in the United States found that 66.5% of all bankruptcies from 2013 to 2016 were tied to medical issues, with 58.5% caused specifically by medical bills. The rest met criteria for medical bankruptcy due to income loss related to illness.[9] Although politically divided, the Patient Protection and Affordable Care Act signed into law on March 23, 2010, was intended to help reduce some of these financial risks for patients in the United States and make healthcare more affordable and accessible. Despite gains in coverage and access to care from the ACA, findings suggest that it did not change the proportion of bankruptcies with medical causes.[9]

In summary, from the perspective of the healthcare delivery organization, three basic types of payers are at play: government-financed and managed programs, insurance programs administered by private entities and patients who pay with personal funds. Add to that the number of potential insurance companies in the market and the differences in payers' health benefits coverage, and the management of accounts receivable can become an incredibly complex task requiring sophisticated administration and automation support.

Interrelations Within and Across Healthcare Organizations

The purposes of interrelationships among healthcare organizations are numerous. Some of the key requirements include enabling comprehensive care, assuring effective transfers of care, ensuring the general portability of information in support of care, reporting public and population health information, obtaining appropriate reimbursement for care and supporting particular organizational models of care.

Enabling Access to Comprehensive Care Services

As noted in the section above, healthcare organizations are reliant upon a number of partners within or outside of their organization to enable the delivery of comprehensive care. Providers in the outpatient setting often rely on external laboratory and radiology services to ensure accurate diagnoses and on the availability of pharmacies to provide prescribed medications to complete the provider's care plan for the patient. Absent effective communications— increasingly electronic today—the care process will break down and patient outcomes could suffer as a result. This is the area in which technology is having the greatest impact. Various public and private initiatives are in place to facilitate the seamless, transparent interchange of patient clinical data. "Interoperability" is the keyword here, as the transferred data must be consumable by the receiving system in order to eliminate duplicate data entry and make the data instantly available to the treating provider.

Assuring Effective Transfers of Care

When a provider determines that the scope of care required for a patient's treatment is outside of his or her capability, care is generally transferred to another provider or healthcare organization. Effectively communicating health information during the transfer of care is exceptionally important to the patient's welfare. When a complete set of information is transferred with the patient regarding the history of the present illness, along with subjective and objective findings that include the results of diagnostic tests performed and medications prescribed and administered, the receiving organization can advance the patient's treatment in a substantially more efficient and effective manner. When such information does not accompany a patient during transfer, precious time is often lost, as that information is re-created through repetitive evaluations and repeat administration of diagnostic tests that are sometimes of an invasive nature. To facilitate the provision of essential health information during transfer of care between providers or facilities, an initiative in the United States encourages the use of Health Level Seven International's (HL7) Consolidated-Clinical Document Architecture (C-CDA), which is a standard for electronically transmitting continuity of care information.[10]

Both the loss of time in treating an acute patient and the need to repeat invasive tests can have adverse consequences for a patient. Not having a clear awareness of the pharmaceutical products a patient may be taking or has been administered in the present course of care can be life threatening and has led to attempts in some countries to ensure that medication reconciliation has taken place. In the United States, medication reconciliation is defined as the process of identifying the most accurate list of all medications that the patient is taking, including name, dosage, frequency and route, by comparing the medical record to an external list of medications obtained from a patient, hospital or other provider.[11]

Ensuring the General Portability of Care

Even when patients are enrolled to a specific clinical organization or provider for care, there are times when they will need care from other providers. This occurs not only under the two scenarios covered above, but also when patients travel away from their routine places of care. If a patient who is several hundred miles away from home becomes ill or is injured in an automobile accident, having the correct health information available can have a powerful influence on the patient's health outcomes from the clinical intervention. The most common example is that of the new provider who does not know a patient's medication allergies. To overcome these challenges, some nations are implementing national health information exchanges (HIEs) that endeavor to provide virtual, real-time access to patients' health information. One such initiative is Canada's Health Infoway, a nonprofit organization made up of the 14 federal, provincial and territorial deputy ministers of health. Infoway's vision is "healthier Canadians through innovative digital health solutions."[12] In the United States, much work is under way to define standards to facilitate ease of sharing health information both through HIEs at the state level and nationally via the Nationwide Health Information Network (NHIN) and, more recently, through the Nationwide Interoperability Roadmap. The United Kingdom has also invested heavily in its NHS Digital (formerly Health and Social Care Information Centre (HSCIC)) through its national health system, which connects England's healthcare organizations to facilitate the availability of clinical information that can be shared to support the continuity of care and safety of patients in the healthcare process.

Reporting Public and Population Health Information

Improving health status at the local or national level requires more than ensuring information availability at the point of care. It requires a sort of information use that is often referred to as the secondary use of health information because the information is used outside of the direct healthcare delivery process, which is viewed as the primary use of health information. The United Kingdom's Secondary Use Services (SUS), through its NHS Digital program, leverages the SUS in support of public health, research and management, among other activities. Similarly, the U.S. Centers for Disease Control and Prevention have been receiving health information from across the country for many years not only to support such public health activities as actively responding to disease outbreaks, but also to work proactively through education on prevention and healthy lifestyles through its Division of Population Health.

Obtaining Appropriate Reimbursement for Quality Care

In most publicly funded healthcare systems, the hospitals and clinicians delivering the care are private entities, so a substantial amount of communication must occur to ensure reimbursement for the care provided. Whether a healthcare organization is a one-provider office, a multispecialty clinic, a hospital or another entity, it must submit claims to be reimbursed for care provided. The exception to this rule, of course, is in those countries, such as the United Kingdom, that have a national health system with both government facilities and a largely government-paid healthcare staff. Claims may be submitted to state Medicaid offices, the Centers for Medicare & Medicaid Services (CMS) for Medicare, or private insurance companies in the United States or to provincial offices in Canada, but no healthcare organization will exist for long absent an ability to efficiently process—and be reimbursed for—claims for care. In multiplayer systems, such as in the United States, this process can be exceptionally complex and require a surprising investment of administrative overhead and systems complexity. Both governments and major employers are increasingly concerned that improved health outcomes are associated with the cost of care. In the United States, the CMS Merit-Based Incentive Payment System (MIPS) will provide incentive payments to eligible professionals who satisfactorily participate in one of two value-based payment models, Alternate Payment Models (APMs) or Quality Reporting under MIPS. Similarly, the Leapfrog Group supports healthcare purchasers and insurers by "mobilizing employer purchasing power to alert America's health industry that big leaps in health care safety, quality and customer value will be recognized and rewarded."[13]

Supporting Particular Organizational Models of Care

While the number of models of care is too great to discuss at length here, a key trend we see in the industry today is the need to share increasing volumes of information among partners in the healthcare system. Such partners in care are often referred to as an integrated delivery system (IDS). Stephen Shortell has defined the IDS as

> administrative entities that bring together a set of organizations that provide a coordinated continuum of services to a defined population and are willing to be held clinically and fiscally accountable for the outcomes and health status of the population served.[14]

While some IDSs are more integrated (from an ownership or a systems point of view) or more complete (providing a broader continuum of services) than others, the trend in the United States has been toward increasing integration. A type of IDS referred to as an accountable care organization (ACO) has been around for a few years and was recently codified in law by the Patient Protection and Affordable Care Act—often referred to as simply the Affordable Care Act. In an ACO, inpatient and outpatient providers of care are administratively organized into a single organization, often including a health insurance company, to provide a full spectrum of healthcare services to large groups of Medicare patients. If the ACO is able to reduce costs to CMS for their enrolled population while improving the quality of care, the ACO gets to share in the cost savings. As might be imagined, proving improvements in quality concurrently with reduction in healthcare costs is an information-intensive process that requires close integration of the partners in an ACO. Many ACOs will likely be developed from existing IDSs, as the IDS model already has many of the components necessary to achieve the quality and cost objectives of CMS.

In summary, interrelations within and across healthcare organizations can be as simple as a GP requesting an x-ray for a patient or reporting a patient disease observation to a public health entity. On the other end of the spectrum, the relationship could be as complex as assembling an integrated network of care providers under an ACO with sophisticated cost and quality reporting requirements. Each of these constructs not only requires effective coordination, but is also increasingly supported by sophisticated automation capabilities that reduce the labor involved while ensuring more reliable process support.

Roles and Responsibilities of Healthcare Information and Management Systems Professions

The number of position titles in the health information management (HIM) and health information technology (HIT or IT) space is quite large. In a single-provider office, the person who performs the broad range of HIM/IT tasks may work less than full-time or double as the office manager. In a large academic medical center or IDS, the IT department could include more than 100 personnel. The top IT position in healthcare organizations is usually referred to as the chief information officer (CIO). The CIO is generally accountable for a broad range of IT activities, including many that are not directly related to healthcare. Among these would be such things as maintaining organizational computing rooms, individual desktop computers, telephone communications (including an increasing variety of mobile and BYOD (Bring Your Own Device) and IOT (Internet of Things) equipment, secure Internet access, local and wide area networks and the organization's website.

In larger organizations, the complexity of HIM and IT functions leads to specialization. The chief security officer (CSO) endeavors to secure the healthcare organization's computing and communications assets from either intentional or unintentional security breaches from inside or outside the organization. Lead IT security personnel may carry the Certified Information Systems Security Professional (CISSP®) credential from the Information Systems Security Certification Consortium, Inc. (ISC²®).[15] Similarly, the privacy officer is responsible for ensuring that personally identifiable data, including protected health information, is accessed exclusively by those authorized to do so under a broad range of laws—in the United States, the Privacy Act and the Health Insurance Portability and Accountability Act (HIPAA), among others. A credential leveraged in supporting this role is that of Certified in Healthcare Privacy and Security (CHPS®).[16]

The chief technology officer (CTO) is generally responsible for the technical architecture of the IT systems supporting the organization and often looks toward the developing market in HIM and IT to try and keep the organization competitive from a technology perspective. This could range across the full spectrum of such things as mobile computing platforms, cloud-based computing and state-of-the-art clinical applications.

Health information managers have held roles in medical records departments for decades, but prior to the common availability of electronic health records (EHRs), there was not a strong relationship between HIM and IT departments. As medical records functions have become increasingly automated over the past few years, culminating in EHRs of advanced capabilities, HIM departments are finding themselves at the center of the IT activities in healthcare organizations. In the HIM area, you will find professionals with the Registered Health Information Administrator (RHIA) or Registered Health Information Technologist (RHIT®)[17] credential in the United States or with the Certification in Health Information Management (CHIM) credential in Canada.[18] Healthcare organizations may also rely on the Certified Professional in Healthcare Information and Management Systems (CPHIMS™)[19] credential to ensure that staff members in the IT department have a broad base of knowledge and experience in healthcare information and management systems.

The role of clinical informatics professionals is also expanding as the practice of medicine is increasingly supported by EHRs and other health information systems. The role of clinical informatics is discussed in depth in Chapter 3.

The American Medical Informatics Association (AMIA) advocates advanced training for clinicians to develop a clinical informatics subspecialty in the practice of medicine.[20] A frequently used title for staff with such backgrounds in the health information space is that of chief medical information officer (CMIO). Popular variants are chief medical informatics officer and chief health information officer (CHIO), and in the area of nursing, chief nursing informatics officer (CNIO). With the increasing use of IT in healthcare processes, effective integration of clinical insights into systems solutions is of great importance.

While the great variety of organizational structures in IT departments is driven by such factors as organization size, geographical distribution and line of business, a sample organization structure a CIO may oversee could include

- Application development and support
- Data center operations
- Database administration
- Desktop support
- Information security
- Network operations

Similarly, the specific roles an IT organization may expect to fill would vary based on the functions the organization supports. These roles could be filled by staff, consultants or contractors. Examples of the more common types of positions one might expect to see include

- Desktop support technician
- Database administrator
- Programmer/application developer
- Web developer
- Network engineer/analyst
- Systems analyst/administrator
- Project manager
- Security analyst

In summary, there is great variation in the size and structure of IT departments within healthcare organizations, which drives the number and specialization of jobs within the IT organization.

Roles of Government, Regulatory, Professional and Accreditation Agencies in Healthcare

Given the importance of healthcare in our lives—including our quality of life, our longevity and even our ability to continue living following life-threatening encounters with disease or accidents—and the incredible expense of delivering high-quality healthcare to very large populations, it is not surprising that a tremendous amount of government oversight and a great number of regulatory bodies are involved in healthcare processes. An overview of these organizations and their associated activities is provided below.

Government

The role of governments in healthcare is quite pronounced, as discussed in the previous section on healthcare organizations. Because most countries continue to experience increases in the proportion of their gross domestic product (GDP) consumed by healthcare activities, they are concerned that these trends will weaken their national economies if not slowed—or even stopped and reversed. Stopping the growth in healthcare costs as a percentage of GDP requires exceptionally difficult decisions for governments in industrialized countries, as citizens have grown accustomed to the existing health benefits programs.

According to the Peterson Kaiser Health System tracker:

> Over the past four decades, the difference between health spending as a share of the economy in the U.S. and comparable OECD countries has widened. In 1970 the U.S. spent about 6% of its GDP on health, similar to spending by several comparable countries (the average of comparably wealthy countries was 5% of GDP in 1970). The U.S. was relatively on pace with other countries until the 1980s, when its health spending grew at a significantly faster rate relative to its GDP. In 2017, the U.S. spent 17% of its GDP on health consumption, whereas the next highest comparable country (Switzerland) devoted 12% of its GDP.[21]

Figure 1.2 further illustrates health expenditure as a share of GDP as reported by the OECD in 2019.

It is easy to see that healthcare is consuming our national economies at an unsustainable rate, making governmental engagement in these factors essential.

To address the growth in healthcare costs, many nations' governments are considering changes to their health programs. Among these are enhancements to the primary care delivery system to manage chronic diseases more effectively in Australia, experimentation with privatization in Canada, global budgeting and competition among sickness funds in Germany, requiring long-term care residents to pay for room and board in Japan and consideration of pro-market

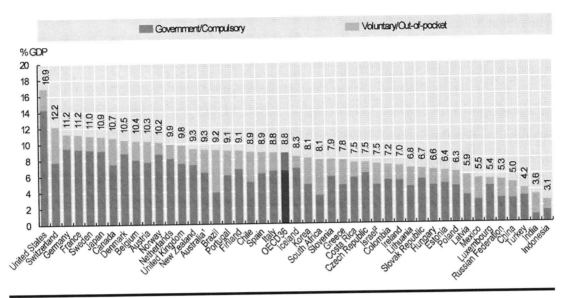

Figure 1.2   OECD health expenditure as a share of GDP, 2018. (From OECD, health expenditure in relation to GDP, in *health at a glance 2019: OECD indicators,* OECD publishing, Paris, https://doi.org/10.1787/4dd50c09-en.[2]).

reforms in the United Kingdom.[22] Similarly, the development of ACOs in the United States is being encouraged with a goal of producing better health outcomes at lower cost. Such trends will continue as we collectively grapple with the best ways to balance quality, access, cost and safety for the greatest proportion of our populations.

Healthcare Regulators

Healthcare regulatory agencies serve a broad range of functions in the healthcare environment, generally by implementing the provisions of a nation's health laws through a more explicit system of regulations. In the United Kingdom, the Health and Care Professions Council (HCPC) is the statutory regulator for 15 professions with nearly 290,000 health and care professionals in the country.[23] The HCPC maintains standards of proficiency and conduct for the professions it regulates. In the United States, the dominating regulatory entity is the CMS. The CMS drafts the rules and finalizes the regulations for the management of multiple federally subsidized healthcare programs for the nation through a complex process of rulemaking involving public engagement. The Food and Drug Administration (FDA) in the United States evaluates and approves medical devices and new drugs used in the treatment of patients. Similarly, medical devices in Canada are regulated by Health Canada's Therapeutic Products Directorate.

While it may be a common belief that regulatory organizations are always government entities, it is not uncommon to find that private-sector organizations, commissions and associations may perform in a regulatory capacity as well. These are addressed in the following sections.

Professional Associations

According to the *Merriam-Webster Dictionary*, a profession is "a calling requiring specialized knowledge and often long and intensive academic preparation."[24] Professional associations in the healthcare environment have proliferated greatly, many serving in a semi-regulatory role. The College of Kinesiologists of Ontario[25] provides a good description of the roles and functions of professional associations, stating that their primary role is to advocate on behalf of its members and promote the profession and may

- Advocate with policy makers in the interest of members
- Market and promote the profession
- Provide continuing professional development opportunities
- Represent members interests by monitoring development which may impact scope of practice, employment opportunities and enhancing relationships with related professionals

Regulatory bodies on the other hand have a purpose of protecting the public by regulating the profession. They may

- Set requirements for entry to the profession
- Maintain a list of individual eligible to practice
- Develop standards of practice
- Receive and investigate complaints about professional practice and administer appropriate disciplinary action when necessary
- Require professionals to participate in continuing professional development

Professional associations exist for nearly every medical specialty, nursing and allied health profession, health administration and IT professions. A sampling of professional associations related to healthcare and healthcare information and technology in the United States is shown in Table 1.1.

Accreditation Organizations

Accreditation organizations (AOs) have substantial interactions with healthcare organizations and generally play a semi-regulatory role in that they often serve on behalf of federal organizations to ensure specific standards or conditions of participation (CoP) are met. The Joint Commission and Joint Commission International (JCI)[26] are perhaps the most recognized AOs utilized for the certification of hospitals in the United States and internationally. The JCI currently operates in more than 100 countries

Table 1.1 Professional Associations Related to Healthcare and Healthcare IT

Clinical	*Administrative and IT*
American Academy of Pediatrics	American College of Healthcare Executives
International Confederation of Midwives	American Health Information Management Association
International Council of Midwives	American Medical Informatics Association
Royal College of General Practitioners	Healthcare Information and Management Systems Society
World Dental Federation	Information Systems Security Association International
World Medical Association	International Medical Informatics Association

around the globe. In the United States, the AOs under CMS are very visible examples of accreditation agencies. CMS AOs determine compliance with Medicare CoP. When a healthcare organization is certified by a CMS AO for compliance with CMS requirements, the organization is deemed to have met the requirements and may then bill CMS for covered services. For participation in Medicare programs, a number of other organizations are authorized to act as AOs, as shown in the Table 1.2.

The interrelationships among government agencies, regulators, professional associations and AOs can be surprisingly complex. For example, in the United States. Figure 1.3 shows the many organizations that play a role in the life of a physician assistant moving through training and into medical practice.

Summary

We have covered the breadth of organizational structures in the public and private domains, defined the nature of their interactions, identified roles of healthcare information and management systems professionals and described the great number of governmental, regulatory, professional and AOs affecting our healthcare delivery systems today. The complexity of the processes can be overwhelming. Fortunately, advances in automation, including inexpensive data storage, increasing network capacities and simplified software programming tools, will allow professionals in healthcare information and management systems to make life simpler for those who deliver care by transferring much of the information processing requirements to automated tools.

Table 1.2 CMS-Approved Accreditation Organizations

Organization	Program Type
Accreditation Association for Ambulatory Health Care (AAAHC)	Ambulatory surgical centers (ASCs)
Accreditation Commission for Health	Home health agencies (HHAs)
Care, Inc. (ACHC)	Hospices
American Association for Accreditation of	ASCs
Ambulatory Surgery Facilities (AAAASF)	Outpatient physical therapy (OPT) providers
	Rural health clinics (RHCs)
American Osteopathic Association/	ASCs
Healthcare Facilities Accreditation Program (AOA/HFAP)	Critical access hospitals (CAHs)
	Hospitals
Center for Improvement in Healthcare Quality (CIHQ)	Hospitals
Community Health Accreditation Program	HHAs
(CHAP)	Hospice
DNV GL-Healthcare (DNVGL)	Hospitals
	CAHs
Institute for Medical Quality (IMQ)	ASCs
National Dialysis Accreditation Commission (NDAC)	ESRD Facilities
The Compliance Team (TCT)	RHC
Joint Commission	ASCs
	CAHs
	HHAs
	Hospices
	Hospitals
	Psychiatric hospitals

Source: Centers for Medicare & Medicaid Services, https://www.cms.gov/Medicare/Provider-Enrollment-and-Certification/SurveyCertificationGenInfo/Downloads/Accrediting-Organization-Contacts-for-Prospective-Clients-.pdf.[27]

- Attend institution accredited by the accreditation review commission on education for the physician assistant (ARC-PA)
- Graduate

Accreditation organization

Take the physician assistant national certifying exam (PANCE) administered by the national commission on certification of physician assistants becoming certified as a physician assistant–certified or PA-C

Accreditation organization serving a regulatory role

Maintain national certification by completing 100 hours of continuing medical education through the american academy of physician assistants (AAPA) every two years and take a recertification exam every six years

Professional association

- Obtain a state license to practice
- Obtain a national provider identifier (NPI) from CMS and become an enrolled provider to allow PA to bill patients covered by federal healthcare programs

State and federal government organizations

Begin provision of care

Figure 1.3   Steps and organizations involved in becoming a practicing physician assistant. (Adapted from AAPA, becoming a PA, Alexandria, VA: AAPA, http://www.Aapa.org/ your_pa_career/becoming_a_pa.Aspx.[28]).

References

1. Preamble to the Constitution of the World Health Organization. Adopted by the International Health Conference, New York, June 19–22, 1946.
2. OECD (2019), *Health at a Glance 2019: OECD Indicators*, OECD Publishing, Paris, https://doi.org/10.1787/4dd50c09-en (accessed February 11, 2020).
3. Makarenko J. Canada's health care system: An overview of public and private participation. *Mapleleafweb*, October 22, 2010. http://www.mapleleafweb.com/features/ canada-s-health-care-system-overview-public-and-private-participation#public (accessed December 1, 2015).
4. U.S. Census Bureau. Hospitals—Summary characteristics: 1990 to 2009. In *Statistical Abstract of the United States*. Suitland, MD: U.S. Census Bureau, Table 172. http:// www.census.gov/prod/2011pubs/12statab/health.pdf (accessed December 1, 2015).
5. Canadian Association of Community Health Centres. http://www.cachc.ca/?page_ id=7 (accessed December 1, 2015).
6. U.S. Department of Health and Human Services, Health Resources and Services Administration. http://bphc.hrsa.gov/about/ (accessed December 1, 2015).
7. U.S. Census Bureau. Health and nutrition. In *Statistical Abstract of the United States*. Suitland, MD: U.S. Census Bureau. http://www.census.gov/prod/2011pubs/12statab/ health.pdf (accessed December 1, 2015).
8. U.S. Census Bureau, Health Insurance Coverage in the United States. 2018. U.S. Census Bureau, 2018, p. 22. https://www.census.gov/content/dam/Census/library/ publications/2019/demo/p60-267.pdf (accessed February 11, 2020).

9. Himmelstein DU, Lawless RM, Thorne D, Foohey P, Woolhandler S., 2019: Medical bankruptcy: Still Common despite the affordable care act, *Am J Public Health* 109, 431–433, https://doi.org/10.2105/AJPH.2018.304901 (accessed February 11, 2020).

10. Health Level Seven International. *HL7/ASTM Implementation Guide for CDA Release 2—Continuity of Care Document (CCD®) Release 1*. Ann Arbor, MI: Health Level Seven International. http://www.hl7.org/implement/standards/product_brief.cfm?product_id=6 (accessed December 1, 2015).

11. Centers for Medicare & Medicaid Services. *Eligible Hospital and Critical Access Hospital: Meaningful Use Menu Set Measures, Measure 6, Stage 1.* Woodlawn, MD: Centers for Medicare & Medicaid Services, November 7, 2010. https://www.cms.gov/Regulations-and-Guidance/Legislation/EHRIncentivePrograms/Downloads/2013Definition_6_Medication_Reconciliation.pdf (accessed December 1, 2015).

12. Canada Health Infoway. https://www.infoway-inforoute.ca/en/about-us (accessed December 1, 2015).

13. Leapfrog Group. http://www.leapfroggroup.org (accessed December 1, 2015).

14. Shortell SM, Casalino LP, Fisher ES. Achieving the vision. In Crosson FJ, Tollen LA, eds., *Partners in Health: How Physicians and Hospitals Can Be Accountable Together.* San Francisco: Jossey-Bass, 2010, pp. 53–54.

15. Information Systems Security Certification Consortium (ISC2®). https://www.isc2.org/cissp/default.aspx (accessed December 1, 2015).

16. American Health Information Management Association. http://ahima.org/certifcation/chps (accessed December 1, 2015).

17. American Health Information Management Association. http://ahima.org/certifcation (accessed December 1, 2015).

18. Canadian Health Information Management Association. https://www.echima.ca/cchim/certification (accessed December 1, 2015).

19. Healthcare Information and Management Systems Society. https://www.himss.org/resources/certification (accessed December 1, 2015).

20. American Medical Informatics Association. https://www.amia.org/education (accessed December 1, 2015).

21. Sawyer B, Cox C. How does health spending in the U.S. compare to other countries? *Peterson-KFF. Health System Tracker.* https://www.healthsystemtracker.org/chart-collection/health-spending-u-s-compare-countries/ (accessed February 11, 2020).

22. Shi L, Singh DA. Delivering Health Care in America: A Systems Approach. 5th ed. Burlington, MA: Jones & Bartlett Learning, 2012, pp. 20–27.

23. Health & Care Professional Council. https://www.hcpc-uk.org/ (accessed February 11, 2020).

24. Merriam-Webster. Profession. http://www.merriam-webster.com/dictionary/profession (accessed December 1, 2015).

25. College of Kinesiologists of Ontario. Regulators vs. Professional Associations. https://coko.ca/CKO_Public/Public_Content_Records/About_/Subcontent/Regulators_vs_Associations.aspx (accessed May 29, 2020).

26. Joint Commission International. http://www.jointcommissioninternational.org/About-JCI/(accessed December 1, 2015).

27. Centers for Medicare & Medicaid Services. https://www.cms.gov/Medicare/Provider-Enrollment-and-Certification/SurveyCertificationGenInfo/Downloads/Accrediting-Organization-Contacts-for-Prospective-Clients-.pdf (accessed February 11, 2020).

28. AAPA (American Academy of Physician Assistants). Becoming a PA. Alexandria, VA: AAPA. https://www.aapa.org/career-central/become-a-pa/ (accessed September 14, 2012).

Chapter 2

Technology Environment

Learning Objectives

At the conclusion of this chapter, the reader will be able to

- Articulate characteristics of applications commonly used in healthcare organizations (e.g., clinical, administrative, financial, consumer, business intelligence)
- Articulate characteristics of technology infrastructure that support the healthcare environment (e.g., network, communications, data integration, privacy and security)

Introduction

The world now is steered by technology and computers—from social networks to IoT (Internet of Things) devices, everything we interact with has a computer in the process. Healthcare may have been a little bit slower than other industries to adopt information technology (IT), but now the electronic health record (EHR) is an essential part of every facility that provides care to patients—from population health to the intensive care unit. Patients are no longer surprised when the provider pulls out a tablet computer instead of a paper chart and pen.

Most hospitals and outpatient sites provide wireless networks for staff to use in caring for patients and a different network for family and visitors to access. It is common to see patients updating their status on Facebook, reviewing their care plan from their hospital beds or checking in for their outpatient visit using their smartphone. Where hospitals used to have policies forbidding employees from accessing social networks during working hours, many institutions now employ staff to monitor and update social media sites. Many patients have

DOI: 10.4324/9780429442391-3

personal health records (PHRs) they manage online, as well as access to a patient portal through the facility's EHR system. Healthcare IT is changing the way that healthcare does business, as well as the way that clinicians care for patients. An understanding of the attributes of healthcare IT, as well as knowledge of the applications and hardware required for their use, is essential in helping to improve the care and the safety of the care provided to patients.

There are three components of the technology environment:

1. Applications—the software used by administrative, clinical and support staff to process and store data, manage patients' records, provide information and knowledge
2. Hardware—the actual servers (virtual, cloud and physical), network connections and devices used to access and generate information
3. Networks—the wired or wireless connections that link the infrastructure together and enable accessibility of the applications and patient data

A healthcare facility requires these three components to function. While this may seem a very simplistic listing, these are essential to providing IT to a healthcare institution. And, while essential, with the rapid changes in technology and improvements in software, the sections of these components change frequently. Decreased access time and increased processor and hard drive speed enables the application to return processed data to the requesting clinician much more quickly. Technology changes are supporting—and changing the applications and the functions of the applications. The illustrations here are not intended to be a complete listing but to provide an overview.

Software in Healthcare IT

Software provides the face of healthcare IT. Hardware is not typically visible to the end users, but the applications that run on that hardware are. Use of the various software applications, along with changes in workflow and processes, can benefit the organization. The software is what the end user interacts with, using interfaces ranging from mobile devices to voice enabled assistants. There are a large number of applications, so we will discuss the major groups of applications and examine some of the newer ideas that are in the pipeline.

Clinical Applications

As with most specialties, healthcare IT has developed its own terminology and acronyms. Some of the terms seem interchangeable when, in fact, they do have different meanings. The EHR, the electronic medical record (EMR) and the PHR are examples of this. The EMR is the continuous, longitudinal electronic record in one specific setting—a provider's office, a hospital or a home healthcare service. The EHR is a longitudinal record covering multiple settings over time.[1-3] The PHR is a medical record often created, edited, maintained and controlled by the patient, and possibly includes importation of clinical data from other sources. Often created online, it is accessible by providers when the patient invites providers to review information in the PHR using secure access.

Clinical applications support patient care wherever it is being delivered. The most apparent clinical application is the EHR. In some institutions, this is a one-vendor application; in others, it is a best of breed, with many different vendor applications performing different functions. The EHR is used by clinicians to document patient care, from medication administration to order entry, as well as to retrieve patient data from the lab or from radiology. The provider's office can send electronic prescriptions to the patient's pharmacy, as well as import and export data from an inpatient stay or outpatient testing from a health information exchange (HIE) system.

EHR systems can also execute algorithms for stratifying various clinical and operational activities. The data points that drive these prediction models can range from vital signs, lab results, to the number of no shows for outpatient visits. Enterprise EHR's can also include population health capabilities, clinical specialty modules and integration with outside regulatory and public health systems. The list of capabilities keeps growing as these systems mature.

The EHR interfaces with specialized systems in different departments. As an example, in the United States, radiology and pathology labs have specific requirements, with formatting and data display governed by different accrediting agencies, such as Clinical Laboratory Improvement Amendments (CLIA), the College of American Pathologists (CAP) and the American College of Radiology.[4,5] In Europe, the European Cooperation for Accreditation[6] covers laboratory certifications. Professional dietitians, case managers and social workers all have specific needs in software functionality, often dictated by professional or regulatory standards.

Some clinical areas, such as the perinatal areas (labor and delivery, nursery, neonatal intensive care and postpartum), the perioperative areas (preoperative unit, operating rooms and post anesthesia care unit), the critical care units, the outpatient centers for primary care and special functions like renal dialysis, have specialized documentation and information needs. The picture archiving and communication system (PACS) stores and displays images from ultrasounds to computed tomography (CT) scans and magnetic resonance imaging (MRIs). These systems require fine-resolution monitors, large storage drives, good bandwidth and large amounts of random access memory (RAM) for image display. Some of the major EHR vendors are able to support all the specialty areas; others do not and require the purchase and interface of a niche system specific to each specialty. The goal of all these systems is to communicate and exchange this patient health information, also known as interoperability. Interoperability is one of the most important attributes of clinical systems, since data should not be entered into systems more than one time. It is essential that these systems exchange data with each other.

The availability of clinical data at the point of care has transformed how clinicians care for patients. They no longer need to go to the radiology department to look at MRIs or CT scans; those images can now be made available in the EHR application, saving time for clinicians, as well as money for the institution, since there are no films to create, store, or retrieve. Perinatal systems archive the fetal monitor strips electronically, saving thousands of dollars in charges for storage of paper fetal strips.

Administrative Applications

Administrative applications provide support for clinicians, as well as the administrative staff in an institution. These applications run the gamut from electronic time cards, intranet, payroll, staff competency record keeping and educational applications, to scheduling both staff for work shifts and patients for procedures and office visits. Bed management systems, which include staff from housekeeping and patient transportation, as well as clinicians, are very helpful in getting patients into a room as soon as possible. Popular applications in the last few years include equipment-tracking applications that use radio frequency identification (RFID) technology, thus saving staff time spent in hunting for needed equipment. Web-based applications that permit staff to bid for understaffed shifts are being implemented, reducing overtime labor costs and increasing staff satisfaction, as do systems that permit self-scheduling.

Financial Applications

Financial applications in healthcare IT cover all the features of any organization's financial needs, but possibly with more variables than most businesses have to entertain. From the solo provider's office to the multihospital, multi-provider health system, there is a need for financial systems. Multiple regulations govern how billing can be done, how bills are submitted and the details that have to be included with a bill, such as diagnosis codes and providers' licenses and billing numbers—the list is incredibly long. Systems have to handle charge posting via both orders and manual charge entry, payment posting and billing based on the providers. Insurance, coinsurance and deductibles have to be part of the calculations, as do revenue codes, supplies, tests and medications. Items that require a provider's order and cannot be billed to patients without an order must be distinguished from items that do not require an order and can be billed to patients. Statements need to be provided to patients and claims to insurance companies. These billing systems are commonly referred to as practice management systems.

A general ledger must accurately track charges, bills and payments. Payroll systems need to accept data from the electronic time card system and convert it to salary costs, correctly matching hours worked, both regular and overtime, and calculate any overtime pay, holiday bonuses, shift differentials, or additional wages earned from professional certifications. It also has to track earnings for paid time off, usually based on the number of hours worked by the employee. The accounts payable portion of the software must also be in sync with all the other systems; financial systems have to communicate in real time. The supply chain mission and support has to include all methods of supply purchasing, as well as invoice payment, and ensure that they are linked correctly.

Consumer Applications

Consumers are becoming more and more involved in electronic records and their patient health information. Not infrequently, patients request electronic versions of their charts from providers. The importance of the consumer's relationship to the record and the information in that record is more apparent. While there used to be discussions about who owned the medical record, this seems to have been decided in the patient's favor. Most EHRs have a patient portal that permits the patient to view test results and clinical notes, ask for prescription refills and send the provider or the office staff a secure e-mail, as well as schedule an appointment. Some portals permit patients to add comments or request amendments to their EHR.[7,8]

Some PHRs are stand-alone and are not connected with an institution's EHR. These applications may be web based, or an application installed on the user's computer or mobile app. In the United States, the Centers for Medicare & Medicaid Services (CMS) encourages the use of PHRs[9,10] and provides a link to Blue Button®, a PHR initiative which originated through the Veteran's Administration and is now being offered through other healthcare organization patient portals. The National Committee on Vital and Health Statistics also provides detailed information on the advantages of a PHR.[10] Convenient guides are helpful to patients around the world.[11] Web-based PHRs give the patient full control of the record's contents, and often offer the opportunity to import prescription medication history from national drug store chains or results from laboratories. According to Gherardi et al., PHRs are becoming very popular in Europe, the United Kingdom and Scandinavia.[12] Vendors are increasing their promotion about the PHR across Europe, the United Kingdom and China.[13]

Some healthcare organizations have partnered with web-based PHR vendors and uploaded records into patients' PHR applications from those healthcare institutions. Some healthcare insurers also provide the ability to create a PHR from their websites.[14] In the United States, a national survey conducted by the California Health Care Foundation (CHCF) provides evidence that PHRs actually support patients in improving their own health.[15] According to the survey, caregivers did note that PHRs were almost a necessity in maintaining knowledge and continuity of care for family members with multiple chronic conditions.

The numbers of patients using PHRs is growing rapidly, with the CHCF survey reporting that most patients want to use PHRs that their physician or insurer provides. The survey also identified security as the major stumbling block to PHR adoption, with patients looking for evidence that any information they enter into the PHR is completely secure. Most websites clearly provide information on how security and privacy of the patients' records is maintained. Most allow the patients to decide who can view their information, often by providing a secure URL or separate login and password for the healthcare provider. Patients have found that after establishing a PHR through their insurance company or other third-party vendor, information could not be easily transferred to a different PHR, resulting in the patients having to reenter the data in their new systems. PHR use has increased with the medical home and accountable care platforms, as they provide incentives for keeping patients healthy.[16] In addition, the use of in-home health monitoring systems and wearable devices has also intensified the need for PHRs. In the United Kingdom, the NHS Summary Care Record (SCR) is an electronic summary of key clinical information (including medicines, allergies and adverse reactions) about a patient, sourced from the general practitioner (GP) record. It is used by authorized healthcare professionals, with the patient's consent, to support their care and treatment. If you are registered with a GP practice in England, your SCR is created automatically, unless you have opted out. 98% of practices are now using the system. The SCR is created automatically through clinical systems in GP practices and uploaded to the Spine. The Spine is a set of national services used by the NHS Care Record Service. In addition to the SCR, these include: The Personal Demographics Service (PDS), which stores demographic information about each patient and their NHS number. Patients cannot opt-out from this component of the spine and the secondary uses service (SUS), which uses data from patient records to provide anonymized and pseudonymised business reports and statistics for research, planning and public health delivery.[17]

Patients are also very interested in communicating electronically with their providers. According to the *Wall Street Journal*,[18] doctors are far behind the rest of the world in using electronic communications, and either patient portals or secure messaging applications can provide security for this increasingly popular communication. Most patient issues can actually be addressed in e-mail by office staff, leaving only a few e-mails that the physician or nurse practitioner needs to address. Patients want the convenience of electronic communication with their providers, but at the same time, both sides of the communication have to be secure. While providers may not have the skill to set up secure communications, there are web-based and application-driven tools that will provide both security and convenience.

The requirement to be able to provide "human-readable" medical records in electronic format is something very new to healthcare. In the past, patients had to go to the health information management department, complete paperwork to request their own records and often pay a per-page fee for a copy of the paper record. As an example, in the United States, Stage 1 of the CMS Meaningful Use requires that a copy of the medical record be available to the patient within 24 hours of the request.[19] While it is not always easy to retrieve data from EHR systems, this requirement has to be fulfilled. Ensuring the EHR can provide this information, whether on a flash drive, or pushed out through an existing patient portal, is essential. In addition, regardless of the regulations, informed patients want copies of their records. Patients want to see their records, as determined by a group of researchers in the United States and Canada.[20]

Clinical Business Intelligence (CBI) and Analytics

According to the HIMSS Clinical and Business Intelligence (CBI) Committee, CBI consists of "technologies, applications and practices for the collection, integration, analysis and presentation of clinical information, for the purpose of better clinical decision-making. In recent times, quality in healthcare is being shaped by evidence-based medicine and the proper utilization of data."[21] Tools of clinical and business intelligence can provide support to clinicians to improve patient safety and patient care, as well as analyzing operating room use and staff overtime patterns. Collecting—and reporting in a meaningful way—supports not only direct patient care, but also all aspects of healthcare, including predictive analytics. Hospitals want to show that they are providing high-quality, low-cost care for their patients; providers want to show that they are doing the same. Data and data analysis are the only keys to providing that information. More and more organizations around the world are implementing clinical and business intelligence, whether by using specific applications or by constructing data warehouses, to document the care they provide, as well as to show trends in patients' conditions and document improvements in patients' status and population health outcomes based on the care that they were given.

Hardware in Healthcare IT

Technology Infrastructure

The basis of any technology has to be the hardware systems that store data, run applications and connect those applications and tools together. The physical routers, switches and virtual and physical servers are some of the integral parts needed to connect clinicians, administrators, providers and patients to essential clinical systems, information and support. Firewalls, both physical and software based, along with virus scanning systems, protect the network from unauthorized access as well as maintain security of the information in the system.

Servers

While the vision that many people have of IT is a data center full of servers, this is no longer completely accurate. Most healthcare IT departments have virtual, physical and cloud servers. What application is installed on which type of server is determined by the vendors' recommendations, as well as the capabilities of the organization to support this technology. Servers are part of the most expensive equipment in a healthcare IT shop and must be managed well and appropriately. Cloud computing provides alternative cost-effective options for those organizations that may not have the appropriate space, resources, or desire to house and maintain their data in-house.

Data Storage

There are, depending on the type of patient, regulations on how long patient data must be maintained. Many healthcare organizations are simply resigned to keeping charts forever.

With paper records, that translates to a large amount of money to store stacks of paper that will probably never be looked at again. Health information management departments have looked for a less expensive and more reliable storage method. Historically, most organizations were forced to store paper charts off-site and have to order them when or if they are needed, thus adding transportation costs to and from the storage area to the record-keeping costs. Some health systems have a practice of scanning paper charts, and then appropriately disposing the paper chart. EHRs have reduced or eliminated the need for paper chart storage. Current practice, where data is stored, backed up and archived, is changing—often to the cloud. The cloud can provide room for storage, even when those storage needs may double every few years.

Mobile Devices

Hardware needs to be designed to support clinical workflow, and increasingly that means portable devices and wireless connectivity. Healthcare institutions are using workstations on wheels (WOWs) with wireless access, as well as smaller handheld devices. These workstations can be configured to meet end users' needs, from drawers for storage to holders for barcode medication scanners and locked drawers for security of medications. Workstations can also be designed for outpatient clinics and other clinical areas that have no need for drawers or scanners, while other workstations can have medical devices mounted on them. It is important to remember that while standardization may be a goal, one documentation device will likely not meet every area or end user needs.

The popularity of smartphones, and their increased functionality, is prompting end users to ask for similar devices for use in healthcare units. Smartphones are one of the most popular handheld devices. Most EHR vendors have updated their applications for use on handheld devices. Devices with touchscreens are being configured for healthcare, with attention to the concern about maintaining good infection control practices while using equipment that is touched by gloved hands. Several devices, such as MRI scanners, employ touchscreens to program the examinations and review the images.

A major concern with any handheld device that connects to the institution's network is security, especially when end users actually bring their own devices (BYOD) to work. Prior to permitting staff's use of their personal devices in the clinical areas, it is important to establish a policy to ensure that protected health information (PHI) is safe, that the institution can wipe a device clean if it is compromised and that passwords are required to access the device. The decision to permit data storage on a personal device must be dependent on maintenance of the data's security.[22,23]

Medical Devices

Many physiologic devices, such cardiac monitors, ventilators, some IV fluid pumps, medication pumps and vital sign monitors, have the ability to send out the data they obtain, often in Health Level Seven (HL7®) format. This integration with the EHR helps staff by decreasing data entry and transcription errors, as well as saving time. Depending on the EHR, this data could be sent directly to preconfigured fields, or a third-party device can be used to translate the data into EHR-acceptable format. It is important to require validation of the information by the clinician prior to permanently storing data in the EHR.

Laboratory devices can conduct tests and export the information to the EHR. Typically, radiologic images are stored in a PACS and viewed via a link from the EHR to the image in PACS or enterprise imaging system. Both areas have specific regulatory agencies that supervise the use of those devices and regulate them. As an example, in the United States, the Food and Drug Administration (FDA) regulates medical devices. Since so many of those devices have incorporated advanced technology, IT must be aware of the laws and regulations from the FDA that apply to hardware and software that is IT supported. In addition to radiologic images, any display of physiologic data, such as heart rhythms, fetal monitor tracings, ventilator or heart waveforms and any implantable device, such as an automatic cardiac defibrillator, are covered by the FDA. In addition, the FDA regulates mobile medical apps. Examples of these are applications that display fetal heart tracings or cardiac waveforms on physicians' cell phones.[24] The institution's biomedical engineering department must work closely with IT to maintain these important systems.

In Europe, the Parliament and the Council of the European Union have developed directives for medical devices and *in vitro* diagnostics. Canada has medical device regulations, as does Japan.[25] In Russia, the Ministry of Public Health and Social Development of the Russian Federation control medical devices.[26] The World Health Organization (WHO) has published a large amount of information about medical device requirements on its web page.[27] According to the WHO, "65% of 145 countries have an authority responsible for implementing and enforcing medical device specific product information."[28] There is discussion that the European Commission's regulations for devices are not strong enough to really protect patients.[29]

Networks in Healthcare IT

Network Infrastructure

The network, while still dependent on network cables, is increasingly connected using wireless points. Putting the information for clinicians at the point of care requires wireless access points, not hard or physical wires. Clinicians want data at their fingertips and do not accept the model of going to the patient's room and then back to the nurse's station to log in to the clinical system and retrieve results. Providers can now take the electronic chart with them to the patient's room, where they can review lab results, x-ray reports and other tests with the patient. Wireless access points can support this workflow, permitting clinicians to work with the information they need when and where they need it. This wireless and cabled access supports more than just documentation stations. Virtual private networks (VPNs), voice over Internet protocol (VoIP) using fiber-optic cables and coaxial cables and supporting protocols, govern the connection of routers and switches. Local area networks (LANs) using Ethernet and a token ring, and wide area networks (WANs) using multiprotocol label switching (MPLS) or asynchronous transfer mode (ATM) are all in use, supporting the hardwired and wireless networks. VPN technology is a safer, more secure method of providing remote access to an organization's network and servers. VPNs, using tunneling protocols and encryption, require authentication to block out unauthorized users.

There are guidelines and rules from regulatory bodies and professional organizations, and standards that require documentation about patients and the care given to those patients, as well as documentation of procedures. One of the major requirements of an EHR is that it must be able to support the documentation, order entry and lab results reporting required by regulations, professional standards and patient need. Ideally, that care is documented when and where it is provided, thereby reducing errors.[30]

There are many areas in an organization that have cabled access to the organization's intranet (internal) and Internet (external). Cabled access is more reliable and faster. Many institutions already have cable that was installed before wireless was within the price range and speed requirements of most IT departments. Clinical departments, as well as administrative and support services, usually have hardwired desktop computers. Some healthcare providers, especially in outpatient settings, have installed a desktop or fixed device in each patient exam room. Specific clinical areas, such as radiology examination rooms, need special hardware, such as larger, high-resolution monitors and high-speed graphic cards that will support detailed images. In addition, hardware devices in patient care areas have to be cleaned with appropriate cleansing agents.

Communications

There are many different types of data communication protocols and media available in healthcare IT today, from the standard telephone landline with conferencing and video capabilities to various devices that use VoIP and broadband access. Data communication protocols allow information to transmit from one point or media to another. One of the most common examples would be the telephone. Some of the devices look like the same cell phones that are used outside the hospital, while some are clip-on, hands-free phones worn by staff members. As with other devices in use in clinical areas, such as tablets and medical devices, infection control is a major concern. Materials for these devices need to be antibacterial and cleanable. While some of these devices can send and receive text messages, there are concerns about the security of using text messages for patient orders and not all providers want to use text messages for orders. Bifurcated workflows such as these can result in missed patient care. Other examples of communication protocols would include broadband access, Ethernet and Wi-Fi for transmitting data across computer networks or accessing the Internet.

Interoperability and Standards

An important facet of all healthcare IT applications is the use of standards. Interoperability is essential to smooth functioning of healthcare IT, and systems that support standards ensure that functionality. Health Level Seven (HL7) is an international standard interface language used in healthcare,[31] HL7 Fast Healthcare Interoperability Resources (FHIR®) is a next-generation standards framework that leverages the latest web standards, Digital Imaging and Communications in Medicine (DICOM®) is used as a standard for images[32] and the Systematized Nomenclature of Medicine—Clinical Terms (SNOMED CT®) is the most comprehensive multilingual clinical healthcare terminology in the world,[33] while the International Statistical Classification of Diseases and Related Health Problems (ICD) provides diagnosis codes for most disease conditions.[34] In the United States, these codes, along with current procedural terminology (CPT®) codes, classify patients' diagnoses and the procedures they had and provide a link between each procedure and the diagnosis that required it.[35] In France, the International Society for Pharmacoeconomics and Outcomes Research (ISPOR) has developed charge codes for providers, including the correct prices that can be charged for a specific procedure.[36] These codes can be entered into the system by clerical staff as well as providers, and in most cases, these codes have a large part in determining if an institution or provider will receive the maximum amount of reimbursement for performing a procedure or the minimum amount.

Interoperability is "the extent to which systems and devices can exchange data and interpret that shared data" and the "uniform movement of healthcare data from one system to another such that the clinical or operational purpose and meaning of the data is preserved and unaltered."[1] With the current movement to exchanging patient data, regardless of the physical location of the patient and the patient's home data, those standards, especially data formats, have become increasingly important and necessary.

Without standards, interoperability is impossible; without standards, healthcare IT would most resemble the Tower of Babel, with no system or device speaking the same language and resulting in duplicative effort and work from clinical and administrative staff as well as patient safety concerns. In the United States, governing standards are included in the Final Rule, published by CMS in August 2012, as well as the Advisory Board for Health Standards in Europe.[37]

Included in the discussion of standards are nursing and other disciplines' terminologies. These terms can be used by nurses, as well as other providers, including physicians, to document patient care. The need to standardize terms affects all parts of healthcare and especially impacts quality reporting. The use of standard words for documentation improves data, research and natural language processing (NLP), since it is clear what the standardized terms mean.

There are challenges to EHR interoperability throughout the world. The integration effort currently in place in Europe is improving the chances of adoption. This integration needs to move quickly, as the number of specialty systems is increasing. The specialty systems are often intended for use by only one discipline, moving away from an integrated EHR.[38]

Data Integration

Data integration and the use of interface engines are essential in healthcare IT. Interface engines permit systems to be connected correctly. It is not enough to simply send data from one application to another—there are many rules that must be followed. If data does not go to the right patient's chart, errors in the patient's care, bill and final report could result. Interface engines in a healthcare IT environment really drive the systems, matching data and patients correctly in near real time. Without data integration and interface engines, a national health information network, connections to EHR's with best of breed systems and EHR app integration using FHIR would not be possible.

Data Warehouses

Data warehouses are highly prevalent in today's healthcare IT landscape. The value of being able to store and mine data from multiple sources, such as the EHR and ancillary systems, is clearly recognized. Storing data in one place—the warehouse—from multiple sources allows it to be queried at the same time. Healthcare institutions have multiple requirements for submission of their data to different organizations, from the Bureau of Vital Statistics to the American Heart Association in the United States or the European Society of Cardiology. Often, these organizations require submission of the same quality improvement data elements, but just want it in a different format. The warehouse can support this type of quality reporting, as well as clinical research and analytics. Data mining can be used to identify populations at risk, search for patterns of illness and identify potential study candidates or those patient populations that are doing well.[39] Defining a data model, deciding if a data mart would be more helpful than a warehouse and determining how to search the warehouse are all decisions that should be made by an experienced database manager.

Privacy and Security

Maintaining patients' information, ensuring that it is kept private and secure, is the first charge for EHR administration. As an example, while patients' data has to be shared through HIEs and Regional Health Information Organizations (RHIOs), it must remain confidential. Increasingly, data regulations are including strong language about privacy and security, emphasizing that the EHR can and must be developed without compromising a patient's privacy. Systems, as part of their design, have to be able to provide the patient an accounting of disclosures. The system must be able to maintain levels of confidentiality. For example, a nurse or physician must be able to see the patient's laboratory results, but a nurse's aide using that same EHR should not be able to see that information.

While disclosures of information can be made to appropriate agencies, such as the patient's insurance provider, those agencies cannot be given complete access to the patient's record, but must be given the minimum amount of information necessary.

Ethically, healthcare providers have an obligation to keep any patient's information private and confidential. The healthcare professions have codes of ethics that clearly detail the nurse's and physician's obligation to protect the patient's information.[40]

Summary

Understanding the basic foundations of healthcare technologies, applications and other tools used in connecting them together provides healthcare professionals and others allied to the field the ability to create, support and maintain healthcare information. Knowledge of these fundamental areas, as well as key issues and especially trends, is the basis of building and designing healthcare IT and supporting healthcare providers in their work of caring for patients in a safe, accurate and timely manner.

References

1. HIMSS. *HIMSS Dictionary of Health Information and Technology Terms, Acronyms and Organizations, Fifth Edition.* Boca Raton: Taylor & Francis Group, LLC, 2019.
2. Office of the National Coordinator, *Department of Health and Human Services. Benefits of EHRs* [Issue brief]. Washington, DC: Office of the National Coordinator, 2012. http://www.healthit.gov/providers-professionals/electronic-medical-records-emr (accessed April 22, 2016).
3. European Commission/Information Society. 2012. http://ec.europa.eu/information_society/activities/health/index_en.htm (accessed April 22, 2016).
4. American College of Radiology. *ACR-AAPM-SIM Technical Standard for Electronic Practice of Medical Imaging* [Resolution ACR-Resolution 35]. Reston, VA: American College of Radiology, 2012. https://www.acr.org/-/media/ACR/Files/Practice-Parameters/Elec-Practice-MedImag.pdf (accessed April 22, 2016).
5. Centers for Disease Control and Prevention. *Certifications, Licenses and Accreditations.* Atlanta, GA: Centers for Disease Control and Prevention. www.cdc.gov/clia (accessed April 22, 2016).
6. European Cooperation for Accreditation. 2012. hhttp://www.european-accreditation.org/home (accessed April 22, 2016).
7. Mayo Clinic Staff. *Personal Health Record: A Tool for Managing Your Health.* Scottsdale, AZ: Mayo Clinic, 2011. http://www.mayoclinic.org/healthy-lifestyle/consumer-health/in-depth/personal-health-record/art-20047273 (accessed April 22, 2016).
8. HIMSS. *Connected Health – It's Personal.* Chicago: HIMSS, 2019. https://www.himss.org/resources/connected-health-its-personal (accessed May 8, 2020).
9. Personal Health Records (PHR). 2011. http://www.medicare.gov/manage-your-health/personal-health-records/personal-health-records.html (accessed April 22, 2016).
10. National Committee on Vital and Health Statistics. *Personal Health Records and Personal Health Record Systems: A Report and Recommendations from the National Committee on Vital and Health Statistics.* Hyattsville, MD: National Committee on Vital and Health Statistics, 2006. http://www.ncvhs.hhs.gov/ (accessed April 22, 2 016).
11. AHIMA Personal Health Record Practice Council. *Helping Consumers Select PHRs: Questions and Considerations for Navigating an Emerging Market.* Chicago: American Health Information Management Association, 2006. http://library.ahima.org/xpedio/groups/public/documents/ahima/bok1_032260.hcsp?dDocName=bok1_032260 (accessed April 22, 2016).
12. Gherardi S, Kensing F, Osterlund C. Personal Health Records: Empowering Patients through Information Systems? *IT and People,* 2012. https://ec.europa.eu/digital-single-market/en/news/personal-health-records-empowering-patients-through-information-systems-manuscript-submission (accessed April 22, 2016).
13. *MMRGlobal Moving into Europe with MMRPro and MyMedicalRecords.* Los Angeles: MMRGlobal, 2012. http://phx.corporate-ir.net/phoenix.zhtml?c=178404&p=irolnewsArticle&ID=1704074&highlight= (accessed April 22, 2016).
14. Aetna. *Aetna's Personal Health Record.* Hartford, CT: Aetna, 2008. http://www.aetna.com/employer-plans/document-library/corporate-wellness-program/aetna-personal-health-record.pdf (accessed April 22, 2016).
15. California HealthCare Foundation. *New National Survey Finds Personal Health Records Motivate Consumers to Improve Their Health.* Oakland: California HealthCare Foundation, 2010. http://www.chcf.org/media/press-releases/2010/new-national-survey-finds-personal-health-records-motivate-consumers-to-improve-their-health (accessed April 22, 2016).

16. Lewis N. Consumers Slow to Adopt Electronic Personal Health Records. *Information Week*, April 8, 2011. http://www.informationweek.com/healthcare/electronic-medical-records/consumers-slow-to-adopt-electronic-perso/229401249# (accessed April 22, 2016).

17. NHS (National Health Service). *Introduction to Summary Care Records*. London: NHS, 2012. http://www.nhs.uk/NHSEngland/thenhs/records/healthrecords/Pages/servicedescription.aspx (accessed April 22, 2016).

18. Should Physicians Use Email to Communicate with Patients? *Wall Street Journal*, January 23, 2012. http://online.wsj.com/article/SB10001424052970204124204577152860059245028.html (accessed April 22, 2016).

19. Department of Health and Human Services. *Health Information Technology: Initial Set of Standards, Implementation Specifications, and Certification Criteria for Electronic Health Record Technology; Final Rule* (45 CFR Part 170). Washington, DC: Government Printing Office, 2010.

20. Wiljer D, Urowitz S, Apatu E, DeLenardo C, Eysenbach G, Harth T, Leonard KJ. Patient Accessible Electronic Health Records: Exploring Recommendations for Successful Implementation Strategies. *J Med Internet Res* 10(4), 2008. http://dx.doi.org/10.2196/jmir.1061 (accessed April 22, 2016).

21. Clinical & Business Intelligence Committee. https://www.himss.org/clinical-business-intelligence-committee (accessed May 8, 2020).

22. HIMSS. Mobile Security Toolkit. 2017. https://www.himss.org/mobile-security-toolkit (accessed May 8, 2020).

23. Wireless, Smartphones and Applications. 2012. http://www.csoonline.com/article/2134942/data-protection/useful-settings-alert–how-to-secure-iphones–ipads.html (accessed April 22, 2016).

24. Food and Drug Administration. *Draft Guidance for Industry and Food and Drug Administration Staff—Mobile Medical Apps*. Silver Spring, MD: Food and Drug Administration, 2011. http://www.fda.gov/MedicalDevices/ (accessed April 22, 2016).

25. Process Quality Associates. *ISO 13485*. London: Process Quality Associates, 2006. http://www.pqa.net/ProdServices/ISO/ISO13485.html (accessed April 22, 2016).

26. Emergo Group. *Medical Device Approval Process in Russia*. Austin, TX: Emergo Group, 2012. http://www.emergogroup.com/resources/articles/russia-medical-device-approval-process (accessed April 22, 2016).

27. World Health Organization. *Medical Devices*. Geneva: World Health Organization, 2012. http://www.who.int/medical_devices/en/ (accessed April 22, 2016).

28. World Health Organization. 2012. http://www.who.int/en/ (accessed April 22, 2016).

29. Fiore K. New Device Rules Criticized at EASD Meeting. MedPage Today, October 3, 2012. http://www.medpagetoday.com/MeetingCoverage/EASD/35119?utm_content=&utm_medium=email&utm_campaign=DailyHeadlines&utm_source=WC&xid=NL_DHE_2012-10-04&eun=g440157d0r&userid=440157&email=mbarthold@umc.edu&mu_id=5537079 (accessed April 22, 2016).

30. Kohle-Ersher A, Chatterjee P, Osmangeyoglu HU, Hochheiser H, Bartos C. Evaluating the Barriers to Point-of-Care Documentation for Nursing Staff. *Comput Inform Nurs* 30(3): 126–133, 2012.

31. Health Level Seven International. 2012. http://www.hl7.org/ (accessed April 22, 2016).

32. DICOM (Digital Imaging and Communications in Medicine). http://dicom.nema.org/ (accessed April 22, 2016).

33. SNOMED CT (SNOMED Clinical Terms). http://www.ihtsdo.org/snomed-ct/ (accessed April 22, 2016).

34. CDC (Centers for Disease Control and Prevention). *Classification of Diseases, Functioning and Disability*. Atlanta, GA: CDC, 2011. http://www.cdc.gov/nchs/icd/icd10cm.htm (accessed April 22, 2016).

35. American Medical Association. 2012. http://www.ama-assn.org/ama/pub/physician-resources/solutions-managing-your-practice/coding-billing-insurance/cpt.page (accessed April 22, 2016).

36. Meyer F, Denis C. *France—Medical Devices*. Lawrenceville, NJ: International Society for Pharmacoeconomics and Outcomes Research, 2011. http://www.ispor.org/htaroadmaps/francemd.asp (accessed April 22, 2016).

37. CEN-CENELEC Advisory Board for Healthcare Standards. 2009. http://www.cen.eu/cen/Sectors/Sectors/Healthcare/Forum/Pages/currentissues.aspx (accessed April 22, 2 016).

38. Lakovidis I. Towards Personal Health Record: Current Situation, Obstacles and Trends in Implementation of Electronic Healthcare Record in Europe. *Int J Med Inform* 52(1–3): 105–115, 1998. http://www.ijmijournal.com/article/S1386-5056(98)00129-4/abstract?showall=true= (accessed April 22, 2016).

39. Wickramasinghe N, Calman RA, Schaffer JL. *Defining the Landscape: Data Warehouse and Mining: Intelligence Continuum* [HIMSS white paper]. Chicago: HIMSS, 2007. http://s3.amazonaws.com/rdcms-himss/files/production/public/HIMSSorg/Content/files/Intel_Continuum06052007.pdf?src=cii20110110 (accessed August 23, 2021).

40. Erickson JI, Millar S. Caring for Patients while Respecting their Privacy: Renewing our Commitment. *Online J Issues Nurs* 10(2), 2005. http://nursingworld.org/MainMenuCategories/ANAMarketplace/ANAPeriodicals/OJIN/TableofContents/Volume102005/No2May05/tpc27_116017.html (accessed April 22, 2016).

CLINICAL INFORMATICS II

Chapter 3

Clinical Informatics

Learning Objectives

At the conclusion of this chapter, the reader will be able to:

- Identify basic clinical vocabulary/terms frequently represented in healthcare informatics (e.g., dosage frequency, dosage routes, body systems)
- Identify basic healthcare IT vocabulary/terms frequently represented in healthcare informatics
- Identify basic clinical metrics frequently represented in informatics (e.g., average daily census, turnaround time, adherence, barcode medication administration)
- Develop and implement system functionality to optimize clinical effectiveness and efficiencies
- Interpret clinical and operational outcomes through the use of various data analytics tools (e.g., reports, tables, graphs, charts, predictive models)
- Develop mechanisms to facilitate ongoing clinical content and decision-support tools

Introduction

Clinical informatics is a vast and diverse study of information technology (IT) and how it can be applied to the healthcare field. HIMSS defines clinical informatics as the promotion of "understanding, integration and application of information technology in healthcare settings to ensure adequate and qualified support of clinician objectives and industry best practices."[1] The field includes[2]:

- Methods to collect, store and analyze healthcare data
- The study of information needs and cognitive processes and optimal ways to meet those needs

DOI: 10.4324/9780429442391-5

- Methods to support clinical decisions, including summarization, visualization, provision of evidence and active decision support
- Optimizing the flow of information and coordinating it with care providers' and patients' workflows to maximize patient safety and care quality
- Methods and policies for information infrastructure, including privacy and security

Globally, clinical informatics has been increasingly impactful to the healthcare world. Diana Nole, the Chief Executive Officer (CEO) of Wolters Kluwer Health, states that in 2018 there was more than US$ 8 billion in digital health deals made.[3] Clinical decision support (CDS) continues to be a powerful tool in providing guidance to today's clinicians. Drug usage and cost is being looked at with new eyes through data, and artificial intelligence (AI) and machine learning adoption are on the rise. With the increased focus on social determinants of health and patient-driven care, AI will development and usage will continue well into the future.[3] And clinical informaticists will be needed to maintain their role as translators in the interprofessional team, as a professional that speaks both informatics and healthcare.

As discussed in Chapter 1, "Healthcare Environment," often considered a hybrid of many different informatics models and theories, clinical informaticists can consist of physicians, nurses, pharmacy, laboratory, radiology and other clinical professions. Physicians and nurses make up the largest group of healthcare professionals, "who have actively contributed to and advanced the theory and practice of clinical informatics."[4] Nurses established an early role as clinical informaticists, with certifications starting in 1992.[4] Physicians later followed with their own certifications through the American Medical Informatics Association (AMIA) in 2013.[5] HIMSS, Certified Associate in Healthcare Information and Management Systems (CAHIMS^SM) and Certified Professional in Healthcare Information and Management Systems (CPHIMS^SM) are listed among the highest recommended informatics certifications for clinicians, as well as board certifications. Acquiring a certification is recognized as a "highly-visible quality indicator and a tool to improve recognition among peers."[4] Table 3.1 takes a look at the differences between nursing and physician certification processes.

Global Aspects of Clinical Informatics

Although many items referenced in this chapter are centered around the United States, clinical informatics is very global. Global clinical informatics is a fast-growing, interdisciplinary field. From privacy and security issues to global population health, clinical informatics professionals have a great impact on the management of patient health data.

Health information data can be stored across borders, which allows for the impact of international law with both the data usage as well as patient's rights.[6]

Table 3.1   Comparison of Informatics Certification Processes for Nurses and Physicians[4]

	Nursing Informatics Certification Informatics Skills/Competencies References	*Clinical Informatics Board Certification for Physician* Informatics Skills/Content Outline References*
Skills and Competencies	Scope of nursing informatics practice: foundational knowledge of metastructures, concepts and tools, functional areas of nursing informatics; evolution of informatics competencies, ethics, the future of nursing informatics including trends in practice roles, technology, regulatory changes and quality standards, care delivery models and innovation. Standards of nursing informatics practice: assessment, diagnosis, problems and issues, outcomes identification, planning, implementation, evaluation standards of professional performance for nursing informatics: ethics, education, evidence-based practice and research, quality of practice, communication, leadership, collaboration, professional practice evaluation, resource utilization, environmental health	Informatics competencies as listed on the outline for board certification: leading and managing change, health information systems, fundamentals of informatics, clinical decision-making and care process improvement, legal, ethical and regulatory issues
Eligibility	Eligibility is limited to nurses with a baccalaureate degree in nursing; current R.N. license; two years' experience practicing as a Registered Nurse; experience practicing as an informatics nurse and/or graduate-level practicum hours in informatics	Eligibility is limited to physicians with MD or DO degree; current, unrestricted medical license in the United States; current American board certification in primary clinical discipline or pathology
Practice Requirement	ANCC certification requires up to 2000 hours of experience in informatics nursing. Practicum hours in a graduate nursing informatics program may also be used to satisfy the practicum requirement.	Accredited fellowship: 2 years Practice Pathway (25% time spent in informatics related activities for at least 36 months in the 5 years or acceptable 24-month informatics master or fellowship prior to taking the examination)

(Continued)

Table 3.1 *(Continued)* **Comparison of Informatics Certification Processes for Nurses and Physicians**[4]

	Nursing Informatics Certification Informatics Skills/Competencies References	*Clinical Informatics Board Certification for Physician* Informatics Skills/Content Outline References*
Validation Domain	Certification validates knowledge pertaining to the informatics nurse role; informatics nurse specialists, those with graduate degrees in informatics, practice at higher levels than that implied by certification	Board certification validates practice-based training and experience and/or formal training in clinical informatics (either advanced degrees or fellowships)
Duration of Validity	Board certification valid for five years	Board certification valid for 10 years
Recertification	A minimum of 30 hours continuing education in informatics required for initial certification. Continuing education also required for re-certification.	Continuing education needs for maintenance of certification; requires examination once every 10 years

This requires not only a strong healthcare system and regulatory knowledge for the country of origin but any foreign locations as well.

Several global initiatives share the mission of increasing clinical informatics education and best-practices. The AMIA leads a global health informatics working group (GHIWG) designed to work with resource-constrained countries. They work to increase overall informatics usage and facilitate collaborative efforts between clinical informatics workers. Their connection forum helps to facilitate the exchange of both informatics experiences, as well as expertise, across the global spectrum.[7]

HIMSS has always had its North American roots. Within that scope, it includes the digital health support of Canada, including its own HIMSS certification (CPHIMS-CA[SM]). Digital health is a term for clinical informatics more commonly used outside the United States. Through HIMSS, "international insights, resources, and audiences" are provided at the ready for the Canadian clinical informatics professionals.[8] The Canadian/HIMSS collaboration currently concentrates in three areas[8]:

1. Strengthening the HIMSS Ontario Chapter (ON Chapter) through increasing the Canadian health association presence in HIMSS activities, volunteer opportunities and project that will aid both Ontario's, as well as HIMSS, global digital health influence.
2. Support existing associations and Canadian digital health initiative by including (and sponsoring) local informatics groups such as the British Columbia Health Information Management Professionals Society (BCHIMPS) and the Canadian Trade commission.

3. And by filling the void. HIMSS has the unique ability to bridge the clinical informatics gap and aid in increasing the knowledge and expertise of Canadian stakeholders. This is evidenced by its recent expansion efforts, including the formation of the Canadian Prairies Chapter of HIMSS to support other areas of Canada in a more local fashion.

Furthermore, since the publication of this chapter, HIMSS has also worked with local constituents to form the Canadian Prairies Chapter and with the BCHIMPS to form the HIMSS British Columbia Chapter.

Finally, there is the EU–US eHealth Work Project, which culminated its project work in May 2018. As a Horizon 2020 project, its goal was to "map skills and competencies, provide access to knowledge tools and platforms and strengthen, disseminate and exploit success outcomes for a skilled transatlantic eHealth workforce."[9] The 21-month project began in September 2016 with funding from the European Commission's Horizon 2020 research and innovation grant program and came to a close in May 2018. Their challenge was to develop something that would expand the foundations already in place for digital skills and push the global boundaries of innovation and resource development. This included making sure that clinical informaticists were engaged and brought into the extensive stakeholder community. They achieved this through the development of the Consortium, which consisted of a network of partners in academia, healthcare associations, as well as healthcare providers, and industry workers. The Consortium included: Omni Miro Systems/Med Solutions (Germany) who served as the project coordinator, European Health Telematics Association (EHTEL) (Belgium), University of Applied Sciences Osnabrück (Germany), Tampere University of Technology (Finland), Steinbeis 2i GmbH (Germany),[9] and the HIMSS Foundation with project fulfillment by the HIMSS Technology Informatics Guiding Education Reform (TIGER™) Initiative. To meet their goals, they conducted a survey (Survey of Current State and Needs of the eHealth Workforce) to identify the "real world" challenges and gaps in informatics. The study, which served as the flagship of the project, considered demographics with over 1,000 respondents globally, primarily from the United States (72%) and Europe (19%). One of the most significant results of the survey was the need for increased clinical informatics education, specifically with nurses, physicians and educators rounding out the top three. They released this as GAP1: eHealth knowledge and skills of healthcare professionals, with there being ten significant gaps identified in total. Other deficiencies consisted of gaps in teacher/trainer knowledge, acceptance and usage of systems, availability of course or programmes for education and the quality of current training materials for any clinical informaticist.[9]

The project also included an update of the Health Information Technology Competencies (HITCOMP) Tool to a 2.0 version. Seen as an innovative solution, this tool is available to the global clinical informatics community and concentrates on eHealth, digital skills research, education development, skills assessment, and career progression. It contains over 1000 competencies, over 250 healthcare roles, in five major European languages.

The HIMSS TIGER Initiative continues its partnership with the project through support in several platforms such as the Foundational Curriculum and the Interactive Web Platform TRIE (tools, resource, information, education) (includes HIMSS TIGER Virtual Learning Environment (VLE)). Also, the skills and knowledge assessment and development (SKAD) framework promotes certification programs such as the HIMSS CAHIMS/CPHIMS.[9]

Domains of Clinical Informatics

With patient safety always paramount, "clinical informaticians transform healthcare by analyzing, designing, implementing and evaluating information and communication systems that enhance individual and population health outcomes, improve patient care, and strengthen the clinician-patient relationship."[10]

According to AMIA (Figure 3.1), "clinical informaticians use their knowledge of patient care combined with their understanding of informatics concepts, methods, and tools to:

- Assess information and knowledge needs of healthcare professionals and patients;
- Characterize, evaluate and refine clinical processes;
- Develop, implement and refine clinical decision-support systems; and
- Lead or participate in the procurement, customization, development, implementation, management, evaluation and continuous improvement of clinical information systems."[10]

In this chapter, we will take a deeper dive into the world for clinical informatics. Starting with the basics, we will review the language and definitions commonly

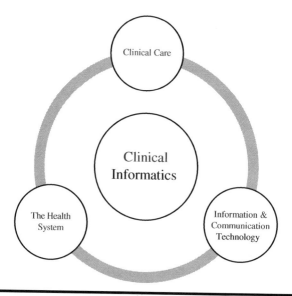

Figure 3.1 Domains of clinical informatics.[10]

used in healthcare. We will also examine clinical metrics frequently represented in informatics such as average daily census, turnaround time, adherence and barcode medication administration. To evaluate these metrics, often informaticists will need to use various analytical tools. It is essential to have a good understanding of clinical and operational outcomes through the use of tools such as reports, tables, graphs, charts and predictive models. Finally, in this chapter, we will review one of the most often used tools, and often debated, clinical content and decision-support tools.

Basic Clinical Vocabulary and Terms

Understanding the basics of healthcare is vitally important for health IT workers and clinicians alike. To be able to speak the same language, and understand each other, common ground must be found. In this section, we will review frequently used clinical terminology found in the healthcare environment. At the root of clinical language is the use of prefixes, letters, words, or numbers placed before a medical term. Any tables listed are merely a sampling of existing terminology; they are not meant to be a complete catalog (Tables 3.2–3.6).

Table 3.2   Frequently Used Clinical Terminology Prefixes[11,12]

Brachi/o	*Arm*	Lapar/o	*Abdomen, loin or flank*
Cardi/o	*Heart*	My/o	*Muscle*
Cyt/o	*Cell*	Neur/o	*Nerve*
Derm/a, derm/o, dermat/o	*Skin*	Ocul/o	*Eye*
Encephal/o	*Brain*	Ophthalm/o	*Eyes*
Gastr/o	*Stomach*	Or/o	*Mouth*
Hemat/o	*Blood*	Ot/o	*Ear*
Intestin/o	*Intestine*	Pulmon/o	*Lungs*

Table 3.3   Common Drug Routes and Abbreviations[13]

Classification	*Drug Routes*	*Common Abbreviations*
Enteral	Oral	PO
	Sublingual	SL
	Per rectum	PR
Parenteral	Injections	SQ, IM, IV, IA, IT, IO, ID
Inhalation	Lungs	Aerosols, steam
Topical	Skin	Enepidermic, epidermic, insufflation, instillation, irrigation, swabbing

Table 3.4 Medical Specialties[14]

Allergy and Immunology	Allergies	A provider that specialized in diagnosis and treatment of allergies, including allergy testing, medications
Anesthesiology	Sedation/ anesthesia	Specializes in anesthesia, sedation and airway management. Typically seen in the operating room working with the patient during their surgery
Cardiology	Cardiovascular system	The provider treats heart and blood vessel issues and disease processes
Dermatology	Integumentary system	The provider delivers care from aesthetics (e.g., laser treatments) to rashes, skin cancers and other skin issues
Endocrinology	Endocrine system	Diseases such as diabetes and thyroid issues
Family Physician	Primary care provider	Providers deliver basic care (typically nonspecialized) for patients across all spectrums (genders and ages)
Gastroenterology	Digestive system	Providers works around the esophagus, stomach, intestinal issues including reflux, gallbladder, colitis, etc.
Infectious Disease	Infections	Difficult to diagnose or treat, such as tuberculosis, Zika, or Dengue
Internal Medicine	Primary care provider	Specialized providers that encompass sub-specialties such as cardiology or endocrinology
Neurology	Neurologic system	Works with spinal issues, brain, nerves. Some examples include Parkinson's and neuropathies
Pediatrics	Pediatric care	The care is given to younger patients, typically infancy through age 18. This includes well-checks, immunizations, physicals, etc.
Oncology	Cancer management	Providers care for cancer, side-effects of treatment, clinical trials and end-of-life care
Obstetrics/ Gynecology	Women's health	Reproductive care, preventive care (annual pap exams, mammograms), pregnancy, menopause, contraception and infertility
Otolaryngology	Ears, nose and throat	Most often, ENTs are also surgeons that cover areas from sinus issues, neck cancers, etc.
Psychiatry	Mental and behavioral healthcare	Providers work with patient counseling, psychotherapy, analysis, hospitalization and medications
Radiology	Imaging	A physician trained at interpreting diagnostic exams/ testing
Surgery	Surgical care	General or specialized surgical providers. Responsible for planning pre-operative needs, the surgery, post-operative needs, as well as any complications that may arise (e.g., orthopedics, general, bariatrics, etc.)

Basic Information Technology Vocabulary and Terms

Table 3.5   Frequently Used Clinical Abbreviations[13]

Abbreviation	Definition	Abbreviation	Definition
AM	Morning	L	Liter
AC	Before meals	LMP	Last menstrual period
AD	Right ear	MCG	microgram
Ad lib	Freely	mEq/L	Milliequivalent per liter
Amp	Ampule	mL	Milliliter
Ante	Before	Mm	Millimeter
AS	Left ear	N/V	Nausea and vomiting
ASA	Aspirin	NKDA	No known drug allergies
AU	Both ears	NPO	Nothing by mouth
BID	Twice a day	OD	Right eye
BMI	Body mass index	OS	Left eye
BP	Blood pressure	OU	Both eyes
BS	Blood sugar	oz	Ounce
CC	Chief complaint	PRN	As needed
Cap	Capsule	PM	Evening
CM	Centimeter	PMH	Past medical history
CXR	Chest x-ray	Q	Every
DC	Discontinue	Q2h	Every two hours
Disp	Dispense	Q6h	Every six hours
ER/EC/ED	Emergency room	Qam	Every morning
G	Gram	Qpm	Every night
Gr	Grain	QID	Four times a day
HR	Hour	QOD	Every other day
H/O	History of	Rx	Prescription
HR	Heart rate	SL	Sublingual
HS	At bedtime	SQ	Subcutaneous
HX	History	STAT	Immediately
ID	Intradermal	Supp	Suppository
IM	Intramuscular	T	Temperature
IN	Intranasal	TID	Three times a day
INJ	Injection	w/o	Without
IV	Intravenous	WNL	Within normal limits

Table 3.6 Frequently Used Healthcare Information Technology Vocabulary[15–19]

Affordable Care Act (ACA)	The comprehensive healthcare reform law in the United States enacted in March 2010, also known as "Obamacare"
Accountable Care Organization (ACO)	A group of healthcare providers who give coordinated care, chronic disease management and thereby improve the quality of care patients receive
Current Procedural Terminology (CPT®)	These codes are used for the billing of medical procedures
Digital Imaging and Communication in Medicine (DICOM®)	The Digital Imaging and Communications in Medicine (DICOM) Standard was developed for the transmission of images and is used internationally for Picture Archiving and Communication Systems (PACS)
Federally Qualified Health Center (FQHC)	Federally funded nonprofit health centers or clinics that serve medically underserved areas and populations
Health Information Portability and Accountability Act (HIPAA)	U.S. law designed to provide privacy standards to protect patients' medical records and other health information provided to health plans, doctors, hospitals and other healthcare providers
Health Level Seven (HL7)	ANSI-accredited, a nonprofit, standard-developing organization that creates methods for interoperability of healthcare data interchange. It focuses on clinical and administrative data
Tenth revision of the International Statistical Classification of Diseases and Related Health Problems (ICD-10)	ICD-10 is a system used by physicians and other healthcare providers to classify and code all diagnoses, symptoms and procedures recorded in conjunction with hospital care in the United States
Logical Observation Identifiers Names and Codes (LOINC®)	Coding system for the electronic exchange of laboratory test results and other observations. LOINC development involved a public-private partnership comprised of several federal agencies, academia and the vendor community. This model can be applied to other standards setting domains
Merit-Based Incentive Payment System (MIPS) (U.S. based)	MIPS was designed to tie payments to quality and cost-efficient care, drive improvement in care processes and health outcomes, increase the use of healthcare information and reduce the cost of care

(Continued)

Table 3.6 *(Continued)* **Frequently Used Healthcare Information Technology Vocabulary**[15–19]

Natural Language Processing (NLP)	Natural language processing (NLP) is a branch of artificial intelligence that helps computers understand, interpret and manipulate human language. NLP draws from many disciplines, including computer science and computational linguistics, in its pursuit to fill the gap between human communication and computer understanding
Systematized Nomenclature of Medicine-Clinical Terms (SNOMED CT®)	SNOMED-CT (Clinical Terminology) has been created from the combination of SNOMED-RT (Reference Terminology) and Read codes
Unified Medical Language System (UMLS®)	Developed by the National Library of Medicine in an attempt to unify disparate medical vocabularies and facilitate sharing medical knowledge across information systems

Common Clinical Metrics in Informatics

Most clinical informatics professionals will credit the birth of clinical metrics with the 1999 publication by the Institute of Medicine (IOM), "To Err is Human." This landmark report brought to light issues within the healthcare system that not only was responsible for significant financial loss but also loss of life.[20] With the field of clinical informatics being vast in scope, certain areas set it apart from other types of IT. One is the focus of healthcare informaticists on the need for identification and adoption of clinical metrics. Since the IOM report, there has been a significant surge in the development of methods to help keep down cost, provide accessible healthcare, as well as significantly improve patient safety.

In the United States, the development of the American Reinvestment and Recovery Act (ARRA), the accompanying Health Information Technology for Economic and Clinical Health (HITECH) Act,[21] and the Patient Protection and Affordable Care Act[22] reinforced the shift in focus even more towards the goal of decreasing government spending on healthcare while also improving patient safety. These public laws, as well as the Centers for Medicare and Medicaid Services (CMS) introduction of Meaningful Use (MU), created a rapidly changing landscape for clinical informatics. Before the introduction of these laws, adoption was slow at best. But with the incentives provided by the HITECH Act, a landslide of implementation of certified electronic health records (CEHRTs) was kick-started.

CMS has had many variations since 2009, of the expectations of meeting their electronic clinical quality measures (eCQMs). These tools were designed to specifically aid in measuring and tracking several aspects of healthcare. The reporting of these measures revolved around working the eligible providers (EPs), eligible hospitals, dual-eligible hospitals and critical access hospitals (CAHs). Per CMS (2019), their current version of meeting the guidelines includes using the 2015 version of CEHRT to meet the requirements of the promoting interoperability program (PIP) (Tables 3.7, 3.8). Each year, CMS provides updates to the eCQMs. These consist of updates regarding evidence-based medicine, code sets and measure logic.[23] The current measurement goals of eCQMs for both Medicare and Medicaid for 2019 include[23]:

- Patient and Family Engagement
- Patient Safety
- Care Coordination
- Population/Public Health
- Efficient Use of Healthcare Resources
- Clinical Process/Effectiveness

With these new standards of cost-saving and healthcare safety, there have been many organizations developed to aid in quality improvement. These groups accomplished this by setting forth guidelines and metrics for facilities and providers to integrate into their care of patients. The tools they provide aid clinical informaticists to develop and implement system functionality to optimize clinical effectiveness and efficiencies. There are many, but two of the more significant ones include the National Quality Forum (NQF) and the Agency for Healthcare Research and Quality (AHRQ).

The NQF is an agency that supports improving overall national health by several methods: setting national standards, recommendation of measure for use in payment and public reporting programs, identification of quality improvement (QI) priorities, advancement of electronic measurement and providing information and tools to help healthcare decision-makers.[25] The tools provided by the NQF are especially helpful to healthcare providers when aiming to meet metrics and achieve both facility and personal goals. Table 3.9 provides a brief explanation of the tools provided.

The AHRQ is a U.S. government agency that functions as part of the Department of Health & Human Services (DHHS). Its primary mission is to support research and produce evidence for the improvement of quality healthcare. To achieve this, they developed quality indicators to determine the standards of healthcare and if certain providers are meeting those standards.[27] Examples of their goals are keeping patients safe, helping physicians and other healthcare providers improve quality, and develop data to track changes in the healthcare system (Table 3.10).

These metrics, such as average daily census, cervical cancer screening and diabetic eye exams, require a thorough investigation of the requirements as well as current and future state workflow assessments to ascertain how the metrics

Table 3.7   Eligible Professionals Objectives and Measures[24]

Protect Patient Health Information	Protect ePHI created or maintained by the CEHRT through the implementation of appropriate technical, administrative and physical safeguards
Electronic Prescribing	Generate and transmit permissible prescriptions electronically
Clinical Decision Support (CDS)	Implement CDS interventions focused on improving performance on high-priority health conditions
Computerized Provider Order Entry (CPOE)	Use CPOE for medication, laboratory and diagnostic imaging orders directly entered by any licensed healthcare professional, credentialed medical assistant, or a medical staff member credentialed to and performing the equivalent duties of a credentialed medical assistant, who can enter orders into the medical record as per state, local and professional guidelines
Patient Electronic Access to Health Information	The EP provides patients (or patient-authorized representative) with timely electronic access to their health information and patient-specific education
Coordination of Care Through Patient Engagement	Use CEHRT to engage with patients or their authorized representatives about the patient's care
Health Information Exchange	The EP provides a summary of care record when transitioning or referring their patient to another setting of care, receives or retrieves a summary of care record upon the receipt of a transition or referral or upon the first patient encounter with a new patient and incorporates summary of care information from other providers into their EHR using the functions of CEHRT
Public Health and Clinical Data Registry Reporting	The EP is in active engagement with a public health agency or clinical data registry to submit electronic public health data in a meaningful way using CEHRT, except where prohibited, and in accordance with applicable law and practice

Table 3.8   Eligible Hospital or Critical Access Hospital Objectives and Measures[24]

Protect Patient Health Information	Protect ePHI created or maintained by the CEHRT through the implementation of appropriate technical, administrative and physical safeguards
Electronic Prescribing	Generate and transmit permissible prescriptions electronically
Clinical Decision Support (CDS)	Implement CDS interventions focused on improving performance on high-priority health conditions
Computerized Practitioner Order Entry (CPOE)	Use CPOE for medication, laboratory and diagnostic imaging orders directly entered by any licensed healthcare professional, credentialed medical assistant, or a medical staff member credentialed to and performing the equivalent duties of a credentialed medical assistant, who can enter orders into the medical record per state, local and professional guidelines
Patient Electronic Access to Health Information	The EH/CAH provides patients (or patient authorized representative) with timely electronic access to their health information and patient-specific education
Coordination of Care Through Patient Engagement	Use CEHRT to engage with patients or their authorized representatives about the patient's care
Health Information Exchange	The EH/CAH provides a summary of care record when transitioning/referring their patient to another setting of care, receives or retrieves a summary of care record upon the receipt of a transition or referral or upon the first patient encounter with a new patient and incorporates summary of care information from other providers into their EHR using the functions of CEHRT
Public Health and Clinical Data Registry Reporting	The EH/CAH is in active engagement with a public health agency or clinical data registry to submit electronic public health data in a meaningful way using CEHRT, except where prohibited, and in accordance with applicable law and practice

Table 3.9   National Quality Forum Tools[26]

NQF Graphics Library	Collection of downloadable graphics that can be used in your work
Alignment Tool	Helps you align, expand, or start your measurement and reporting efforts in ways that fit with key national programs
Health IT Knowledge Base	Provides answers to some of the most technical questions surrounding NQFs health IT and eMeasures initiatives
My Dashboard	Helps track what is happening at the NQF and lets you personalize your experience on the web
NQFs Action Registry	Online collaboration space designed to help people on the frontlines of making care sage connect with others, find new resources and help distribute proven ideas
Field Guide to NQF Resources	Dynamic, online resource designed to help those involved with measurement and public reporting more easily access basic information and NQF resources related to quality measurement

Table 3.10   Agency for Healthcare Research and Quality Areas of Focus[27]

Project ECHO (Extension for Community Healthcare Outcomes)	AHRQ funded an innovative model, Project ECHO, for training and supporting primary care clinicians in rural communities to provide specialized care for their patients. This model has flourished and expanded from its initial focus on hepatitis C into new clinical areas, including mental health and substance abuse and HIV. It has also been adopted by the Veterans Health Administration as a tool for expanding access to high-quality care for veterans across the country.
Re-Engineered Discharge (RED)	RED is a structured protocol and suite of implementation tools that help hospitals rework their discharge processes to reduce readmissions by determining patients' needs and carefully designing and communicating discharge plans. Hospitals using these tools have seen a 30% reduction in hospital readmissions and emergency rooms visits.
Centers of Excellence	Three Centers of Excellence were funded to study how high-performing healthcare systems promote evidence-based practices in delivering care. The AHRQ project will help close this research gap and produce information that can be used by health systems throughout the United States to improve patient outcomes.

can be met within a CEHRT. The subsequent reporting on to government agencies for either reimbursement incentives or avoidance of penalties often becomes the primary goal. But workflow and ease of usability are factors that also need to be considered when asking providers and other healthcare professionals to aid in meeting these metrics. To accomplish this, often times the use of CDS systems will be brought into play.

Clinical Content and Decision Support Tools

Clinical informaticists and clinicians in general, have been making a significant impact in HIT since the late 1950s. Since then, there has been the development of mathematical models used to aid providers in diagnosing various medical conditions[28] to the present-day use of AI, application programming interfaces (APIs), substitutable medical applications reusable technologies (SMART), the fast healthcare interoperability resources (FHIR®), or a combination of several of these such as SMART on FHIR.

CDS is defined as "a category of concepts and methods designed to provide patient-specific clinical information to a healthcare provider at the point of care."[29] The ultimate goal in the use of CDS is, of course, patient safety and improved patient experience. But, it can also serve other purposes. Establishing a robust and reliable process for developing best-practice maintenance of a CDS is paramount. Good build design and implementation can not only provide better patient outcomes but improved overall quality, reduced cost, improved documentation consistency and reliability, as well as an enhanced clinician experience. This is where clinical informaticists are paramount. They have the skills to translate workflow into the CDS design and build. Clinical informaticists have the ability to better communicate and understand all the challenges that clinicians face and that come along with new CDS, new implementation of any kind, within an electronic health record, "acceptance and adoption of CDS is critical for successful implementation."[4] CDS is typically implemented within an EHR, in the form of order sets, condition-specific clinical alerts, access to reference information (also known as info buttons) and passive/active generalized alerts. But, it can also be seen in use with patient portals, health information exchanges (HIEs), mobile applications and other HIT systems.

Considering it takes up to 17 years for translational research to make its way into clinical practice, maintaining current, evidence-based clinical content can be a challenge but is required for any successful use of CDS in the healthcare setting.[30] To maintain this rapidly changing use of not only technology, but medicine as well, skilled workflow assessments, governance and maintenance is a must. According to Butterfield, "medical knowledge doubles approximately every eight years, so a physician's knowledge base is outdated very quickly after graduation from medical school. Keeping up with current knowledge by reading

Table 3.11   Advantages and Disadvantages of Computerized Provider Order Entry[33]

Advantages	Disadvantages
Averting handwriting issues	Perceived as more work for clinicians
Drug/drug, drug/food, drug/allergy alerts	Provider coding requirements
Formulary recommendations	Bad use of CDS; design, maintenance
Safer or lower cost	Duplicate alert drop-down issue
Economic savings	Never-ending system demands
Better billing turn around	Hybridized paper/electronic workflows
Faster order transmission to lab/pharmacy/ radiology	Constantly changing evidence and technology
	Overdependence on CDS

journal articles is impractical due to the volume of material and lack of time for reading it."[31]

To quote Dr. W. Edwards Deming of The Deming Institute, "a bad system will beat a good person every time." No matter the amount of governance management, or expert opinion of the project informaticist, if the design and build are "bad," the implementation will fail. Here, we look as some of the advantages and disadvantages of CDS[32,33] (Table 3.11):

Advantages of CDS:

■ Increased quality of care and enhanced health outcomes
■ Avoidance of error and adverse events
■ Improved efficiency, cost–benefit and provider and patient satisfaction
■ Computerized practitioner order entry

Disadvantages of CDS:

■ Alarm/alert fatigue
■ Clinical burnout, documentation burden
■ Delegation of order entry to other clinicians
■ Data integrity
■ Auto-population
■ Design and implementation issues
■ Lack of maintenance and governance

According to Bresnick, "CDS tools are designed to help sift through enormous amounts of digital data to suggest next steps for treatments, alert providers to available information they may not have seen, or catch potential problems.... "[34]

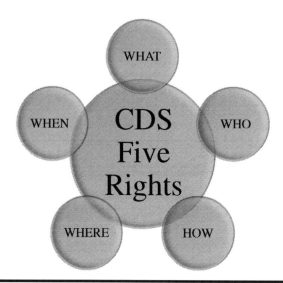

Figure 3.2   The five rights of clinical decision support[36]

Osheroff et al. recommends a five-rights framework for CDS that has been adopted and promoted as best practice by the AHRQ[35] (Figure 3.2). There is also a need for increased usability. This relates directly to CPOE. The less a physician or advanced practice provider (APP) uses the order systems as designed, the less impactful CDS is. It will be alerting in the face of the incorrect people. So, our providers have to be well trained, well informed and satisfied with the usability of the system.

The five rights include (Table 3.12)[37]:

■ The right information
■ To the right person
■ In the right intervention format
■ Through the right channel
■ At the right time in the workflow

Table 3.12   Explanation of the Five Rights of CDS[36]

Right Information	Right Person	Right Format	Right Channel	Right Time
Have the right decision-makers involved	Include the end-users and the healthcare team	Alerts; passive or actionable?	EHRs	When should the CDS be presented in the workflow?
Evidence-based, recognized guidelines	Determine who needs to actually see the CDS	Order sets, HIEs, patient portals	CPOE	Workflow analysis
Actionable, not too much information	Is the person seeing it qualified to use it?	Infobuttons	Forms, etc.	Close the loop

Ultimately, CDS is not going anywhere, anytime soon, "CDS tools are increasingly leveraging machine learning and artificial intelligence to sophisticated power analytics. Machine learning algorithms can ingest large quantities of data, identify patterns, and return detailed results to users."[34]

Clinical Data Analytics Tools

To put all of this together, clinical informatics is all about the clinical data; how do we enter it, where do we store it, what can we do with it? Whether it is a retrospective look at the data or more towards the future with predictive analytics, clinical informatics plays a vital role in healthcare. Considering what has been discussed related to data, CDS and quality measures, outcomes are a top goal and are necessary in order to meet the goals you have set for providers and facilities, including lowering cost and improving the patient experience. This consists of defining and understanding both clinical outcomes as well as the operational outcomes. Later chapters discuss the systems life cycle and data management in more detail. With all the regulatory and accreditation requirements (e.g., Joint Commission, DNV GL), the ability to develop and maintain a functional system of data management is challenging. According to McBride & Tietze, "data management, measures, and analytics are the foundations of improvement."[6] Data warehouses, retrospective storage of data, can include clinical and operational data.[38] See Chapter 2 for more discussion surrounding data warehouses.

Clinical Outcomes

Clinical outcomes are somewhat different from typical outcomes measures. The clinical measurements are related to specific changes in health or health quality, as it relates to the healthcare a patient has received. They are measurable and can be evaluated through activity metrics such as hospital re-admission rates, or catheter-associated urinary tract infections (CAUTIs), as well as many other metrics.[39] Often times, facilities will benchmark or compare themselves to other comparable facilities based on a shared standard. This ranking is usually available to the public. It is easy to see why keeping up with data, and clinical outcomes would be considered vitally important.

Operational Outcomes

Operational outcomes are defined as outcomes that are specific and measurable statements about improvements a facility would like to make to its processes or services, "each outcome should flow directly from a more general goal of the unit." For example, if an academic department has a goal of increasing diversity, then the department might have separate outcomes addressing the recruitment of more diverse students and recruitment of more diverse faculty.[40]

In the development of outcomes, the use of the acronym SMART is often recommended to assure a measurable outcome is designed.

Outcomes should be **SMART**:

Specific
Measurable
Attainable
Realistic
Timely

Common Data Analytics Tools

Now that you have all this data, how do you go about making it work for you? The process starts with learning about your data, manipulating it, creating information from it and then distributing that knowledge and wisdom to others. By determining what kind of data you have (nominal, ordinal, interval, ratio), you can examine or explore the data set. There are many tools available for data analysis, including Microsoft Excel, IBM SPSS, Tableau, business intelligence software and many more. When you have identified and opened your data file, you can start with a visual inspection[6]:

- What rows and columns do the data set reflect?
- How are the data structured?
- Are there visibly missing data apparent in the file?
- Do they appear to be sorted in some order?
- What variables in the data set represent dependent, independent and grouping variables?

In healthcare, it is not uncommon for there to be data integrity issues or problems with the accuracy or validity of the data over its lifecycle.[41] This can often occur for various reason. Some of the more common ones are listed here:

- Wrong patient data
- Height/Weight inaccuracies impacting drug calculations
- Allergies and medications documentation inaccuracies or omissions
- "Fat finger" errors, physical typing/entering the wrong data
- Overall missing data; forgetting, time constraints, fraudulent documentation
- Not documenting real time (e.g., sepsis alert dependent on vital signs data entry)

Table 3.13   Common Data Analytics Tools and Terminology[38]

Tool	Purpose/Definition	Example
Fields	Vertical column in a database that contains data with common characteristics for the entire record	"First Name" "Last Name" "Date of Birth"
Records	Horizontal rows in a database containing different pieces of data belonging to a given entity	All of the fields related to the row of "Billy"
Tables	Consists of all records; combinations of all fields and records together	All horizontal and vertical rows together
Reports	Alternate view of data; typically assembled from a query	Generally generated on paper, can also be electronic for distribution of data
Query	Process of selecting desired records; pulling the data	Pulling data related to all female patients older than 50 with a history of colon polyps
Graphs and Charts	Tool for examining and presenting data	Scatter plot, pie charts, bar charts, flowcharts
Control Charts	Tool for looking at a process over time	Common and special-cause variation, upper and lower control limits
Predictive Modeling	Instead of retrospective data analytics, the data is used to predict future outcomes	Pulling last five years of financial data to predict next years' budget needs

Based on these examples, it is not hard to understand the value of inspecting your data prior to presenting it. With that, the ability to recognize clinical and operational outcomes through the use of various data analytics tools (e.g., reports, tables, graphs, charts, predictive models) is a necessary skill set for any clinical or healthcare informatics specialist. Here are some examples of the more common data analytics tools and terminology (Table 3.13).

Summary

The future of healthcare and clinical informatics is wide open. Like medicine, informatics and technology is ever-changing in its day-to-day advancements. Big data is booming, and we are all running to keep up. This, along with project management, evidence-based CDS and mobile technology will keep this profession chaotic and busy for many years to come. It can be anticipated that the field of clinical informatics will continue, and certified nurses, physicians, radiologists, respiratory therapists, pharmacists, as well as other healthcare professionals will be the ones to lead this aspect of healthcare into the future.

References

1. HIMSS (Healthcare Information and Management Systems Society). 2019. HIMSS Dictionary of Health Information and Technology Terms, Acronyms and Organizations. 5th ed. Chicago: HIMSS, p. 40.
2. Columbia University. n.d. *Clinical informatics*. Retrieved from https://www.dbmi. columbia.edu/research/research-areas/clinical-informatics/ (accessed July 21, 2019).
3. Nole D. 2018. 5 Healthcare trends to watch in 2019. *Becker's Hospital Review.* Retrieved from https://www.beckershospitalreview.com/healthcare-information-technology/5-healthcare-trends-to-watch-in-2019.html
4. Cummins MR, Gundlapalli AV, Murray P, Park HA, Lehmann CU. 2016. Nursing informatics certification worldwide: History, pathway, roles, and motivation. *Yearb Med Inform.* 264–271 (accessed August 2, 2019).
5. Lehmann CU, Gundlapalli AV, Williamson JJ, Fridsma DB, Hersh WR, Krousel-Wood M, Ondrula CJ, Munger B. 2018. Five years of clinical informatics board certification for physicians in the United States of America. *Yearbook of Medical Informatics* 27 (1): 237–242. doi:10.1055/s-0038-1641198.
6. McBride S, Tietze M. 2019. *Nursing Informatics for the Advanced Practice Nurse: Patient Safety, Quality, Outcomes, and Interprofessionalism.* New York: Springer Publishing Company.
7. American Medical Informatics Association [AMIA]. n.d. Global health informatics working group. Retrieved from https://www.amia.org/programs/working-groups/global-health-informatics (accessed March 1, 2020).
8. Pettit L. 2018. Why Canada? Health Information Management Systems Society. Retrieved from https://www.himss.org/resources/himss-in-canada (accessed March 2, 2020).
9. EU*US eHealth Work. 2018. Welcome to EU*US eHealth Work: Measure, inform, educate, advance. Retrieved from http://www.ehealthwork.eu/ (accessed March 11, 2020).
10. Gardner RM, Overhage JM, Steen EB, Munger BS, Holmes JH, Williamson JJ, Detmer DE. 2009. Core content for the subspecialty of clinical informatics. *J Am Med Inform Assoc* 16 (2): 153–157. doi:10.1197/jamia.M3045.
11. American Institute of Medical Sciences & Education. *All Essential Medical Terms in One Place.* Retrieved from https://www.merriam-webster.com/dictionary/prefix (accessed July 16, 2019).
12. Merriam-Webster. Prefix. Retrieved from https://www.merriam-webster.com/dictionary/prefix (accessed July 16, 2019).
13. Drugs.com. Prescription Abbreviations. n.d.. Retrieved from https://www.drugs.com/article/prescription-abbreviations.html
14. Fogoros RN. *The Most Common Physician Specialties.* Retrieved from https://www.verywellhealth.com/types-of-doctors-1736311 (accessed July 6, 2019).
15. National Health Information Infrastructure. n.d. Standards and standards organization. Retrieved from http://www.aspe.hhs.gov/sp/nhii/standards.html
16. CMS.gov. 2018. ICD-10. Retrieved from https://www.cms.gov/Medicare/Coding/ICD10/

17. U.S. National Library of Medicine. 2019. Unified Medical Language System. Retrieved from http://www.nlm.nih.gov/research/umls/

18. SAS Institute. n.d. Natural Language Processing: What it is and why it matters. Retrieved from https://www.sas.com/en_us/insights/analytics/what-is-natural-language-processing-nlp.html

19. MIPS. n.d. Retrieved from https://qpp.cms.gov/mips/overview; Medical Definition of HIPAA (2018). Retrieved from https://www.medicinenet.com/script/main/art.asp?articlekey=31785

20. Institute of Medicine (IOM). 2000. *To Err Is Human: Building a Safer Health System.* LT Kohn, JM Corrigan, and MS Donaldson, eds. Washington, D.C.: National Academy Press. Retrieved from http://www.nationalacademies.org/hmd/~/media/Files/Report%20Files/1999/To-Err-is-Human/To%20Err%20is%20Human%201999%20%20report%20brief.pdf

21. Health Information Technology for Economic and Clinical Health Act. 2009. Public Law 111-5 American Recovery and Reinvestment Act of 2009, Title XIII Health Information Technology for Economic Clinical Health Act. Retrieved from https://www.hhs.gov/sites/default/files/ocr/privacy/hipaa/understanding/coveredentities/hitechact.pdf

22. Patient Protection and Affordable Care Act. 2010. Public Law 111–148 Patient Protection and Affordable Care Act, Title X and Health Care and Education Reconciliation Act of 2010. Retrieved from http://housedocs.house.gov/energycommerce/ppacacon.pdf

23. Centers for Medicare and Medicaid Services. 2019. Clinical quality measures basics. Retrieved from https://www.cms.gov/Regulations-and-Guidance/Legislation/EHRIncentivePrograms/ClinicalQualityMeasures.html (accessed July 22, 2019).

24. CMS, 2019. Medicaid Promoting Interoperability Program Eligible Professionals Objectives and Measures for 2019. Retrieved from https://www.cms.gov/Regulations-and-Guidance/Legislation/EHRIncentivePrograms/Downloads/TableofContents_EP_Medicaid_2019.pdf

25. National Quality Forum [NFQ]. n.d. *Measures, reports, and tools.* Retrieved from https://www.qualityforum.org/Measures_Reports_Tools.aspx (accessed August 4, 2019).

26. National Quality Forum [NFQ]. n.d. *What we do.* Retrieved from https://www.qualityforum.org/what_we_do.aspx (accessed August 2, 2019).

27. Agency for Healthcare Research and Quality [AHRQ]. 2017. *About AHRQ.* Retrieved from https://www.ahrq.gov/cpi/about/index.html (accessed July 20, 2019).

28. Ledley Robert S, Lusted Lee B. 1959. Reasoning foundations of medical diagnosis. *Science*, 130(3366): 9–21. Retrieved from http://www.jstor.org/stable/1758070 (accessed April 22, 2016).

29. Sittig DF. 2017. *Clinical Informatics Literacy: 5000 Concepts Every Informatician Should Know.* Cambridge, MA: Academic Press, pp. xiii–xx.

30. Morris ZS, Wooding S, Grant J. 2011. The answer is 17 years, what is the question: Understanding time lags in translational research. *J R Soc Med*, 104 (12): 510–520.

31. Butterfield B. 2013. Who is liable for EHR, clinical decisions support mistakes? *EHR Intelligence.* Retrieved from https://ehrintelligence.com/news/who-is-liable-for-ehr-clinical-decision-support-mistakes/

32. HealthCare.gov. *Glossary.* Retrieved from https://www.healthcare.gov/glossary/ (accessed July 16, 2019).

33. Koppel R, Metlay JP, Cohen A, Abaluck B, Localio AR, Kimmel SE, Strom DL. 2005. Role of computerized physician order entry systems in facilitating medication errors. *JAMA*, 293 (10), 1197–1203. doi:10.1001/jama.293.10.1197

34. Bresnick J. 2017. Understanding the basics of clinical decision support systems. Health IT Analytics. Retrieved from https://healthitanalytics.com/features/understanding-the-basics-of-clinical-decision-support-systems (accessed July 16, 2019).
35. Agency for Healthcare Research and Quality. 2013. Plan-do-study-act (PDSA) cycle. *Quality Tools.* Retrieved from https://innovations.ahrq.gov/qualitytools/plan-do-study-act-pdsa-cycle
36. Osheroff JA, Teich JM, Levick D, Saldana L, Velasco FG, Sittig DF, Jenders RA. 2012. *Improving Outcomes with CDS: An Implementer's Guide* (2nd ed.). Chicago, IL: HIMSS.
37. Centers for Medicare and Medicaid Services. 2014. Clinical decision support: More than just 'alerts' tipsheet. Retrieved from https://www.healthit.gov/sites/default/files/clinicaldecisionsupport_tipsheet.pdf
38. Englebardt S, Nelson R. 2002. *Health care Informatics: An Interdisciplinary Approach.* St Louis, MO: Mosby, Inc.
39. National Health Service [NHS]. n.d. *Clinical Outcomes.* Retrieved from https://www.gosh.nhs.uk/conditions-and-treatments/conditions-we-treat-index-page-group/clinical-outcomes
40. Appalachian State University. 2019. What are operational outcomes? Institutional Research, Assessment, and Planning. Retrieved from https://irap.appstate.edu/institutional-effectiveness/assessment/educational-support-and-administrative-units/faqs-2
41. Brook C. 2019. What is data integrity? Definition, best practices & more. Digital Guardian. Retrieved from https://digitalguardian.com/blog/what-data-integrity-data-protection-101

HEALTHCARE INFORMATION AND SYSTEMS MANAGEMENT

Chapter 4

Analysis

Learning Objectives

At the conclusion of this chapter, the reader will be able to:

- Apply appropriate concepts of systems development (e.g., systems development life cycle or SDLC)
- Apply and utilize project management methodology components (e.g., needs analysis, gap analysis, defining and prioritizing requirements)
- Apply appropriate concepts of process improvement (e.g., DMAIC, PDCA)
- Utilize standard visualization tools to analyze and improve current business and clinical processes (e.g., process mapping, flow diagramming, gap analysis)
- Interpret and analyze disparate data sets
- Formulate alternate processes and potential solutions for new or improved applications and/or systems
- Evaluate if a proposed solution aligns with the organization's strategic and operational plans
- Perform cost–benefit analysis to evaluate impact on issues related to healthcare systems (e.g., customer satisfaction, patient care quality, economics, access to care, business process improvement)
- Develop proposals that include recommended approaches and solutions, and plans for realizing benefits
- Analyze and interpret business documentation to promote system changes and/or implementations (e.g., RFPs, RFIs, SLAs, SOWs, NDAs, etc.)

Introduction

Different industries have adopted the use of information technology (IT) in their various operations in order to enhance growth, conform to emerging standards, attract new customers, maximize profitability and acquire business intelligence. Different sectors, however, have adopted IT use in different capacities. The health sector, like all others, is striving to enhance the acceptance of better and easier techniques available through an IT implementation, yet the average use of IT in healthcare has lagged behind other industry sectors for the better part of the last decade. According to Deloitte's 2018 Global CIO Survey, only about 4.26% of revenues were spent on technology in the healthcare services industry. This is up three quarters of a percent since the previous survey in 2017.[1] In early 2019, Forrester Research and Gartner both released predictions that spending on healthcare would increase to nearly 9%. Gartner's report though further broke down the spending, which continues to show that, although spending is up, monies are allocated mainly on supporting and maintaining the current infrastructure, not on growing and transforming the business through IT.[2] Healthcare has many potential benefits from IT implementation in both managerial operations and patient-related operations. These benefits may be realized through systems implementation. A common methodology that may be followed during this pursuit is the systems development life cycle (SDLC). The SDLC is a process used to develop an information system, including requirements, validation, training and user ownership through investigation/planning, analysis, design, implementation and maintenance.[3] During the planning phase of the SDLC, the phase prior to the analysis phase, the initial idea for an health information system project is first developed. The feasibility, objectives and scope are examined, current problems with the existing situation are considered and a recommended solution is proposed. If the project appears to be worth pursuing the project then moves to the analysis phase. The purpose of the systems analysis phase is to understand the business requirements and to build a logical model of the new system. Requirements modeling is going to be completed, business processes are going to be described and defined, data, process and object modeling will take place, and ultimately a systems requirements document describing the management and user requirements, alternative plans and costs and an analysis of the recommendation will be produced. During the systems analysis phase, the following objectives should be met:[4]

- Gather, analyze and validate technical, functional and nonfunctional requirements.
- Evaluate the alternatives and prioritize the requirements.
- Examine the information needs of end users and establish the systems goals.
- Create software, hardware and network requirements documentation.

Requirements gathering in this phase is key. Lack of end user input can mean a weak analysis. A weak analysis leads to poor design, which can lead to failed projects.

Healthcare Problems and Opportunities for IT Implementation

Healthcare globally is going through dynamic changes in several ways. Improvements to healthcare information systems emerge from a need for change. Either the existing system does not meet the evolving needs of the program or there is an understanding that emerging technologies allow for radically better systems. In response, a small group, or a project champion, identifies this need and then tries to mobilize a larger group of stakeholders. During this phase, systems analysis, the perceived gaps and opportunities are documented, with a strong focus on describing the desired benefits and why. It may include the development of a high-level business case that compares the benefit with estimated costs. To begin, let's look generally at problems plaguing traditional healthcare systems and then potential opportunities to address these issues.

Problems with Traditional Healthcare Systems

Overall, there are some general problems with the traditional healthcare systems. These may include:

- Poor quality of health information including redundancy and inconsistent standards for the collection and sharing information.
- Inability to obtain health information at the time and place where it is needed.
- The data collected in health records is limited.
- Some registers in health exist only in paper form, which limits quick access to them.
- Inadequate procedures for the implementation of information systems not related to the relevant organizational changes.
- Existing solutions do not ensure interoperability and the lack of co-operation between systems makes management of information impossible and adversely affects the accuracy, integrity, comparability and completeness of data.
- To this point, systems have been developed primarily to support the work of the administrative unit, while to a small extent adjusted to the needs of patients, doctors and other users.
- Lack of computerized practitioner order information and histories for drugs and other substances, medical supplies, catalogs and lab test results.
- Lack an integrated, interoperable electronic health record, image and film archiving and associated communication systems, the result analysis

mechanism for ordinary patient processes such as lab tests and drug prescriptions, prescription error alert systems and electronic monitoring of high care patients.

Opportunities with Advanced Healthcare Systems

As we look toward advanced healthcare systems, there are many opportunities. Hospital information system (HIS), healthcare information system and patient data management system (PDMS), all these terms refer to the integrated information systems in the healthcare sector. They are complete solutions for managing medical, administrative, financial and legal data. The overall aim of a HIS is to provide support for patient care, achieve optimal financial performance and streamline administration. These systems include the integration of clinical systems, financial systems and administrative systems. Benefits of integrated healthcare systems include:

Operational

■ Increases productivity, reduces cost, improves data quality, improves data sharing/flow, provides better access to data, provides easier exchange of data, improves data presentation, reduces medical errors and helps achieve satisfaction.

Managerial

■ Improves managerial control, provides more understanding and control of processes, supports decision-making, improves allocation of resources, improves quality of care provided, improves work efficiency, increases performance and increases return on investment.

Strategic

■ Supports more effective planning, increases synchronous-asynchronous collaboration among actors (actor refers to all human and non-human users that interact with the healthcare system), improves relationships with suppliers, improves knowledge sharing, improves population's health and increases survival rates and quality of life.

IT Infrastructure

■ Promotes reusability of objects, reduces development risk, supports the use of e-healthcare and telemedicine-based patient support models, achieves non-invasive solutions, achieves process integration, provides object/

components integration, provides data integration, provides real-time integration, integrates custom systems and integrates packaged systems and integrated e-business solutions.

Organizational

■ Reduces need for hospitalization or length of stay, reduces waiting times, reduces cancelled operations, achieves effective clinical and administrative management, increases business efficiency, supports clinical decision-making, results in reliable data, increases data analysis and reduces paper work processes.

The major avenues of opportunities for change are spread across clinical, administrative and financial functions as well as infrastructure.

Clinical Functions

A significant percentage of modern healthcare facilities are using IT systems in clinical operations. However, the majority of units are still dependent on traditionally used systems, such as physical patients' document keeping, lab reports, drug administration history and other functions. While much progress has been made in these areas over the past couple of decades, we still have a long way to go before we achieve a global, interoperable healthcare system in all types of healthcare settings.

Applications for Clinical Functions

Electronic health records (EHRs) involve standardizing the way in which patients' records are entered, stored and retrieved, not just within an organization, but across different hospitals, caregivers, government-controlled organizations and other interested parties. The biggest challenge regarding EHRs has been the establishment of an industry standard so that an efficient workflow can be realized that would allow for seamless retrieval and use of records for patients, even when patients are moved to units or facilities other than where they were initially treated.

This kind of data pool would imply a dedicated system with necessary checks and balances to prevent unauthorized access to and manipulation of patient records, while, at the same time, enabling data entry by different care providers when patients make additional visits to any facility. This concept is delicate due to the potential of malicious addition or manipulation of patient data by different staff in different facilities. Moreover, a lack of universal standards in proper coding and categorization of prescriptions and procedures has hindered the implementation of interoperable EHR systems in the last two decades. This problem can now be sufficiently handled by high-end software applications that are being developed by individual and corporate research entities.

An example of one type of system being pursued is computerized practitioner order entry (CPOE). CPOE may replace conventional order cataloging and fulfillment in a manner that will enhance tracking, logistic synchronization and cost-effectiveness. Another example of a system is a clinical decision-support system (CDSS), which, in its basic form, will give informative guidelines to practitioners regarding medication and procedures, including warning systems relating to high-risk medications and processes. In addition, the picture archiving and communication system (PACS) integrates inputs from multiple radiological and diagnostic tools to allow easy, consistent and accurate treatment of different conditions, while radio frequency identification (RFID) may help to track patients within a medical unit without the need to restrict them to a particular location or allocate a nurse to them. There are also monitoring systems that may collect vital signs which may include pulse rate, temperature level, blood pressure and other metabolic/respiratory signals. Benefits of such a system, if properly collected, stored and secured, when integrated with other dedicated software applications, may shorten treatment time, allow more freedom and lead to cost efficiency and better resource utilization within a hospital or other healthcare facility. Automated dispensing machines (ADMs) will aid in drug dispensing, while electronic materials management (EMM) systems will operate like the resource planning systems used in other sectors to manage information processing regarding pharmaceuticals, new drug development and coding, among other functions. Such a system could reduce medication errors, which, per a report from 2016 found that adverse drug events (ADEs) account for more than 3.5 million physician office visits and 1 million emergency department visits each year. This same report also stated that it is believed that preventable medication errors impact more than 7 million patients and cost almost $21 billion annually across all care settings..[5]

Administrative and Financial Services

Functions that could be enhanced through investment in IT in the administrative category include general ledger operations, such as revenue and cash flow, expenses, purchases and other day-to-day transactions. Other functions are billing, cost accounting systems, payroll, personnel management and integrated human resource functions, patient registration and booking and electronic management of materials, among others.

Applications for Administration and Finance

IT may find many basic as well as advanced applications in administrative and financial services. Human resource management has experienced radical changes in operational methods as a result of IT implementations. Systems for employee management, role definition, reward and recognition support and performance development have been successfully automated thanks to dedicated software such as enterprise relational database management systems (RDBMSs). Such systems allow easy, timely and accurate workflow management in human resource mobilization and development, saving time and costs that would otherwise be allocated for additional staff. Other functions, such as payroll, budgeting, internal audits and strategic planning, have also been made easier, more precise and tailor-made for specific analytical objectives without incurring additional monthly or yearly charges due to the use of IT systems. Patient registration and tracking can become more enhanced and efficient, and access to the online statistics of every facility within an area may be useful in referrals and in discharge notification, enabling time saving and better emergency handling.

Infrastructure

Infrastructure is a broad category that incorporates various equipment with diverse applications, both general and specific. Current security standards have shifted toward biometric sensors for movement and access control in many major private and public buildings and premises. These security standards enhance accountability in system access and support user logging, which enhances safety and responsibility among authorized personnel. The healthcare sector could, perhaps, benefit the most from such systems, given the delicate nature of confidentiality requirements involved in patient records access and dissemination. Biometric sensors typically used include fingerprint or palm scanners, voice recognition systems and eye scanners, among others. Other more dedicated systems include bar coding systems for medication grouping, ordering, cataloging and stock control. Security infrastructure may also include closed-circuit TV cameras and night infrared cameras.

Security-Related Applications

Since IT relates to healthcare security, it may find many uses, some of which may not be achieved in other ways. Patient information access logging is important in ensuring confidentiality and professionalism in the way patients are treated. It increases patients' confidence in their practitioners and boosts their trust levels. In addition, the use of biometric systems will eliminate to a large extent, ambiguity in accountability in delicate cases due to their high precision levels and extremely low chances of identity theft or manipulation, unlike conventional security protocols when any person with forced access to pass codes may steal information. In addition, healthcare research facilities may hold expensive machinery that, if it falls into wrong hands, may be used in ways detrimental to society. For instance, ultra-modern DNA synthesis machines, if used by experts, may find applications in the terrorist underworld. Other chemicals and drugs in healthcare facilities may also be abused or sold to unsuspecting people as legitimate prescriptions and lead to catastrophic consequences. Such security measures cannot be overlooked, and government control is restricting the use of certain machinery and equipment to high-security facilities, limiting the range of services that healthcare units with lower security may offer.

Another broad category of infrastructure has to do with network development and all associated controls. Medicare processes large amounts of information internally, not to mention the external linkage requirements associated with referrals and national accountability reports that must be processed and sent to government control and data collection agencies and other industry regulatory bodies. The baseline network infrastructure includes servers, end user computer stations, switches, network access points, all associated cabling and external access infrastructure. While very elaborate high-level applications have been incorporated into network infrastructures in a significant number of healthcare facilities, the majority of care units are using their network support equipment for only slightly more than baseline uses, such as record keeping and document sharing.

Needs Analysis in Healthcare Facilities

In order to develop a proper proposal for sustainable IT supplementation in the core processes of the healthcare sector, it is important to identify the main challenges in the sector and specifically those needs that can be sufficiently met by the implementation of sustainable, secure and cost-efficient IT practices. This section will give a detailed needs analysis to lay the foundation for the chapter. The analysis focuses on requirements that may be categorized as operational, administrative, or industry related. During the needs analysis, the problem will be further characterized, a cost–benefit feasibility study will be performed, the scope and value will be defined and the framework for what the system will do is established. The needs analysis may also be referred to as a gap analysis. A gap analysis is a method of assessing the differences in performance between an organizations systems to determine whether business requirements are being met and, if not, what steps should be taken to ensure they are met successfully.[6] These gaps help inform the overall needs assessment. The following text will also describe a number of processes and tools that will aide in establishing the gaps and informing the new system requirements.

Operational Needs

Healthcare facilities need to streamline their core administrative and financial operations with the current global standards in order to foster interoperability in record keeping and analysis with other stakeholders, investors and business partners. Currently, healthcare as an industry is behind average industry standards in IT acceptance. Such processes as payment processing, e-bill systems, human resource systems, stock intake, auditing and other similar functions can be sufficiently integrated with the use of developing software.[7] In order for a system to be sustainable and standard, it is necessary to select a universally accepted platform for data storage and analysis in which organizations may pool data relating to logistics and facilities. Financial as well as private human resource information does not need to be pooled in a central storage facility, but adopting software dedicated to easing these functions on a private level is necessary in order to reduce costs, enhance operational efficiency and increase profitability. Operational needs may be broken down into several areas.

Staff Productivity and Satisfaction

The use of IT may reduce time wasted by operational staff performing administrative work and enhance patient attendance time, which is the key need for patients. It will also reduce unnecessary routines in patient care and reduce work of clinical staff due to rigorous, non-work-related duties. Additionally, it will improve employee satisfaction and reduce fatigue due to extensive overtime schedules. Better productivity will invariably lead to increased patient volumes.

Increased Revenue and Cost Optimization

Increased visitor capacity per unit may boost revenues for a care unit due to a larger number of admissions and discharges per month following shortened lengths of stay, reduced unit costs for bulk purchases and improved capability to meet overhead expenses. Cost optimization needs to be realized through bulk purchases, efficient stock control and reduced cost per day for each patient. In this regard, IT practices will save costs for the unit as well as daily treatment and accommodation charges to the customer.

Patient Safety

A significant number of deaths and serious medical malpractice cases are reported each year due to errors in treatment, procedures or prescriptions. The major cases involve ADEs due to wrong prescriptions that affect patients negatively, admissions following adverse drug events, errors in surgical procedures, blood transfusions and malpractice expenses such as corrective procedures, court litigations and compensations. There is an urgent need to reduce such occurrences, many of which can be satisfactorily handled by the application of proper IT processes.

Quality of Care

Patient quality of care deals with the satisfaction that patients get from care providers' efforts to resolve their problems. It may involve time of delay, time of treatment, appropriateness of procedures used and drugs administered and the levels of professionalism, confidentiality and courtesy of the staff. Moreover, it may involve specific professional services, such as recognition and accreditations, complication management, physician or nurse time with patients and reduced length of stay.[7]

Patient Access to Services

Apart from the length of stay, patients are concerned with delay time for such processes as lab reports, billing, online services such as viewing and scheduling, preventive care management and outpatient care appointment bookings. There is a need to upgrade systems that can be automated to handle most of the routine work not requiring case-specific diagnosis, such as remote patient appointment bookings and all associated alerts on scheduling, integrated lab linkage with other hospital systems that eliminates the need for extended physical queues at facilities, and electronic procedures for alternative bill settlement by customers. If proper systems are established to meet the outlined objectives, other needs relating to healthcare that cannot be quantified but lie at the core of healthcare provision will also be realized. This will lead to nonmonetary benefits such as good patient–physician relationships and improved community health.[7]

Tools for Accomplishing the Needs Analysis

Needs analysis can be conducted through a variety of tools. The most common include observation, interviews, review of documentation, surveys and data analysis.

Needs Summary

The foregoing discussion highlights the need for all-around IT supplementation to help healthcare catch up with other sectors in terms of modernization and integration. In essence, what is required is sufficient planning to implement safe, sustainable and cost-effective IT practices to help healthcare in (1) administrative, (2) operational, (3) patient-related and (4) industry-related functions. There is a need for a seamless backbone IT platform that integrates these four needs, as well as sustainable controls for the IT implementation to ensure it remains secure, serves the maximum purpose possible and is practical for universal adaptability in order to satisfy the core concern within various healthcare institutions, which is the integration of policy implementation.

Needs Prioritization

While all the needs listed above are urgent and important, there are certain ones that must be prioritized in order for IT acceptance in healthcare to stand. These processes are the backbone of healthcare, and all other requirements

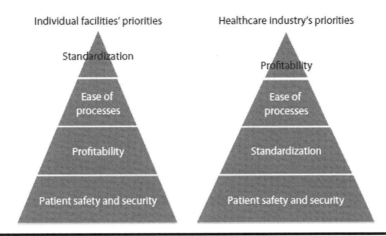

Figure 4.1   Differing priorities of individual facilities and the healthcare industry.

are built on them. For instance, patient security and safety are core driving factors for any practitioner, and they surpass the need for good bookkeeping or profit optimization. Without proper observance of fundamental safety concerns, healthcare units are likely to face legal implications that could cause them to lose their license, rendering futile any advancement they may have in their other operations. This section will therefore seek to address the need for prioritization of IT acceptance in healthcare facilities based on the hierarchy of the needs model. The needs prioritization process helps drive the likelihood of project acceptance. The primary priority from an individual facility's perspective is patient safety, followed by profitability, then ease of processes and lastly, industry standardization. From the healthcare industry's perspective, the priorities are likely to be patient safety and security, professionalism, standardization, profitability and ease of processes. Obviously, the ease of processes is in most cases tied with profitability.[8] The project must therefore address IT implementation issues from both perspectives and attempt to strike a balance. Figure 4.1 illustrates the differing priorities of individual facilities and the healthcare industry.

Workflow and Process Mapping

Workflow and process mapping serve as mechanisms by which to understand current processes and how work is performed to begin the change management process and serve to support the functional data and technical strategies.[9] These two methods can also help identify broken processes and provide an opportunity to address them before a system automates them. This also helps recognize the need for process improvement through automation. Process mapping guides functional specifications where a product may not address all functionality an organization may need or want. It helps visualize the need for standard data structures.[9] This can also be termed process redesign or process reengineering. Workflow aids system configuration during implementation, provides scenarios to create test cases from and guides new users of the system regarding how the process with change with the new system. Workflow and process mapping identify how work is currently performed and the sequence of steps involved. There are a variety of forms these diagrams. Some tools include activity diagrams, swim lane charts, data flow diagrams, system flowcharts, entity relationship diagrams, class diagrams and uses cases.

Current Clinical Processes

Operations and processes in the healthcare sector can be analyzed in four broad categories: administrative and financial, operational, process flow and standardization.

Figures 4.2 and 4.3 present typical process flow diagrams that aid in identifying areas of two healthcare processes that are manageable using IT.[10] Process diagrams and flowcharts are a visual representation of a process that show the boundaries of the process, the steps and the sequence in which the steps take place. These visual representation will use standard symbols, but different approaches and different symbol sets may be used, e.g. ISO 5807 and Unified Modeling Language (UML).

Figure 4.2 shows the process flow for a typical client briefing about lab reports. A nurse will usually try to reach a patient more than four times in stated durations, usually from a few hours to a day. This process takes time, delays other functions and consequently leads to fewer patients served per day. The proper IT implementation, even on the internal level, may allow convenient patient briefing and follow-up using trusted e-mail services, among other channels. Patients can usually be given the option to choose their preferred channel of communication before leaving the hospital or other care facility.

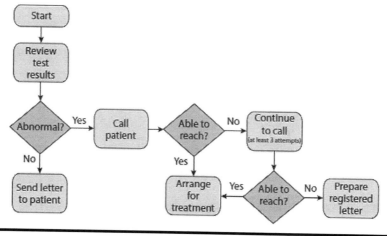

Figure 4.2   Process 1: Laboratory results patient information process.

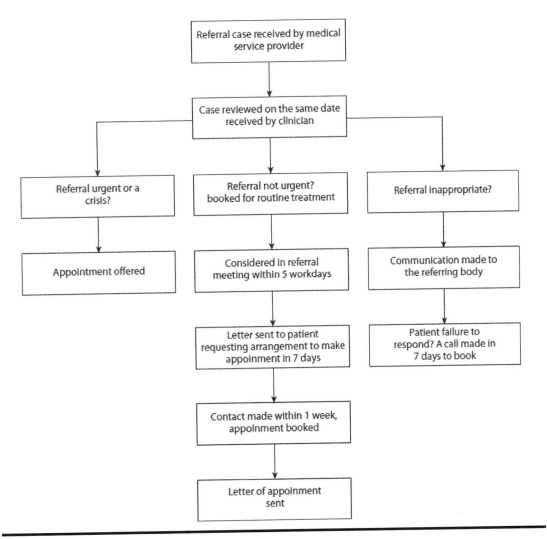

Figure 4.3   Process 2: Referral-patient booking process.

A typical referral process involves even more delay. The referral-patient booking process is diagrammed in Figure 4.3.[11] The figure clearly demonstrates delays introduced in current healthcare systems due to lack of integration between the communication and decision-making systems involving care providers, referral centers and patients. In the workflow diagram, it may be noted that a referral patient may wait up to two weeks between the date of referral and the date of appointment booking solely due to communication and work arrangement delays. Referrals may not appear urgent on the reported data sheet, but patients' situations may become aggravated during the waiting period when they are unable to obtain help. As a result, patient services may be greatly compromised due to the systems' inefficiency. In addition, the lengthy waiting period can be greatly reduced if proper IT policies that incorporate remote meetings, such as video and audio conferencing, are implemented. The time spent between contacting a patient and receiving a response constitutes service degradation for the patient and revenue loss for the care provider.

A reduced number of patients are seen per day; therefore, customer satisfaction levels may also decline. While authentication issues may be cited as the reason for insistence on the use of official letters by care providers, the bulk of the processes requiring care provider–client correspondence involve non-vital documents, such as requests for bookings. A possible method of bypassing this hindrance through the IT-based communication implementation is to develop a web-based communication and client support system that would allow secure communication between the customer and the care provider. In this platform, customers would be able to receive e-mails and respond to booking notifications. Modern day patient portals are beginning to address this need, but the implementation and use of these systems is still lagging.

In addition, digital signing is a standard that is progressively being adopted by many industry sectors and is a concept that may be beneficial to healthcare providers when they send documents requiring authorization or authentication. As an alternative, the use of registered mailing services may greatly reduce the feedback duration for sensitive medical cases. Apart from the operational perspective, billing systems and other workflow routines in most facilities are also very inefficient. The entire process, which includes a medical history review, booking to be attended by the physician, physician duration, prescription, queuing at the pharmacy and bill settlement, involves avoidable delays. These work stages can be sufficiently improved by computer-aided work management and decision-making.

As workflows begin to be examined naturally other key factors to the analysis process will begin to take form. This really begins the requirements gathering processes as well.

Functional Needs Assessment

The functional needs assessment describes the key capabilities or application requirements for achieving the benefits of the system as the organization has envisioned it.[9] This process is important because every organization begins from a different starting point, every organization has different needs and every vendor offers a different approach.

This process is best achieved through surveying users and reviewing use cases. Users should be asked to identify what functionality they need and perhaps rank/prioritize them. Although in the early stages of the project a user's understanding of what may be possible may be limited, it is still important to understand this as you may need to plan for additional functionality in later phases of the project. Knowing this helps ensure that you are selecting a product that will best meet all these needs, including current and potential future needs. You may also be able to identify users who have had exposure to different systems and will be able to provide feedback regarding their experiences. This also allows users to be more engaged in the process which is a critical component of implementation success.

The use case approach is often easier for clinicians to understand. A use case is a scenario that essentially describes a system behavior as it responds to a request that originates outside of that system. It will describe the interaction between the actor who initiated the interaction (such as a clinician) and the system itself. Clinicians can began to form these use cases as they consider patient care events. From these depictions of scenarios, additional visualizations can be created, e.g. process diagrams, but ultimately it will result in a listing of functional requirements to achieve the patient care use case. As part of this, current functional capabilities can be inventoried which will help users see the scope of current capabilities, as well as establish a foundation on which to understand what essential functional capability may be missing and is needed in support of other, more robust capabilities.

Requirements Analysis

The requirements analysis is going to be the documented record of what the system actually does. It is a critical component to keep the project aligned with the identified scope. It is essential to the testing process, as the information gathered in the requirements analysis will produce test cases that can then be used to validate that the system meetings the project requirements. These use cases will begin with a high-level description of the process and will furthermore include a detailed description of each requirement. Often use cases will also include a graphical depiction. This document will describe the future state and is the primary input document for estimating resources, cost and time needed for the project. It will also take into account the needs assessment and further inform the needs prioritization. Requirements are often categorized as follows: functional and workflow, reporting/analysis capabilities, regulatory requirement, data/database, security, system performance and response time, disaster recovery, platform compatibility, interface and interoperability, physical plant consideration, client devices and network.

Document Analysis

In addition to documenting the sequence of steps and decision points in the process, workflow and process mapping should also be accompanied by a collection of all of the associated documents and a documents analysis should be performed. This will also help define the data requirements associated with each process. When working with a vendor they will sometimes provide organizations with a tool to conduct this, while other times a spreadsheet is just as efficient and effective.[9]

Additional Inventories

In addition to the various information-gathering techniques described previously, some additional inventories to be considered include an applications inventory and a reports inventory. In the applications inventory the organization identifies all of the applications that currently exist and how they may or may not be related to one another. This too will help identify the functional requirements of the new system as it leverages and interacts with current applications. It may also help to identify additional applications that could be replaced by the new system. The reports inventory serves as a document of all of the current reports being used/produced by current systems. Again, this too can inform the functional assessment regarding what may need to be produced from the new system.

Process Improvement

These various steps may also lead to process improvement opportunities throughout the analysis phase, and the project as a whole. As workflows and processes are examined and evaluated any improvement opportunities that can be addressed prior to the system design may save time in the long run and produce a better system. Process improvement involves the business practice of identifying, analyzing and improving existing business processes to optimize performance, meet best practice standards, or simply improve quality and the user experience for customers and end users. Process improvement can have several different names such as business process management (BPM), business process improvement (BPI), business process re-engineering and continual improvement process (CIP).[12]

Everything everyone does in an organization is part of a process. To improve the organization, you must focus on the processes. Process improvement is a fundamental step in business management and here are many different accepted ways to improve process. A couple of examples are the DMAIC and PDCA models.

DMAIC

DMAIC stands for define, measure, analyze, improve and control. The DMAIC model is a data-driven quality strategy used to improve processes.

- Define the opportunity for improvement
- Measure the performance of the existing process
- Analyze the process to find any deficiencies
- Improve the process by addressing the root causes uncovered
- Control the improved process and future processes performance to correct deviations before they result in defects and to prevent reverting back to the "old way"

PDCA/PDSA

There is also the PDCA/PDSA model, which stands for plan, do, check/study and act. This is a cyclical model that is also iterative, following a four-stage management method used for the control and continuous improvement of processes.

- Plan
  - Identify and analyze the problem or opportunity
  - Develop hypotheses about the cause of the problem
  - Decide which to test

- Do
  - Test the potential solution on a small scale
  - Measure results

- Check/Study
  - Study results
  - Measure effectiveness
  - Decide whether the hypotheses are supported by the data or not

- Act
  - If the pilot solution is successful, implement it

Deficiencies in Current IT Healthcare Practices

From the discussion provided above regarding process flows in the healthcare sector's IT policies and practices, it can be seen that there are still some obstacles to customer satisfaction, healthcare business profitability and industry integration. These obstacles, which are restricting the sector's potential growth, will be analyzed in this section based on the industry's key performance indicators (KPIs). Client satisfaction through good services and support, business growth through revenue generation, efficient service process arrangement and proper implementation integration can be attained through the corporate initiative.

Patient Support and Satisfaction

Unnecessarily high numbers of patients leave healthcare units without treatment due to long waits for service. Physicians see fewer patients per day when lengthy delays are caused by lack of proper equipment. Such slow systems also lead to extra work for the available personnel, which causes degradation in service quality. Proper patient support and safety also have a correlation with employee retention and employee satisfaction. When healthcare workers are overwhelmed, they tend to perform more poorly and have higher exit rates than workers in places where IT supports workflow management.

Reduction in Revenue Generation

Many healthcare systems are not efficient in revenue generation, and there is a possibility for improvement through IT innovation. Delays in customer service lead to low numbers of attended patients per day, which results in revenue losses. In addition, many patients leave unattended, which leads to business loss. On top of this, healthcare facilities lose potential clients who might have been referred by existing customers if they had not been annoyed by long wait times. In addition to losing business, healthcare units incur extra expenses due to overtime work by doctors and nurses when workloads are heavy. These increased operational expenses and reduced business revenue contribute to overall reduction in business profitability. Inefficient facilities also require a significantly higher number of workers to cope with the physical workflow and lack of integration, which results in extra costs.[13]

Prescription Errors

The current healthcare system does not fully utilize software-supported decision-making for medication orders, even though it would greatly enhance the checking of prescriptions to ensure proper diagnosis support, drug type and dosage. This has resulted in numerous prescription errors, which may lead to adverse patient reactions and deaths. Improper prescriptions have also led to an increase in drug-related claims, legal penalties, license withdrawals and other challenges that could be avoided by proper IT support.

Industry Standardization

Continued lack of healthcare IT standards has led to the loss of tremendous opportunities to improve interoperability, data sharing and transitions of care. This situation will be significantly changed when sustainable policy frameworks can be agreed upon and implemented by IT experts and enforced by government to expand the implementation of IT integration.

Alternative Approaches to Current Healthcare Processes

To increase revenue, provide a seamless link between facilities and regions and improve the patient experience in healthcare workflows, certain IT-based procedures can be implemented. The following sections explore these alternatives according to the deficiency area.

Industry Standardization

The Healthcare Information Technology Standards Panel (HITSP) and the Office of the National Coordinator (ONC) have made many positive achievements in IT integration over the last couple of decades. While there are numerous challenges in such an attempt and many success stories, we continue to work toward this accomplishment through different avenues.[14] Future initiatives might include a new integrated architecture that would meet a cross section of market needs. This platform would be such as to link with all major existing software and hardware configurations in the market, such as EHRs, data management systems (DMSs) and imaging programs, among others.

Alternative Ways to Reduce Prescription Errors

Unlike the global integration challenge, prescription errors can be handled from a local perspective while awaiting the market integration standards. Many software applications are dedicated to prescription information and decision-support systems. Avoidance of ADEs is one major KPI that can be addressed by IT implementation in the healthcare sector. One such software category is a CDSS, which provides updated information regarding recommendations for prescriptions to nurses, physicians and other qualified healthcare workers. This system is typically integrated with the EHR and CPOE systems in order to perform a proper scenario analysis with appropriate patient backup before a provider writes a prescription. Many commercially available software options offer this functionality.

Alternative Processes for Revenue Generation

Financial processes are, perhaps, the easiest to simulate in IT process integration due to their general nature and resemblance to other industries' financial processes. Revenue generation draws primarily from workflow optimization, which mainly seeks to reduce query time and thus queue time, reduce waiting time through the implementation of fast patient data retrieval and diagnostic support and reduce laboratory scheduling and patient briefing time by enhancing fast decision-relay procedures and online client information alternatives. Online support may be an easy way for patients to obtain their lab results electronically signed by their care providers without having to wait in queue. Such a system is not out of reach and may be developed by most modern web applications. In addition to saving time and encouraging more customers, an IT-based process would lead to higher levels of perceived efficiency, productivity, better customer experiences and satisfaction and therefore more referrals.

This chain of flow would, in turn, generate more revenue and lead to higher growth rates. Many software applications have support for workflow management, and most of them do not require very high initial investments in comparison to the average capital requirements of a modern healthcare facility.

Comparative Analysis of Alternatives

This section summarizes the current versus expected status of various aspects of a healthcare IT implementation.

Intended achievements attributable to the new system implementation are presented in Table 4.1 and supported by various research into IT-related healthcare practices. While the extent to which key industry players may benefit from the implementation of these new IT practices may vary, it is likely

Table 4.1 Comparative Analysis of Core Processes in Healthcare

Variables	Current Status	IT-Enhanced Status
Patient service	Lengthy queue times, typically 20 minutes Long durations for record retrieval Long wait times for lab reports, prescriptions and correspondence	Queue times reduced by up to two times Instant record retrieval Shortened lab report delays, instant prescription information and instant messaging
Service processes	Manually coordinated Delays and inefficiency in processes Duplicated work and delayed completion Lack of feedback and rigid decision-making	Computer simulated and optimized Very efficient monitoring Proper process scheduling Decisions based on feedback with continuous dynamic optimization
Erroneous prescriptions	Prevalent errors, with numerous legal and financial implications High admission rates for ADEs Capacity limited by number of prescription-related admissions	Greatly reduced number of prescription errors and minimal revenue loss Greatly reduced admissions due to ADEs More capacity for new cases due to reduction of ADEs
Industry standardization	Highly localized Business losses due to lack of interoperability Limited data access	Universally available Enhanced business due to interoperability Optimized data access and improved quality of care

that the net results will be beneficial.[15] In addition, the capital implications of implementing IT-based healthcare support systems are within investment range. Long-term investment costs should be recoverable from the benefits obtained from healthcare interoperability.

Work Plan Development

Also part of this phase is the start of the development of the work plan. A work plan is aimed at establishing a step-by-step implementation setup for a project, including materials and equipment layout, intended workflow processes, managing the time, analyzing processes and evaluating outcomes. In the healthcare IT implementation plan, a proper work plan involves putting in place procedures to realize the needs for IT acceptance by healthcare facilities, starting with the primary priorities and proceeding to other priorities.[6] Sample elements of a work plan are presented below.

Executive Summary

This project is aimed at analyzing the efficiency of the current systems in healthcare and assessing the situation with the purpose of providing a working alternative that is IT enhanced and will lead to the realization of target objectives of the sector. The plan will provide the project implementation phases as well as define specific operations to be carried out during each phase.

Introduction and Background

The implementation of IT policies in healthcare has been faced with many challenges, rendering the process complex and nonstandardized.[15] Establishing a comprehensive industry standardization process has been impossible due to various individual interests among care providers, drug and device manufacturers, pharmaceutical companies and regulating bodies. Thus, there has been a diverse range of new drugs and other medication practices localized in small market segments without proper administration and regulation. In addition, a wide network of healthcare facilities operating in different geographical, economic, technological and cultural settings has made it difficult for the various stakeholders to come together and develop an enhanced global EHR system that will ensure standardization of procedures, leading to a net lag in technology acceptance in the healthcare sector. The IT sector, however, has advanced and infiltrated all major sectors on the global platform, forcing all industries to confirm or become outdated. This is the case in the healthcare sector as well, prompting stakeholders to start seeking urgent and sustainable methods in preparation for standardization and alignment with emerging trends on the global IT platform.

Goals and Objectives

The goal of this work is to find a structure for IT integration in the healthcare sector's main processes, which includes cost-effectiveness, patient safety and care, ease of processes and industry standardization. To this end, specific objectives must be identified initially that include the following:

- Evaluation of the current operational situation in each healthcare facility. This step will include analysis of current clinical processes such as process mapping. It will also document the current trends that can be found in healthcare procedures, including administrative and operational trends and integration of workflows.
- Identification of the major problems in these processes with respect to the optimization of the IT use. This stage will involve comparing the efficiency of the current processes with the efficiency typically achievable in a similar setting with IT implementation.
- Identification of alternative solutions to these problems through the implementation of IT policies. This process will involve providing alternative solutions to the current processes and include software and hardware recommendations, as well as a proposal for a working interface with existing resources.
- Carrying out a comparative analysis of the alternative processes and the original routines. Flow charts, tables, process flows and other analytic tools will show relationships and deviations between the systems, thereby guiding the policy implementation decisions.
- Evaluation of alternative solutions in alignment with the specific objectives set out in the plan. This stage will involve rethinking the project intentions and comparing them with realized outcomes to assess efficiency.
- Evaluation of the ethical, legal, social and economic implications of the alternatives through a comprehensive cost–benefit analysis.
- Developing a proposal for implementing recommendations and following up after the project to enable quality improvement.

Resources

The plan will usually involve the purchase of additional materials, as well as the hiring of support staff. The major resources should be assigned as follows:

- Personnel - The category will involve all people contracted in the rollout process, including software support teams, simulation teams, project evaluation teams, engineers in various capacities, technical teams and other necessary personnel.
- Partners - These may be governments, government-sponsored partners, nongovernment organizations and private investment agencies, among other stakeholders.

- Equipment - This includes facilities and computers, software and related capital purchases.
- Legal and regulatory infrastructure intended for the implementation of IT.

Work Plan Accountability

The resources available for the implementation of a proposal will be regulated and governed by a project management or steering committee that will be responsible for budgetary allocations, expenditure monitoring and accounts reconciliation. In addition, time management will be essential in order to complete the phases of the project implementation within the specified timeframe.

Proposal Evaluation

The organizational business plan for most healthcare facilities has four major objectives: patient satisfaction, revenue generation, efficient processes that cut costs and increase profits and conformity to industry standards. The proposed solution model should meet all those requirements. First, patient satisfaction is achieved through efficient processes that reduce delay time, enhance the customer experience and offer a good follow-up on patient issues. Second, revenue generation is enhanced through shortened staff time spent per patient, which leads to increased daily patient attendance figures. Third, efficiency in the process flows reduces work duplication and improves service quality, both of which increase revenue generation through cost cutting. Fourth, the proposal expressly seeks to establish a platform for standardization of healthcare IT processes. In summary, the proposed solution enhances the general business requirements and objectives for the average healthcare provider and ultimately the patient. Additionally, the following tools may also strengthen the proposal.

Cost–Benefit Feasibility Study

The stakeholders who stand to gain or lose due to this policy implementation are healthcare facilities, patients, medical practitioners' representative bodies, drug and medical equipment manufacturers, state and federal governments and related authorities and computer equipment and software manufacturers and vendors. The expected cost–benefit elements include finance, service quality, control and time, among others. The important variables to be considered in the analysis are the time of implementation, cost of implementation, alternatives to the proposal, impact on stakeholders, impact on external parties, sustainability versus ongoing operating costs per year and value of time to be used in the implementation.

Table 4.2 provides a sample of a cost–benefit feasibility study for the enhanced IT project.

The anticipated outcome of the cost–benefit feasibility study predicts a continuous reduction in investment costs and a net increment in revenue generation for manufacturers of products that support or can be adapted to the

Table 4.2   Cost–Benefit Feasibility Study of Proposed Healthcare IT Implementation

Variables	Costs	Benefits
Financial implications	• Internal equipment and software upgrade • Licensing fees • Loss of investment for users of nonstandard applications	• Increased revenues of up to 50% per year • Access to the global interoperability platform
Customers	• Possible compromise of privacy and safety due to malicious information access and manipulation	• Improved services, care and access to records • Reduction of prescription errors and resources wasted due to ADEs
Drug and medical equipment manufacturers and related bodies	• Possible losses in equipment standardization, but generally minimal negative effects	• Better policy implementation due to globalization of standards • Less counterfeiting and associated losses • Possibility of forming stronger representative bodies
Governments standards	• Reduced control of medical and healthcare practices for member states • Possible realignment of the structure to include international representation	• Increased diplomatic ties • Better availability of globally competitive healthcare standards for citizens • Achievement of core objective of standardization of healthcare
Hardware and software developers and manufacturers	• Possible loss of business for companies whose products fail to support the new standards	• Numerous opportunities for new developments and increase in sales

new standard, healthcare facilities and drug and medical equipment manufacturers. Similarly, the net long-term outcome for the patient is better service, improved quality of care and greater satisfaction.

Proposal Sensitivity Analysis

Any proposed IT implementation may exhibit various levels of sensitivity to different stakeholders at different times and also to all stakeholders over the course of time. The project's sensitivity to these challenges or changes in the environment will rely on the establishment of a support team to ensure conformity of a project's various elements and initiatives.

RFI/RFP/RFQ

The various processes of systems planning and systems analysis including determining the strategic objectives, defining the usability requirements, completing the various aspects that contribute to the functional needs assessment and determining the buy vs. build strategy, all contribute to the acquisition strategy. If a decision is made to buy a product, a formal selection process takes place and this is discussed more in Chapter 6. However, in these earlier phases the information gathering regarding viable products and vendor selection begins with the request for information (RFI) and request for proposal (RFP) processes. Through these two processes, the organization should be seeking to understand:[9]

- Does the vendor share the same vision for the product as the organization?
- Does the product meet the key functionality needed to achieve the organizations strategic objectives?
- Does the product/vendor utilize the appropriate technology?
- Does the vendor qualify in regards to the organizations acquisition policies?
- Can the vendor support the organizations implementation strategy?
- What is the vendor's track record for operations and maintenance support?
- What is the vendor's viability in the market?

Request for Information

RFIs are not utilized today as much as they used to be. With the popularity of information sharing through web services and trade shows, much of the information that has traditionally been requested through the RFI process is largely available on a company's website and through demonstrations. However, a RFI is intended to be an informal request for information that does not require commitment from either party. It is a collection of documents designed to collect information regarding prospective vendors and their ability to meet the defined need or high-level requirements. Should an organization still desire to execute the RFI process, it is generally a two or three page set of questions on the following areas:[9]

- Company background (size, years in business, number of employees, product lines)
- Product information (product name, product history, technical platform, overview of product capabilities)
- Market information (major competitors and identification of key differentiators)
- Installed base and clients (number of products the company has sold, how may they are currently implementing, number fully installed)
- Special criteria (anything that the vendor has identified as unique or established as critical)

This information in combination with website research should result in a pool of about 10 to 20 products/vendors, with the intent to narrow this list down to only a handful to further evaluate. Tools like a vendor comparison map, which can be used to plot responses to key criteria and help narrow down the large list of vendors to the smaller list to pursue further.

Request for Proposal

Once the list has been narrowed, the organization should then complete the RFP process. The RFP is a formal request sent to vendors that ultimately leads to a contract between the organization and the selected vendor(s). This process is used to obtain more detailed information with more specificity placed on what the organization has identified as their system requirements. All vendors are asked the same questions, which helps foster a more consistent review and selection process. It would be most appropriate to send the RFP to the four of five vendors that seem to best fit the organization's overall criteria. Note here that the number of RFPs sent may also be dependent on the type of organization. Public organizations may be required to send RFPs to every eligible vendor. In general, RFPs have some fairly typical components including:[9]

■ Organizational profile (describes the organization seeking the new vendor including; basic demographics, mission and goals, vision for the product(s), current information infrastructure, any specific constraints, instructions for responding to the RFP, how many copies will be sent and how vendor questions will be directed)

■ Vendor information (description of its demographics (size and longevity, years in business, revenues, profitability, number of employees), product research and development history and plans, types of installations (number, size, status), corporate composition, references, user group information and contract history)

■ Functional specifications (description of functional capability and processes and workflows the product supports)

■ Operational requirements (data architecture, analytical processes supports, necessary interfaces, reliability and security features, system capacity, expansion capabilities, response time, downtime and other system maintenance issues)

■ Technical requirements (vendor should propose the appropriate technical architecture to meet the organization's functional specifications and operational requirements, specific hardware and networking and software requirements)

■ Application support (the proposed implementation schedule describing data conversion, acceptance testing, training and documentation, ongoing support and maintenance, which may include information regarding any service level agreements (SLAs) and upgrades)

■ Licensing and contractual details (supply the specific bid for one-time and recurring costs based on the organization's requirements, standard contract,

financing arrangements, proposed relationship with hardware vendors, warranty information, any clauses that protect the organization should the vendor go out of business)
■ Evaluation criteria (provided to let the vendor know up front the most important elements of the evaluation and how certain factors are weighted)

Request for Quotation

Although a RFP may include pricing information (as described above in the licensing and contractual details description), it has also become more commonplace to also complete a request for quotation (RFQ) or a request for bid to obtain a price from which to negotiate.[8] This approach can help minimize the influence of cost from the other critical evaluation factors obtained through the RFP process. The RFQ can be more suitable than the RFP if the organization has thoroughly studied products and concluded that a small number are very similar.

Non-Disclosure Agreement

As part of these processes, organizations should also consider sending a non-disclosure agreement (NDA) or confidentiality agreement to each vendor. The purpose of an NDA is to protect both companies from disclosing confidential information. An NDA includes legal terminology that, in effect, states that the vendor cannot disclose information about your company to anyone without your express permission. It may also be written as a two-way NDA, meaning that the organization cannot disclose information either.[16] Any vendor who is being sent confidential information about your company should be sent the NDA and this should be signed and executed prior to releasing any information about your organization. In some cases, similar terms regarding confidential information that is exchanged between parties may be included in a master client agreement rendering an additional NDA unnecessary. Breaching these types of agreements can be very costly, so it is very important to understand the terms on agreement and identifying what is considered confidential.[16] Your organizations legal counsel should be involved in reviewing the terms of any agreements that are signed.

Cost–Benefit Analysis

The information obtained from these processes, more so the RFP or RFQ, can also be used to inform a cost–benefit analysis (CBA). A CBA is a process that uses quantitative techniques to evaluate and measure the benefit of providing products or services compared to the cost of providing them.[9] The CBA is going to evaluate both the costs (considering things such as hardware, software, installation and training, maintenance and support) and the benefits (considering things such as cost savings or avoidance that are achieved by the new functionality [e.g. charge capture, decision support, diagnostics studies, financial management, medical record operations, nursing department, referral management, etc.]). Taking into consideration the costs and achieved benefits, the net impact is determined for each year by subtracting the cost from the benefits (in Figure 4.4 below this in depth CBA factored in the present value (PV) and determined the accumulated net present value (NPV)). A typical period is established, such as five years, and the exercise is repeated for each year identifying both the costs and benefits for each year. The CBA also visually shows how costs change over time, e.g. many being front-loaded with lower ongoing costs or some being one-time costs and how and when benefits are realized. Once the costs and benefits are mapped, it becomes easier to identify how long it will take to achieve the payback period of the investment and furthermore when the organization will actually see a financial benefit from the implementation and provides that validation that the benefits of the recommended solution are equal to or greater than the costs.

Figure 4.4 provides a sample of a cost–benefit analysis.

All of this information is used to inform the system selection process, which is discussed in more detail in Chapter 6.

Item	2006 (0)	2007 (1)	2008 (2)	2009 (3)	2010 (4)	2011 (5)	2012 (6)	2013 (7)	Total
Cost									
System costs									
System infrastructure	1,241	-	-	-	98	93	88	84	1,604 (10.0)
System application	1,006	1,274	315	192	188	184	179	174	3,512 (21.9)
Office supply	306	286	-	105	102	98	95	91	1,084 (6.7)
Sub-total	2,554	1,560	315	296	388	375	363	348	6,199 (38.6)
Induced costs									
Paper-charts scan	-	-	724	519	-	-	-	-	1,243 (7.7)
MTs support	166	1,186	1,107	1,118	1,185	1,313	1,255	1,281	8,612 (53.6)
Sub-total	166	1,186	1,831	1,636	1,185	1,313	1,255	1,281	9,854 (61.4)
Total PV of annual costs	2,720	2,746	2,146	1,934	1,573	1,687	1,618	1,630	16,054 (100.0)
Benefit									
Cost reductions									
Supplies for paper-charts	11	52	258	100	248	91	231	3	1,076 (5.5)
Chart storage space	-	-	14	145	142	139	135	129	703 (3.6)
Chart management FTE	-	-	180	782	799	847	816	807	4,231 (21.5)
Clerks decreased	-	-	165	165	165	165	165	164	990 (5.0)
Supplies for MDIS	7	67	78	415	168	165	161	155	944 (4.8)
Sub-total	18	120	695	1,335	1,522	1,408	1,507	1,339	7,945 (40.4)
Additional revenues									
From remodeling storage	-	-	-	17	26	35	25	21	125 (0.6)
From temporary storage	-	-	261	300	280	275	269	262	1,646 (8.4)
From MT support	-	-	551	1,411	1,421	2,747	1,928	1,899	9,956 (50.6)
Sub-total	-	-	811	1,728	1,727	3,056	2,223	2,182	11,727 (59.6)
Total PV of annual benefits	18	120	1,506	3,063	3,249	4,465	3,731	3,521	19,672 (100.0)
Accumulated NPV	(2,702)	(5,329)	(5,969)	(4,839)	(3,163)	(385)	1,726	3,617	
Benefit-cost ratio									1.23
Discounted payback period									6.18

Figure 4.4   Cost–Benefit Analysis (Unit: 1,000 US$)[17]

Applied currency exchange rates: 1US$= 1,100K.

Summary

Implementing a new system requires a thorough analysis of current processes and workflows, documentation of requirements and identification of future-state workflows, with careful consideration given to usability and end user acceptance. Project planning and control helps to ensure the project will meet objectives and be completed on time and within budget. In some cases, requirements will lead to the generation of an RFI and RFP, which are used to inform the system selection process. Planning for the implementation is a critical step and must factor in migration, either from paper or from one system to another. If the project involves an EHR, the IT staff must remain abreast of both regulatory and technological developments to ensure that the clinical system remains current to achieve goals of improved efficiency, quality and patient safety, increased patient engagement, improved care coordination and better measures of population health management.

References

1. Deloitte.Reinventing tech finance: The evolution from IT budgets to technology investments. CIO Insider. January 2020. https://www2.deloitte.com/content/dam/insights/us/articles/6300_CIO-insider-tech-finance/DI_CIO-Insider_Tech-Finance-Budgets.pdf (accessed August 25, 2021).
2. Rave Mobile Safety. Healthcare IT Budgets Forecasted to Increase by 8.8%. https://www.ravemobilesafety.com/blog/healthcare-it-budgets-forecasted-to-increase (accessed August 11, 2020).
3. HIMSS. *HIMSS Dictionary of Health Information and Technology Terms, Acronyms and Organizations, Fifth Edition.* Boca Raton: Taylor & Francis Group, LLC, 2019.
4. Tutorial Points. Systems Analysis and Design – Quick Guide. https://www.tutorialspoint.com/system_analysis_and_design/system_analysis_and_design_quick_guide.htm (accessed June 4, 2020).
5. Journal of Community Hospital Internal Medicine Perspectives. *The alrming reality of medication error: a patient case and review of Pennsylvania and National data.* 2016; 6(4) https://www.ncbi.nlm.nih.gov/pmc/articles/PMC5016741/ (accessed August 25, 2021).
6. TechTarget. *Gap Analysis.* https://searchcio.techtarget.com/definition/gap-analysis (accessed June 4, 2020).
7. Armoni A. *Effective Healthcare Information Systems.* Hershey, PA: IRM Press, 2002.
8. Spekowius G, Wendler T. *Advances in Healthcare Technology Shaping the Future of Medical Care.* Dordrecht, Netherlands: Springer, 2006.
9. Amatayakul MK *Health IT and EHRs, Principles and Practices, Sixth Edition.* Chicago: AHIMA, 2017.
10. National Council of State Boards of Nursing. New nurse toolkit. Chicago: National Council of State Boards of Nursing. https://ncsbn.org/QI-FlowChar.pdf (accessed April 22, 2016).
11. Hertfordshire Partnership NHS Foundation Trust. Schedule 4—Patient booking. Hertfordshire, UK: Hertfordshire Partnership NHS Foundation Trust.

12. White SK What is process improvement? A business methodology for efficiency and productivity. https://www.cio.com/article/3433946/what-is-process-improvement-a-business-methodology-for-efficiency-and-productivity.html (accessed June 5, 2020).

13. Duplaga M, Zielinski K, Ingram D. *Transformation of Healthcare With Information Technologies*. Amsterdam: IOS Press, 2004.

14. Bates D, Gawande A. Improving safety with information technology. *N Engl J Med* 348(25): 2526–2534, 2003.

15. Tyrell S. *Using Information and Communication Technology in Healthcare*. Abingdon, UK: Radcliffe Medical, 2002.

16. Eskelin A Identifying and Contacting Vendors. https://www.informit.com/articles/article.aspx?p=21774 (accessed June 11, 2020).

17. Choi JS, Lee WB, Rhee PL. Cost-benefit analysis of electronic medical record system at a tertiary care hospital. *Healthcare informatics research* 19(3): 205–214, 2013. https://doi.org/10.4258/hir.2013.19.3.205 (accessed June 11, 2020).

Chapter 5

Design

Learning Objectives

At the conclusion of this chapter, the reader will be able to

- Ensure interoperability of software, hardware, network components and medical devices
- Ensure compliance with applicable industry, regulatory and organizational standards
- Ensure a process exists to incorporate industry, technology, infrastructure, legal and regulatory environment trends
- Design an information infrastructure that supports current and anticipated business needs (e.g., business continuity, disaster recovery)
- Evaluate existing and emerging technologies to support organization's future growth and strategy
- Employ and implement effective data management using an established data governance protocol

Introduction

The *Dictionary of Computing* defines *system design* as "the activity of proceeding from an identified set of requirements for a system to a design that meets those requirements."[1] System design depends upon the definition of *system*, which, according to the *Oxford English Dictionary*, means "a set or assemblage of things connected, associated, or interdependent, so as to form a complex unity."[2] Healthcare information technology (HIT) systems today take that complexity to a new level in function and interoperability. These systems must support advanced clinical functionality, patient accounting and financial accounting and have been

DOI: 10.4324/9780429442391-8

doing this for years. The systems must also support functionality demanded by new healthcare regulations, medical devices, mergers and acquisitions, as well as address changes and advances in the information technology (IT) industry.

Compatibility and interoperability are two key aspects of system design. Considering the complexity and criticality of enterprise IT systems in healthcare, it is essential to ensure any new medical devices, software, hardware, or network components are compatible and interoperable.

Compliance with applicable industry, regulatory and organizational standards is a fundamental aspect of system design. Healthcare organizations could face severe implications for not adhering to these standards. A key best practice in system design is the development of a comprehensive technical specification. The design team documents design specifications regarding the infrastructure, network, security, application and use cases based on the requirements uncovered during system analysis. For more information on defining and prioritizing system requirements, refer to Chapter 4 "Systems Analysis."

Compatibility and Interoperability of System Components

Any healthcare enterprise today owns and continually purchases a plethora of hardware, software, network components and medical devices. The hardware may include laptop computers, servers, mobile devices and tablets, each running its own operating system (OS) that is not necessarily compatible with other operating systems. The application software that runs on these devices serves a variety of purposes from patient accounting to payroll, laboratory, pharmacy, radiology, dietetics, digital pathology and so on. Network components include routers (wired and wireless), firewalls, cabling and Internet connectivity. Networks today must support connectivity of devices within the enterprise as well as Wi-Fi access for patients and visitors. Medical devices such as ultrasounds, magnetic resonance imaging (MRIs), patient monitors, ventilators and even blood pressure cuffs all provide information digitally and must connect to the network as well. For more information on hardware, software and networks, refer to Chapter 2, "Technology Environment."

Organizations should define a process by which the IT department reviews purchases of any of these components for compatibility and interoperability. Remember that not all devices or software will work out of the box. There may be system upgrades involved to incorporate the device onto the network. For example, a new patient monitor may connect to the existing network from a physical standpoint, but may not be compatible with the existing patient monitoring system used to aggregate and distribute waveform data to the electronic health record (EHR). This process dictates close cooperation between the IT department and the procurement/purchasing department so IT has a chance to review purchases, thus avoiding such hidden costs of system and/or device upgrades and potential delays.

Compatibility of medical devices and systems is just one dimension of systems design. Interoperability is equally important. HIMSS defines interoperability as "the ability of different information systems, devices, or applications to connect, in a coordinated manner, within and across organizational boundaries to access, exchange and cooperatively use data amongst stakeholders, with the goal of optimizing the health of individuals and populations."[3] In the patient monitor example above, interoperability may translate to a Health Level Seven (HL7®) interface to the patient monitor to enable admissions, discharges and transfers (ADT) notifications from the existing EHR system.

Standards Compliance

Healthcare providers face a huge number of external standards from government and industry, in addition to their own internal standards. Some of these affect the entire organization, and others affect just one department. Some countries even dictate which vendor IT system the organization must purchase. ASTM International, HL7, Digital Imaging and Communications in Medicine (DICOM®), and other international organizations publish many standards related to healthcare IT. The Institute of Electrical and Electronics Engineers (IEEE) publishes standards for wired and wireless networking used by most countries in the world. Just as an enterprise must have a process to address compatibility of system components, it must also develop a process to address standards compliance. Given the number of standards, this is not a simple effort. There must be an overlap between business process and compliance management. System design should attempt to address standards by the clear definition of technical specifications.

Process to Address Industry Trends

With the extensive changes occurring in healthcare and technology, a process must exist or be created to evaluate and incorporate industry, technology, infrastructure, legal and regulatory trends. This process must address areas that in the past were governed by departments other than IT. The digitization of telephone systems means that these systems generally share the same networks as IT and have become a part of the IT organization. Medical devices such as electrocardiographs, ultrasound and MRI devices now generate millions of bytes of medically relevant data and must be integrated into the electronic patient record. The purchase of such devices must include IT participation to ensure compatibility and interoperability with existing systems.

One of the most critical trending issues facing healthcare IT is cybersecurity. The greatest threat to healthcare networks comes from medical devices. Many computerized medical devices connect to hospital enterprise networks. In the development of these medical devices, enterprise security was not included in the product requirements. In many cases, generally accepted IT security practices like anti-virus software, firewall software and frequent password changes are not compatible with medical devices or the medical devices have significant restrictions on the use of these generally accepted security practices and tools. For example, some medical device vendors discourage customers from using anti-virus software to scan files associated with medical devices. Other medical device vendors hard-code passwords or use obsolete commercial operating systems.

Many healthcare organizations have invested in Innovation Centers within their organization to develop and deploy healthcare technology innovations. An example of this is the Emory Healthcare Innovation Hub (https://www.emoryhub.com). "The Emory Healthcare Innovation Hub is a premier health care advancement and commercialization program that connects all the pieces of the health care continuum to validate, accelerate and realize ideas. Our mission-realize improvements in health outcomes, increase access to quality care, lower overall costs to the system and improve health care provider experiences in Georgia and across the nation." These innovation centers are developing solutions to address problems in the dynamic healthcare environment.

Structure of the System Design Team

The members of the system design team may vary based on the complexity and scope of the project. A project sponsor, one of the team's key members, should kick off the project with the team and help determine the business goals and how those goals should be measured. Once the team has been established and the goals clearly defined, the sponsor may not need to be involved in more detail-oriented design meetings. Below is a list of potential team members:

- Project sponsor
- Project manager
- Solution architect[4]
- Enterprise business architect[4]
- Biomedical engineers
- Application developers
- Quality assurance analysts
- Information security officer
- Stakeholders/users

Detailed Technical Specifications

The design team must create comprehensive and detailed technical specifications that not only cover the function of the system or applications, but also address nonfunctional issues, such as information infrastructure. Some of the key areas of technical specifications that should be addressed are:

- System and wired/wireless network architecture—Does the system have to fit into the organization's existing architectures or may it vary?
- Security and data encryption—Does the system integrate into the organization's security standards?
- Disaster recovery—What is the recovery time objective (RTO) or the time it will take to recover the system in a disaster? What is the recovery point objective (RPO) or to what point in time must the system be restored?
- Data conversion—What are the data conversion options if converting from one system to another with different data models?
- Response times—What are the expected response times and how will they be measured?
- System backups—What are the backup options? How long will backups run?
- System monitoring—How will the system be monitored? Will it fit into the organization's existing monitoring infrastructure?
- Change management—How does the vendor of a newly purchased system handle changes? Is there a regular schedule? Or, is it done at customer convenience?
- Availability—What are the availability requirements? What is the downtime associated with system upgrades?
- Time zone and daylight savings time support—Does the system support multiple time zones, especially if the organization has facilities in different time zones? Are system outages required for spring or fall clock changing?
- Standards—Does the system support integration standards such as HL7, International Statistical Classification of Diseases and Related Health Problems, 10th Revision (ICD-10) or DICOM?
- Government regulations—Does the system meet current government regulations? What is the vendor commitment for turnaround of new regulations?
- System integration—How will the system integrate with the other HIT systems and medical devices in the enterprise?
- Usability—Much focus is being placed on usability today, and that topic will be discussed in more detail below. Usability should include accessibility for persons with disabilities as well as the use of mobile devices.
- Workflow definitions—The definition of desired workflows is another key area of the design that will be discussed in more detail later in the chapter.
- Data management—Does the system fit the organization's data management policies and procedures for such functions as backup, recovery and archiving?
- Antivirus/OS patching policy—Which anti-virus application and versions are supported by the system? Is automated OS/security patching allowed?

Usability

As previously mentioned, interest in usability has grown significantly over the past decade due to increased EHR adoption. HIMSS has created various tools and forums to help clinicians and health IT professionals overcome some of the more common challenges with usability, including the Usability Maturity Model (UMM).[5] IT examines three nonhealthcare usability models and uses common themes from those models to create a healthcare model with five phases:

- Phase 1: Unrecognized—lack of awareness of usability
- Phase 2: Preliminary—sporadic inclusion of usability
- Phase 3: Implemented—recognized value of usability and small teams using it
- Phase 4: Integrated—benchmarks implemented and have dedicated user experience team
- Phase 5: Strategic—business benefit well understood, mandated, budgeted and results used strategically in the organization

The UMM documents how an organization can take itself from one phase to another and recommends the following tactics to expand usability within the organization:

- Include usability in contracts
- Create feedback loops from users to vendors
- Talk about tasks and workflows
- Educate about return on investment related to usability
- Engage organizational leaders in usability
- Include usability metrics on one project
- Interview users to determine key usability issues
- Compile evidence from usability assessments
- Look for and document usability wake-up calls
- Find a business/organization driver supporting need for usability

Information Infrastructure

The information infrastructure must be able to support today's business requirements and anticipate emerging or future business requirements. A continuing trend, known as bring your own device (BYOD), is one example of a requirement prompted by doctors, nurses and other employees who want to use their own notebook computers, tablets or smartphones on the enterprise network. Most healthcare organizations have made investments in secure mobile communications platforms and network infrastructure to support a BYOD strategy. A good example of a future business requirement is the 11th Revision of the International Classification of Diseases (ICD-11).[6] Most healthcare organizations today utilize ICD-10. While today's applications do not support ICD-11, healthcare organizations should consider how new system/applications will support it the future. Overall, an organization should have a process in place to examine or evaluate emerging trends and technologies. This evaluation should be done on a regular basis as new technologies emerge or existing technologies begin to be adopted. As part of the process, the organization should decide where it wants to be on the technology adoption curve (Figure 5.1).

As more and more healthcare records are electronic, business continuity emerges as a key part of the IT infrastructure. Organizations must plan for various types of disasters, whether natural or man-made. Off-site storage of data becomes a minimal requirement. Many sites negotiate contracts with disaster recovery vendors to retain not only copies of data, but also the capability to restore entire systems. Larger organizations may own multiple data centers in which they may mirror their data. Networks must be in place to access these remote sites. The business continuity plan must not only ensure that the remote sites are in place, but also test the plan at frequent intervals to make certain that it can be executed.

Many healthcare organizations now utilize cloud-based applications, which enable on demand availability of computing resources. Cloud computing refers to the provision of applications over the Internet where customers do not have to invest in the hardware and software resource needed to run and maintain the applications. Of particular concern in healthcare, is the security of all application data and customer information. With cloud computing, data is stored on servers/infrastructure not owned by the healthcare organization. The security requirements of the healthcare organization need to be well understood by the cloud vendor and incorporated into the system design.[7]

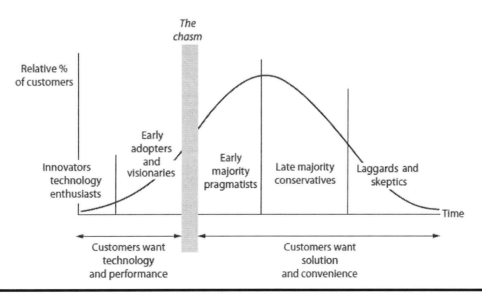

Figure 5.1   Technology adoption curve.

Data Management

Healthcare organizations must address a wide variety of issues related to their data. Data Management International (DAMA®) created a framework for data governance that defines 11 data management knowledge areas[8]:

1. Data Governance—planning, oversight and control over management of data and the use of data and data-related resources
2. Data Architecture—the overall structure of data and data-related resources as an integral part of the enterprise architecture
3. Data Modeling & Design—analysis, design, building, testing and maintenance
4. Data Storage & Operations—structured physical data assets, storage, deployment and management
5. Data Security—ensuring privacy, confidentiality and appropriate access
6. Data Integration & Interoperability –acquisition, extraction, transformation, movement, delivery, replication, federation, virtualization and operational support
7. Documents & Content—storing, protecting, indexing and enabling access to data found in unstructured sources (electronic files and physical records) and making this data available for integration and interoperability with structured (database) data
8. Reference & Master Data—Managing shared data to reduce redundancy and ensure better data quality through standardized definition and use of data values
9. Data Warehousing & Business Intelligence—managing analytical data processing and enabling access to decision support data for reporting and analysis
10. Metadata—collecting, categorizing, maintaining, integrating, controlling, managing and delivering metadata
11. Data Quality—defining, monitoring, maintaining data integrity and improving data quality

The organization must define a process for addressing those data management functions. Then, the system design team must ensure that the system fits into that process.

Summary

Successful system design centers on the design team, which must include the proper members. The design team should create clear, documented technical specifications. Two ways in which the design team can produce such requirements are by examining usability and data management. It is fundamental that the system design ensures the compatibility and interoperability of medical devices, software and hardware components. The system must also comply with industry, regulatory and organizational standards. As healthcare practices are constantly changing and evolving, a process should be in place for evaluating emerging technologies to support the healthcare organization's strategy and mission.

References

1. Daintith J. System design. In *A Dictionary of Computing*. Oxford: Oxford University Press, 2004. https://www.encyclopedia.com/computing/dictionaries-thesauruses-pictures-and-press-releases/system-design (accessed July 19, 2019).
2. System. In OED Online. Oxford: Oxford University Press, 2012. http://www.oed.com (accessed August 11, 2012).
3. HIMSS (Healthcare Information and Management Systems Society). Interoperability Definition. Chicago: HIMSS. https://www.himss.org/library/interoperability-standards/what-is-interoperability (accessed August 1, 2019).
4. The Open Group. TOGAF 9.1: 52.6.2 Characterization in Terms of the Enterprise Continuum. San Francisco: The Open Group https://pubs.opengroup.org/architecture/togaf91-doc/arch/chap52.html (accessed August 3, 2019).
5. HIMSS (Healthcare Information and Management Systems Society). Promoting Usability in Health Organizations: Initial Steps and Progress Toward a Healthcare Usability Maturity Model. Chicago: HIMSS. https://rdcms-himss.s3.amazonaws.com/files/production/public/2013-HIMSS-Usability-Maturity-Model.pdf (accessed April 17, 2020).
6. WHO (World Health Organization). Classification of Diseases (ICD). Geneva: WHO. https://www.who.int/classifications/icd/en/ (accessed August 3, 2019).
7. Hoffer, J. A. Designing distributed and internet systems. Modern Systems Analysis and Design (8th ed) (pp. 425–433). Boston, MA: Pearson, 2017.
8. Data Management International. DAMA-DMBOK2 Framework. Data Management International, 20014. https://www.datasqlvisionary.com/wp-content/uploads/2018/06/DMBOK-Framework.pdf (accessed August 24, 2021).

Chapter 6

Selection, Implementation, Support and Maintenance

Learning Objectives

At the conclusion of this chapter, the reader will be able to:

- Conduct solution selection activities (e.g., identify organizational stakeholders, demonstrations, site visits, reference checks)
- Employ effective technical change management practices
- Identify and execute effective training and support methods (e.g., computer-based learning, classroom training, train the trainer, at-the-elbow support from superusers)
- Implement solutions while managing scope, schedule, budget and quality
- Maintain healthcare information systems (e.g., operate, upgrade)
- Analyze data for problems and trends (e.g., error reports, help desk logs, surveys, performance metrics, network monitoring)

Introduction

The systems selection process begins with the identification of a need and subsequent approval of a project proposal. The successful implementation and adoption of a new application or a system is dependent on an organized system selection process, followed by a well-planned and executed implementation strategy. Once a need has been identified within an organization, an effective governance committee evaluates it against the organizational mission, goals, objectives, information technology (IT) strategic plan, budget and available resources.

DOI: 10.4324/9780429442391-9

Once the decision is made to move forward, objectives, goals and measures of success should be clearly defined. Once the high-level strategy is defined, the team is assembled to analyze and further define the requirements. It is important to have the appropriate team members to ensure the analysis includes all parts of the organization affected by the new solution. Through this analysis, opportunities for process improvement and workflow efficiencies are identified.

Chapter 4 discussed in detail the items that should be included in a request for information (RFI) or request for proposal (RFP). To summarize,

A RFI

- Is an informal request for information that does not require commitment from either party
- Is a collection of documents designed to collect information regarding prospective vendors and their ability to meet the defined need or high-level requirements
- May or may not include budget or cost information

A RFP

- Is a formal request that leads to a contract between the organization and the selected vendor(s)
- Is a collection of documents that outline the detailed requirements and how each responding vendor will be compared for a final decision
- Always includes timelines and budget or cost information

Evaluating the vendors that respond to the RFP includes on-site visits, reference checks, demonstrations and sometimes a trial version or trial period for the system. After the list of possible vendors is narrowed down to a few, contract negotiations allow the organization to get the best possible deal based on price, payment plan, support levels and ongoing support. It is important to include a step to verify any regulations as part of any standard selection practice.

After the application and vendor have been selected, it is time to begin implementation. Understanding the different implementation strategies will help the organization choose the one that best fits its culture, objectives and available resources. Proper planning and a defined methodology will help decrease project risk and lead to a successful activation. For a smooth transition to support, the implementation project should include planning for post-live activities, such as configuration management, user communication, user support and new employee training, along with operations and maintenance, to ensure continuous performance of the system.

Solution Selection Criteria

As mentioned earlier during the analysis phase, system selection begins with a defined need based on the organization's strategic objectives or a solution to a problem that blocks achievement of an organizational or departmental objective. The selection and implementation processes are built around fulfilling the need and realizing the solution that will meet the organization's expected outcomes. There is quite a bit of overlap with the information identified/defined in the systems analysis phase and the solution selection process as much of the analysis information helps inform this process. The process defined below should be used as a template and modified as needed to fit the specific situation and satisfy the current regulatory requirements.

As was described in Chapter 4, the need and justification for a project are often described in a formal business case, project proposal, or a needs assessment. This document outlines the goal and objectives of the request, along with the high-level resources required to meet them. Most organizations request a business case prior to approving the proposed system selection process. If the organization does not require a business case, it is imperative that the IT governance committee request one. The challenge comes from defining the required resources this early in the process. Most often, they are defined through scientific guesses. If time allows, market research can provide more accurate estimates. Market research starts with high-level requirements, not the detailed ones identified later in the process, and may be conducted formally or informally. Formal market research is completed through a process similar to the RFI process. With market research, however, it is clearly stated that the RFI is for research only, with no intent to purchase at this time. The informal process is completed through vendor exhibitions, Internet searches and contact with other similar organizations.

The business case or project proposal should present the need and requirements, not necessarily the solution, but again, it informs the solution selection process. This document should avoid the identification of a single solution, but rather several solutions or recommendations. The governance committee reviews the business case and decides whether to move forward based on the system's fit within the organization's strategic plan or operational goals and the availability of resources to complete.

Once approval to move forward is received, the selection criteria are built on the defined need and high-level requirements that the business case identified as necessary for the solution. Whether the need is to improve office-scheduling processes through automation or to create a paperless environment in an acute care setting, the requirements go beyond end-user functionality to include nonfunctional necessities also.

A list of requirements could include the following:

Functional requirements

- Application with organization-specific functionality
- Security and privacy requirements
- Regulatory requirements
- Reporting capability, including standard and custom reporting
- Integration with other applications or devices
- Interoperability requirements
- Access from multiple locations (acute care, long-term care, clinics, etc.)
- Access from mobile devices
- Redesigned workflow

Decision support functionality/nonfunctional requirements

- Cloud infrastructure
  - Capacity requirements
  - Separate cloud environments for production, development, testing and training
  - Load balancing configuration and requirements
  - Software as a service or platform as a service requirements
- Facility IT infrastructure
  - Space, cooling and power
  - Hardware for production, development, testing and training environments
- Hardware for disaster recovery or high availability
- Hardware for reporting
- Backup and recovery plans and procedures
- Workstation and printer requirements and hardware
- Wired and wireless networks
- System installation, configuration and maintenance documentation
- Supplemental staffing for implementation, training and post live support
- Independent verification and validation to reduce risk by providing impartial reviews of business and technical aspects of the project
- Processes for issue resolution and requests for enhancement
- Maintenance and support process and procedures
- Expected procurement and implementation timeline, along with any constraints that would affect the timeline
- Expected availability, reliability and scalability
- Training requirements

The gap analysis might be the first step in defining these requirements. What is the status of your current application(s)? Are you planning to replace or enhance those systems? What manual processes can and must be improved

through automation? Throughout this process, it is important to focus the analysis on the identified need. Requirement creep can occur very quickly if the team is not focused. The governance committee and executive sponsors are there to help with ensuring the requirements fit within the defined goals and objectives.

Once the requirements are defined, they should be ranked to show which are required, preferred, or optional. It is rare for vendors to be able to meet every requirement, so clarity about which ones are absolutely necessary helps during the evaluation of responses. The rankings should be agreed upon by all committee members and used consistently for all vendors. The requirements and rankings feed into the RFI or RFP documentation as defined earlier in this chapter.

Through this process, a decision to build versus buy should be made. There are many factors that influence this decision. Does the organization have the skill set to build and support the new solution? Is there room in the budget to buy? What is the expected timeline? Which option fits with the organizational IT strategy? Is there a vendor who can meet the need and defined requirements? Based on these factors, the decision to build or buy may occur early in the process, after reviewing the RFI/RFP responses, or anytime in between.

One more analysis to perform is whether a cloud-based technology is preferred over an on premise solution. The analysis should include several criteria such as personnel requirements to install and maintain the software, hardware purchase and maintenance, proper monitoring and auditing and evaluating how well the system aligns with privacy and security requirements in the cloud.

Having the appropriate people involved in the selection process is key to being successful. The governance committee and executive sponsors have already been introduced. A facilitator should be identified early on to ensure that the activity progresses as expected, the defined process is followed and the right people are involved in the review team.

Selecting Review Team Members

The selection of the review team should be completed as early as possible. It is possible that the entire team might not be needed at the very early stages of the process or that some members may not be as actively involved as others. Team members should be identified early so they will be ready to participate when needed. Decisions about team membership should balance the importance of including the right people with the need to keep the size manageable.

The exact members will depend on what is being selected and should include representatives from clinical, organizational operations, IT and the business department to ensure all affected areas are involved. Below is a list of who might be involved in the selection team:

- Facilitator—Provides overall leadership and coordination of the system selection process.
- Executive sponsor—Provides support, clarifies the mission, facilitates necessary resources and acts as champions within the organization.
- Technical representative—Provides technical expertise, such as IT, biomedical and telecommunications.
- Business representative—Provides business or clinical end-user expertise. These individuals are highly knowledgeable about the current business and workflows and represent the end users.
- Program/project manager—Provides implementation and methodology expertise.
- Contracting representative—Provides contracting, negotiation and process expertise.
- Financial representative—Provides budgetary expertise.
- Organizational change leader—Provides expertise related to facilitating change within the organization.
- Governance committee—Provides oversight but is often not directly involved in the team. The selection team reports to this group. Once implementation begins, this group will remain intact to monitor and ensure the project's success. In some organizations, this group is called a steering committee.

The role of team members is to represent their specific area within the organization. It is very difficult to include everyone who will be affected by the new system on the team. Members should be expected to gather information from their peers to bring back to the team. This process helps to ensure that the right information will be reviewed and included where needed throughout the selection process. All requirements should be reviewed and approved by the team.

Solution Selection Activities

Once the requirements have been approved and the decision to buy has been made, it is time to look for vendors that are able to meet them. It is important to consult with your contracting or legal representative to understand the organizational rules and regulations about contacting vendors prior to a signed contract. Some regulations are in place to avoid giving any one vendor an advantage. The contract representative will be able to guide you through the selection activities. The following elements may be involved in solution selection:

- RFI: The request for information provides a format for gathering information about which vendors are able to meet the high-level requirements. The responses are compared with the documented requirements, which may be modified prior to posting the RFP if it is clear some required items are not available or require more definition.

■ RFP: The request for proposal provides the official request for vendors to submit how they will meet the requirements, which are more defined and include timelines and budget details.

■ Evaluation of RFP responses: Responses should be reviewed and scored based on ability to meet required, preferred and optional requirements. This step is accomplished with the entire team doing independent scoring of each response, followed by team discussion and consensus on a final score. This process helps identify which vendors can meet the organizational need and provides the first opportunity to eliminate any vendor that cannot.

■ Comparison to IT strategic plan: When evaluating the responses, it is important to understand how a vendor's solution or planned implementation will fit with the organization's IT strategic plan. Is the IT roadmap leading in the direction of virtualization, to simplification of technologies, or to a decreased number of vendors? How does the offered solution fit with this roadmap? It might be OK if the solution does not fit, but that fact should be considered during selection.

■ An evaluation of a vendor's interoperability capabilities is another important factor to consider: To adopt best of breed solutions, it is absolutely critical to have interoperable systems that doesn't add burden to the end user workflow. The systems need to integrate seamlessly with the existing solutions to provide greater insights with data integration and efficient workflows with system-level integration. Interoperability capabilities span a wide spectrum from core data integration, standard based data sharing such as using Fast Healthcare Interoperability Resources (FHIR®) or Health Level Seven (HL7®) Version 2, to optimal application integration using Substitutable Medical Applications, Reusable Technologies (SMART) on FHIR or CDS Hooks standards.

■ Compliance with regulatory requirements: Pertinent regulations should be part of your requirements and listed as essential. All vendors should be evaluated against any government, regulatory or security requirements.

■ Background checks: Once the list of possible vendors is decreased, some research should be done. This would include evaluation of their financial stability, market share and customer satisfaction. How long a product has been on the market and how many other customers are using it should be matched to your organization's risk tolerance level. Are you an early adopter who can tolerate some issues with the application if you are able to work with the vendor on new features and functionality? Or, would you prefer a solid, reliable application that the vendor has had time to refine? The outcome of this activity should be included in the scoring of each vendor.

■ Demonstrations: Requesting a demonstration allows vendors to show how they can meet the request. This provides a visual that is very beneficial, but it is often done with a generic version of the product. This does not reflect how it can be customized to fit the organization's workflows or processes. Prior to the demonstration, it is suggested that a list of scenarios be provided to the vendors so they will show how their product can meet your needs, rather than highlight only the features that they choose. All vendors should be guided to demonstrate the same scenarios to ensure they can be compared with one other. Whenever possible, the same people should be invited to all scheduled demonstrations. Having each vendor demonstrate how their product fits within the same scenarios and having the same people attending each meeting make it easier to properly compare and score each option prior to final selection. It is important to control the agenda very tightly, making sure all scenarios are covered and, if you choose, allowing vendors to demonstrate additional functionality at the end. Demonstrations should be scheduled closely together, if possible, so the information is fresh when they are scored.

■ Trial period or trial version of the software: With many cloud-based solutions, it is becoming easier to offer trial versions of the system or the system for a trial period. If available, facilities should take advantage of it to run through the end user scenarios in the system to see its fit for the requirements. This also provides for an ability to identify various roles and responsibilities needed for real implementation and to assist in additional implementation planning activities.

■ Site visits: Visiting a site that has already worked with a vendor and implemented their solution provides an opportunity to speak with people directly, ask specific questions and see how the solution works within their workflows and processes. This helps to demonstrate how the system can be customized during the implementation to fit defined workflows and processes. Questions to ask during site visits would range from what it is like to work with the vendor, how they respond to requests for support during the implementation or after go-live and how easy it is to customize the application or to integrate it with other systems. The number of site visits is often dependent on the number of vendors remaining at this point in the process. The decision on who should participate often depends on who will be affected by the implementation and the distance to be traveled for the visit. It is optimal if the organization, and not the vendor, chooses what sites to visit, but this is not always an option.

■ Client references: If a site visit is not possible, a call with the reference site would still provide the ability to ask questions. While the selection team will not be able to actually view the system live, the same questions can be asked. Through use of remote web meeting technologies, it is possible to have a demonstration of how a client is using the system without the travel. This provides the ability to understand the implementation process, so remember to ask about any lessons learned from their experience. Just like a demo, there should be predefined questions to be asked of each reference site. Simple web searches and informal contacts with peers can also provide some good reference information.

■ Selection meetings: Throughout this process, the team is meeting regularly to continuously evaluate and score the remaining vendors against the new information obtained through the research, demonstrations, site visits and original proposal scores. Through this process, the number of vendors should be decreased to two or three. The team's comments and final evaluations of each of the remaining options are provided to the contracting representative for negotiations.

■ Negotiation: The contract representative negotiates with the remaining vendors to obtain the best solution for the organization. This would include cost, software, hardware, implementation services, support and maintenance. The selection committee, as well as a legal representative, should carefully review all documents sent to the organization from the vendors because once the papers are signed, they are a binding contract. During the negotiation, there may be multiple requested modifications to the documents that require back and forth communication. This process can take a while since each modification needs to be properly reviewed by the other party before they come back with their modifications and so on. The cost tables should include costs for items such as software licenses, integration, data conversions, training, implementation services, hardware and third-party software licenses.

■ Selection: Based on the negotiations and the final offer from each of the remaining vendors, the team makes a selection. Each step of this process, along with the justification of the selection, should be documented in case any vendor chooses to contest the award. The final agreements often include items such as payment schedule, vendor and client responsibilities, delivery schedule, system installation and configuration documentation, specific deliverables, standard project plan, penalties for not meeting deadlines, termination process, assignment of licenses and process for upgrades or updates.

■ Budget development: During the negotiations, the budget is developed based on the costs defined during negotiation and selection. The budget often needs to include costs beyond the system vendor. Other items that might be included in the project budget are contractors to supplement the organization's staff; business change management requirements; hardware not purchased through the software vendor, such as new workstations or printers; costs from other vendors for integration services; training; travel; and standard fixed or variable costs, such as space and staffing. The budget is typically finalized within 30 days after the final contract is awarded.

The formality, steps included, and length of this process can vary greatly. There are various reasons for this beyond the organizational contracting process. The contract size, a time constraint, or the desire to stay with a single vendor might shorten this process. With each step, a document or process that is cut brings some level of risk. The organization needs to balance the risk versus the benefit of shortening the process.

Implementation Process

Now that a system has been selected, it is important to define how it will be implemented. While the phases of an implementation are fairly standard, there are a variety of defined methodologies that differ only in the terminology they use or the number of phases. The basic phases which implementation projects go through include: planning, analysis, design, build, test, train, implementation and closeout. It is important to remember that they all start with gathering information and planning what work is required, along with when and how it will be done. Most projects fail due to lack of planning, poor planning, or not following the plan. If the organization does not have a defined project management strategy, it would be important to take the time to decide what processes will be followed throughout the project. This includes defining the project team's roles, categorizing which tasks need the facility project team vs the vendor implementation team, the project manager's authority, the documentation and deliverables expected throughout the project and the role of the governance or steering committee.

The initial activity is to plan how the project will be accomplished. This includes defining what is within and outside the scope of the project. The project sponsors will approve the scope prior to any other plans being finalized. Also, the risk management plan, the change management plan, the training plan, the testing plan, the issue management plan, the work breakdown structure and the communication plan all need to be prepared. All of these documents make up the project management plan and define the tasks to be scheduled to successfully complete the project. When preparations begin for the activation (go-live), the activation plan is developed and approved.

At the end of the planning phase, after the sponsors approve the project management plan, a kickoff meeting is conducted to communicate the project to all stakeholders. The agenda often includes the following:

- The project scope
- The project management methodology, or how the project will be managed
- The change management process, or how changes are requested, analyzed and approved
- Identified risks and their mitigation strategies
- Introduction of the project team and their roles
- High-level milestones and schedule
- The communication plan

This meeting and conversation then kicks off the remaining work, following the phases as identified in the systems development life cycle (SDLC) and using typical project management processes.

Change Management

Any new system will have an impact on the organization, and some change will need to occur. It is not good enough to just automate a process; the process should be improved through automation. Changes affect everyone from top management to end users. Planning for these changes and evaluating the different options for managing them should begin during the procurement process. It is important to have top-level support, as well as a member of senior leadership on the change management team, to show commitment and provide strong leadership. The team should also include members from all affected areas, so they have a sense of ownership and commitment to the project's success. The team should also identify clinical champions as well as IT champions who can serve as the decision makers and point of contact for various change management and risk-management activities, along with other implementation activities.

The team should define a strategic plan similar to the project plan used for implementing the software. The strategic plan should take into consideration the organizational culture and politics related to how staff handle change. The types of resistance that might occur should be identified, along with the strategy to break down the resistance and move on to acceptance. A clear communication plan will ensure the information is properly disseminated throughout the organization.

Adoption is often affected by users' perceptions of how the system fits with their workflow. Does it provide efficiencies or appear to be extra work? Does the system functionality cause a perceived negative change in processes, or can the system be made to fit within the processes and even improve them? Often, the adoption is based on perceived benefit by the end users. The staff has to be ready for the change, which is why stakeholder involvement in the workflow redesign is critical. Having end users involved in hardware selection, such as workstations on wheels or mobile devices, provides feedback to the project team about the usability of the devices being evaluated. Some additional change management principles and strategies will be discussed in Chapter 9.

Implementation Strategies

There are multiple strategies for implementing a new system. Early in the project, they should be evaluated to determine which one is the right fit for the organization and right for the current system implementation:

- Big bang—Going live with all functionality to be implemented in all locations at the same time. If there is a legacy system being replaced, this might be the only option. This strategy requires a considerable amount of coordination to ensure that all areas are ready, with hardware in place, training completed and enough support staff available.

- Phased by location—Going live with all functionality to be implemented in one location at a time. This strategy extends the duration of the activation activity, but provides some benefits. The staff from the areas that are already live can assist with providing support to the ones that follow. Holding a meeting after each phase to discuss lessons learned could provide continuous improvement for later phases.
- Phased by functionality—Going live in all locations with one feature at a time. An example would be to bring the admissions process live first for admission, discharge and transfer and patient demographic information, followed by computerized practitioner order entry (CPOE) and then clinical documentation. This strategy also extends the duration of the activation and allows users to gradually get accustomed to the system before utilizing it fully. As above, meeting after each phase to discuss lessons learned could provide continuous improvement for future phases.
- Pilot—Going live initially with one location as a pilot test, and then following with everyone else in a phased big-bang process. This allows the team to learn from a small group before going live with the entire user community.
- Like for like—Going live with functionality to support the same processes that were in place prior to the project. Extra functionality is often added later through configuration management (discussed later in this chapter) or a later project. This strategy is often used when replacing a legacy system or during an upgrade. It helps to decrease the complexity of the activation and decreases the impact on the end users. There will always be some users who perceive this approach to be useless since they do not see an improvement.

Implementing Solutions

You have taken enough time to properly plan how the system will be implemented. You have selected a project team with the right skills, chosen the right implementation strategy, identified what features will be implemented, and developed an outstanding communication plan. Now all you have to do is follow your plan.

This is when the project team takes the basic vanilla application the vendor provides and customizes it to meet the organization's needs. The vendor should provide training to the project team on how to make these changes. This includes configuring the clinical documentation data entry into notes or flow sheets, as well as the output as reports. Each order that can be placed for a patient, such as medications, diagnostic tests, diets and consults, has to be configured in the system. Other items range from drop-down lists for a patient's religion during admission to how surgery will be scheduled. If there is a legacy system, the data conversion or loading of data also happens during this time.

Even if data is migrated early, some data migration will have to occur during activation to ensure that all data is in the new system when it goes live. Care should also be taken to avoid duplication of data during the migration. Data validation after each migration is an important step that should be combined with an action plan to resolve duplicate records if they occur. Vocabulary mapping process should also be implemented to align with industry standards such as RxNorm®, SNOMED® and LOINC®.

Part of the methodology should include how changes are handled during the project. There will be some requests to change the scope of the project or some requirements during the execution phase. Having a defined process for evaluating each request to determine its impact on the project helps prevent scope creep. The change management plan should identify who can submit changes, how changes are evaluated, what documentation is required and who makes the final decision. A request may be approved, denied, or deferred to a later time. The project sponsors usually make the decision with the project manager facilitating the impact analysis.

Testing activities occur throughout the execution. A test plan, which should have been started during the planning and analysis phases, describes all the different testing activities to be completed during the project. Often, the first testing activity is verifying that the hardware and application were installed correctly. Each of the initial environments, such as development, testing, or training, is required to ensure that the installations were successful. Testing will occur throughout the project based on the test plan and the different types of testing to be performed. For additional information on systems testing, refer to Chapter 7.

System Integration to Support Business Requirements

It is rare in healthcare today to have a stand-alone system that does not share data with another in some way. The electronic health record (EHR) should include data from the lab and radiology systems so those who need to make medical decisions can view the results. Patient demographic information should be shared between the outpatient clinic, or office system, and the inpatient EHR so the patient does not need to provide the same information over and over again. Integration allows data to be in multiple systems without manual data entry. Some types of integration to be considered include the following:

■ Real-time data integration—Sharing of data nearly simultaneously when it is entered or modified or when another defined trigger occurs. The standard for this type of integration is HL7, which defines the specifics surrounding the interface messages so what is sent from the source system is acceptable by the destination system.

- Scheduled data integration—Sharing of data in a batch according to a predetermined time frame, such as nightly at midnight or every so many hours. The data feed can be accomplished through formatted files or HL7 messages.
- Integration of data from devices—Feeding of data from a specific device into an application. These devices can range from hemodynamic monitors to vital sign monitors and anesthesia machines to ventilators. This type of interface helps decrease manual data entry, but may require the data to be verified before it becomes official within the system.

Integration utilizes an interface engine that receives information from the source system and either passes it directly to the destination system or makes some modification to the data before passing it along. For example, a modification would occur if the source system sent a patient's name as first name and last name, but the destination system could only accept a full name. The interface engine would accept the first and last names, combine them and send the full name on. Different systems have different requirements for how the data is structured and where in the interface message they expect the specific data to be located. The interface message has sections, and a mapping document describes where each piece of data is expected to be and if the interface engine needs to do any manipulation.

User and Operational Manuals and Training

As a project nears activation, it is necessary to educate the end users through documentation and training. If hands-on training is required, a training environment should be set up early in the project to allow the training team to develop materials and hypothetical patient data for any practice exercises that might be included. Training activities are tricky to schedule because they need to take place on the system that will actually be in use. As a result, the training environment cannot be fully set up until the entire configuration is completed and a copy created.

There are many factors that lead to the decision on what type of training should be provided. These include the organizational culture, extent of the change, number of users, users' work hours and even the staff's comfort level with computers. Training can be done through computer-based training modules, lectures, demonstrations, hands-on exercises, or a combination of these.

Training should occur right before the activation so the users will retain what they were taught. The timing depends on how many users need to be trained and how long the training classes will be. Experience shows that the best planning will not eliminate the need for just-in-time training. Inevitably, someone will not make it to class or will not remember how to do something. End-user manuals and quick reference guides along with the presence of support staff during the initial week or two will help fill this gap.

Activation Planning and Immediate Post-Activation Activities

Planning for the system to go-live begins with the decision on implementation strategy discussed earlier in this chapter and continues through the remainder of the project. The organization should work with the vendor to define which activities can be completed in advance and which have to occur on the go-live day. The actual activities will depend on the specific project. If the organization is moving from a manual process to an automated one or is implementing a new system, the activation could be as simple as having users start using the system. When migrating from a legacy system or upgrading an existing system, the activation activities are more complex and include a period of time when the system is down, or unavailable. A detailed checklist of tasks that occur before and during the activation, whether downtime is scheduled or not, helps to ensure nothing will be missed or forgotten. A rehearsal of the activation provides an opportunity to test the process and fix any mistakes that occur. Evaluating the rehearsal helps to refine the process and the checklist to make the actual activation go more smoothly. It also boosts the project team's level of confidence because they have already done the tasks at least once, depending on how many rehearsals are conducted.

The planning for activation goes beyond the actual tasks that will occur to bring the system up. Other considerations should include where everyone will sit; if a command center will be set up so the entire team will be in one location; if food and drink will be available, especially if the activity will go beyond a few hours; if there will be a place for the staff to rest; what forms of communication will be available for anyone not in the command center; and how status updates will be communicated to the end users. How will issues requiring escalation be handled, and will the vendor be on-site or on the phone to provide assistance?

The type and duration of post activation support will depend on the impact of the change and the amount of just-in-time training expected. When implementing a new system in a clinic, the support staff might be available just before and during clinic hours for the first week. When implementing a new EHR in an acute setting, the support staff might be available around the clock for the first few weeks.

The users will almost immediately have suggestions for changing the system. Having a clear process for submitting requests for change will help users know their input is valuable. With that said, it is important not to make changes too early. Often, the suggestions are just because the system, workflows, or processes are new and different from the ways the users have always done things. Unless suggestions are critical to patient care, they should just be documented for now.

Critical issues should be taken care of right away, but should still follow a defined change management process as discussed previously. The rest of the suggested changes should be evaluated one to two months after activation to see if they are still needed.

Managing Healthcare Information Systems

Once the system is live, it moves into operations and maintenance mode. During this time, the IT department must ensure that it continues to support the mission and goals of the organization and remains reliable and stable. During the implementation project, various processes should be put into place in preparation for this phase. These processes include configuration management, release management, customer support through a service desk and resolution of any issues entered as trouble tickets. Documentation about how the system was configured feeds into good operations and maintenance documentation for resolving issues when they arise. Examples of operations and maintenance documentation include the following:

- Communication plan—Defines how end users communicate with the IT department about the new system. How will they request help for an issue? How will they request modifications to the system? How will they request help for general questions about how to use the system?
- Service desk knowledge base—Explains how to identify and resolve issues when a user contacts the service desk. This includes questions to ask and decision trees to help identify the resolution or the escalation process if an issue cannot be resolved. The escalation process should include how to approach the vendor if an issue cannot be resolved internally, as well as who has the authority to contact the vendor.
- Data flow documents—Identifies where and how data flows from one system to another or from one location in the system to another, along with the dependencies between systems. This includes the triggers that prompt the data to flow, such as a change in the patient's location would trigger the information to be sent to update the lab system.
- Workflow documents—Explains end users' workflows and how the system fits into users' daily activities.
- Configuration management process—Defines how changes are made and what levels of approval and documentation are required for each change.
- Downtime procedures—Identifies which procedures end users will follow when the system is unavailable and what procedures the technical staff will follow to identify and resolve an issue causing downtime.
- Manuals—A group of documents ranging from end-user manuals to training guides and the configuration manual that provides step-by-step directions on how to make changes in the system.

Configuration management and release management are processes to control changes to the system, including software and hardware. They involve how changes are requested, the process for review and approval of changes, how changes are made and tested and the process for releasing changes to the different environments to ensure that they are kept in sync and that each migration is verified. It is important that changes are made in a development environment, tested in a test environment and finally verified in production. Conducting regression testing after the changes are made ensures the new modifications did not break something else. Controlling how and when changes are made in each environment is critical in avoiding unexpected negative results.

Working with the vendor on scheduling updates for small fixes, sometimes called hot fixes, to major upgrade releases will keep the system current while minimizing unexpected downtimes. Each new update should be evaluated prior to moving it through the configuration management process. If the update is large enough, it should be managed as a separate project.

Customer support is often provided through a help desk or a single phone number that goes to someone who can listen and help to resolve the issues the end users have. The calls may pertain to a an issue with the system; a problem with the usability of the system; or a training or how-to question. Having a good knowledge base that allows the help desk staff to ask the right questions and provides enough information to resolve the issue during the first call can keep customer satisfaction high. For times when the service desk cannot resolve an issue, it is important to have a process for providing second-tier support. Often, this is done through a help desk or ticket management system, but a custom database with workflows and notifications could work also. Timely feedback to the customer is important until the problem is resolved.

Analyzing Data for Problems and Trends

Throughout the life cycle of any application, it is good practice to look for trends in usage as well as problems. Within the first year after an application goes live, analysis should occur to see if it actually met the need that was identified prior to its purchase. This is an evaluation of how well the goals leading to the investment were met and if the expected return on investment was realized. The results should be brought back to the governance committee for possible action, especially if the need was not met.

There are many reasons to collect data and look for trends. A researcher may want to look for levels of new system adoption over the months or years, evaluate user satisfaction with a system, or understand trends in system performance. The ways to collect data can be through surveys, user groups, or visits to the users. On the technical side, looking for trends in error reports, help desk logs, monitor logs, or unexpected downtimes will help the technical staff plan for improvements in system performance.

Ensuring Critical Functions Are Repaired, Maintained or Enhanced

The technical staff receives many different kinds of requests for change. These include feedback from users through help desk calls, rounds, user groups and direct change requests. Some of these requests raise issues that must be fixed by the vendor or seek enhanced functionality not currently available. Vendors often provide updates, as mentioned earlier. Each change, or group of changes, should be evaluated and, if approved, prioritized. The smaller changes move through the configuration management process and are assigned and migrated according to the release management schedule. Larger requests or groups of requests should be managed as separate projects and follow the project management process.

Business Continuity and Disaster Recovery Plans

As was also discussed in Chapter 5, the criticality of the system within the organization will define the disaster recovery and business continuity plans. The business continuity plan defines how an organization prepares for and maintains the business functions related to the defined system. This includes the operations and maintenance of the system to ensure stability, the process of resolving issues that could or do cause the system to be unavailable, how the business will continue without the system and how to recover from an actual disaster.

The disaster recovery plan focuses on the technical aspects, such as data backup and recovery after the system goes down. Backups of the data are often done nightly and stored off-site on redundant servers or through a cloud-computing provider, typically for an indefinite amount of time. There are also hardware configurations that provide some level of continuity, such as automatic failover between clustered servers. Vendors can provide some options for how their systems can be configured. For critical systems, some organizations have off-site facilities where they can recover the system from backup if needed. Part of the disaster recovery plan, or a separate technical downtime plan, should include the steps to follow when the system goes down from causes other than a disaster. How the issue is identified and resolved, who is involved, and the process for a root cause analysis should all be included in this plan. These processes should be tested on a regular basis and updates should be made as needed.

The downtime plan focuses on business aspects, such as how to continue to operate without the electronic system. It includes procedures for communication, hard-copy forms for documentation and plans for how data will be entered into the system once it becomes available again. Once users become dependent on the system for their work processes, they are reluctant to use manual processes. Regular reviews of the downtime plan and communication before any scheduled downtime will help with adoption, but support staff should be available to provide assistance whenever the downtime plan is required.

Summary

Technological advances such as cloud computing and the complex healthcare processes require a systematic approach to proper selection and implementation of products within the healthcare environment. Evaluation and selection criteria should be established in alignment with the organization's strategic requirements, privacy and security requirements and regulatory requirements. Sometimes, a best of breed solution might be a better option than a single vendor solution. Solid project management principles need to be applied during the implementation of the solution. Successful implementation is key to end user satisfaction and effective utilization of the new system. Not only is the initial implementation critical, but also the continued support and maintenance of the system is very important to keep up with the updates and new workflows.

Bibliography

1. HIMSS (Healthcare Information and Management Systems Society). *HIMSS Dictionary of Health Information and Technology Terms, Acronyms and Organizations*. 5th ed. Chicago: HIMSS, 2019.
2. Schwalbe K. *Information Technology Project Management*. 4th ed. Cambridge, MA: Course Technology, 2006.
3. Houston S, Bove L. *Project Management for Healthcare Informatics*. New York: Springer, 2007.
4. Houston S. *The Project Manager's Guide to Health Information Technology Implementation*. Chicago: Healthcare Information and Management Systems Society, 2011.
5. Green M, Bowie M. *Essentials of Health Information Management Principles and Practices*. 2nd ed. Clifton Park, NY: Delmar Cengage Learning, 2011.
6. Project Management Institute. *The Guide to the Project Management Body of Knowledge*. 4th ed. Newtown Square, PA: Project Management Institute, 2008.
7. Morris P, Pinto J. *The Wiley Guide to Project, Program, and Portfolio Management*. Hoboken, NJ: John Wiley & Sons, 2007.

Chapter 7

Testing and Evaluation

Learning Objectives

At the conclusion of this chapter, the reader will be able to:

- Administer a formal testing methodology (e.g., unit test, integrated test, stress test, acceptance test)
- Implement and monitor compliance with internal controls to protect resources and ensure availability, confidentiality and integrity during testing (e.g., security audits, versioning control, change control)
- Validate implementations against contractual terms and design specifications
- Evaluate that expected benefits are achieved and report metrics (e.g., return on investment, benchmarks, user satisfaction)

Introduction

Healthcare organizations rely on information systems to manage clinical, administrative, financial and legal aspects of daily operations. As technology advances and new healthcare systems are developed and marketed, stakeholders must weigh the risks of implementing or modifying systems and mitigate those risks as much as possible. A critical element of that risk-mitigation strategy is testing and evaluating any new or modified component or system.

Purpose of Systems Testing

The fundamental purpose of system testing is to provide knowledge to assist in managing the risks involved in developing, producing, operating and sustaining systems and their capabilities. Specifically, system testing provides knowledge

DOI: 10.4324/9780429442391-10

of capabilities and limitations to the stakeholders for use in improving the system performance, and to the user community for optimizing system use and sustaining operations. Furthermore, system testing identifies the technical and operational limitations of the system under development so they can be resolved prior to production and deployment.[1] Information systems have become an integral part of healthcare operations and, as such, often have a direct impact on patient safety. With this in mind, identifying and testing for areas that are likely to be major patient safety risks is very important.

System testing and evaluation are performed on both hardware and software. Hardware testing includes evaluation of the physical components of the system (e.g., circuits, drives, internal components, etc.). Software testing is an investigation of the quality and validation of the functionality of a software product or service with the goal of finding any defects or "bugs" and fixing them before the product is released. Software testing can also provide an objective, independent view of the software that enables the business to appreciate and understand the risks of implementation. Test techniques include, but are not limited to, executing a program or application with the intent of finding software errors or other defects. Comprehensive testing is a process of validating and verifying that a system:

- Meets the requirements that guided its design and development
- Responds correctly to all kinds of inputs
- Performs its functions within an acceptable time
- Is sufficiently usable
- Can be implemented and run in its intended environments
- Achieves the general results the stakeholders desire[2]

Appropriate testing is critical for the success of any new or upgraded system. A study conducted by the National Institute of Standards and Technology (NIST) released in 2002 reported that software bugs (coding issues as well as integration challenges) cost the U.S. economy $59.5 billion annually.[3] It also found that more than a third of these costs could have been avoided if better testing was performed to enable earlier and more effective identification and resolution of defects; the earlier a defect is found within the product development life cycle, the cheaper it is to fix. In 2017, the estimated cumulative cost of software bugs and failures worldwide grew to $1.7 trillion, affecting at least 3.7 billion people.[4]

The first step in executing a successful test is creating a test methodology.

Test Methodology

Different types of methodologies are used in the field of systems testing and quality assurance for today's complex healthcare information technology (IT) systems. Whether testing an enterprise-level system, an individual workflow or application, or a specific piece of code, the methodology is equally important. Due to the complexity of healthcare systems, many healthcare organizations adopt a buy-not-build strategy, outsourcing development to or purchasing off-the-shelf solutions from companies that specialize in that area. As a result, their IT staff often has only a partial picture of their system's development history. In such cases, a well-defined testing methodology is critical to ensure that the delivered system meets the needs of the healthcare organization. Testing methodologies are the strategies and approaches used to test a particular product to ensure it is fit for purpose. Testing methodologies usually involve testing that the product works in accordance with its specification, has no undesirable side effects when used in ways outside of its design parameters, and, in a worst case, will fail safely.[5] Testing scenarios vary widely among healthcare systems and are tailored for each organization by the test teams and stakeholders, but a sound testing methodology generally includes the following key steps:

- Define the test strategy
- Develop testing tools
- Execute testing
- Employ test controls
- Report on testing results
- Perform final evaluation

Each of these steps will be discussed in further detail in the following sections.

Test Strategy

The test strategy is a formal, high-level description of how a system will be tested. It is developed in order to address all facets of the testing process and ensure testing objectives are achieved. The test strategy, also referred to as the test approach, may include testing scope and objectives, current business issues to consider, testing roles and responsibilities, status reporting methods, test automation and tools, a list of test deliverables, applicable industry standards, testing measurements and metrics, risks and mitigation, defect reporting and tracking and change/configuration management. The more specific test plan, which may live within the test strategy or as its own document, is derived from the documented business requirements and may contain test cases, conditions, scripts, testing schedules, test environments, pass/fail criteria and risk assessments.[6] The test strategy may be developed by a project manager, with the more detailed test plan created by a test lead or team, and once completed are shared with the project team, various end users and other stakeholders for review and approval before testing begins.

Test Tools

Testing tools are widely available in the commercial market; the specific tools required will depend on the testing method(s) employed. Generally, system testing is performed either manually or through the use of automated tools. Manual testing is simply direct human interaction with a system, testing to identify defects or unexpected outcomes. A member of the test team plays the role of an end user and tests most features of the application to ensure correct behavior. To ensure completeness of testing, the test team often follows a written test plan or script that leads them through a set of important test cases. Tools required for manual testing include a written test plan, test script or scenarios to follow and a method of recording and reporting the results. Although manual testing may find many defects in a system, it is a laborious and time-consuming process. In addition, it may not be effective in finding certain classes of defects not immediately apparent to the end user.

Automated testing may be performed through the use of special software (separate from the software being tested) that controls the execution of tests, compares actual outcomes to predicted outcomes, sets up test pre-conditions and performs other test control and test reporting functions. The use of automated testing tools in healthcare is expanding, and there are many automated tools available that can be tailored specifically to an individual system's testing needs. One of the most significant benefits of test automation is the ability to duplicate the testing process. Once tests have been automated, they can quickly be run and repeated. This is often the most cost-effective method for systems that have a long maintenance life; even minor patches over the lifetime of a system can cause features to break that were working at an earlier point in time, so repeated testing is required for each patch or upgrade.[2]

Test Execution

Performing and documenting the test activities is the primary focus of the testing methodology. Test professionals can use any number of methods to execute test events, and most fall into one of two categories: white-box testing or black-box testing.[2] These approaches are based on the point of view a test engineer takes when executing test cases. White-box testing (also known as clear-box testing, glass-box testing, transparent-box testing, or structural testing) is a method of testing the *internal structures* or workings of a system, as opposed to its functionality; the tester is not concerned with how the system is supposed to behave or function, but rather with how the system is supposed to operate on an internal level. Black-box testing (also known as functional testing) is a method of software testing that tests the *functionality* of an application, as opposed to its internal structures or workings; the tester is only aware of what the system or application is supposed to do and has no knowledge of the internal operations of the system. A hybrid of the two approaches is known as gray-box testing, which is a combination of white-box and black-box testing approaches; the tester has some knowledge of internal structures and also understands the expected system functionalities. Gray-box testing is most useful when performing tests on existing systems that have been upgraded, patched or modified.

Test methods are classified and executed based on the level of the test or the specific objective of the test. During system development, tests are performed at specific levels of development: unit-level testing, integration testing and system testing. Test methods that are not associated with a specific level of development are classified by the testing objective, such as stress, user acceptance and regression testing.[2]

- *Unit testing* is performed by checking individual units of source code and sets of one or more computer program modules together with associated control data, usage procedures and operating procedures to determine if they are fit for use. Intuitively, one can view a unit as the smallest testable part of an application. Unit tests are created by programmers and white-box testers during the development process. They cannot validate overall functionality on their own but are used to ensure that individual pieces function independently.

- *Integration testing* involves combining individual software modules, applications or units and testing them as a group to identify any issues in how the integrated components interface and interact with each other. Integration testing takes as its input, modules that have been unit tested, groups them into larger aggregates, applies tests defined in an integration test plan to those aggregates and delivers as its output the integrated system ready for system testing. Integration testing can be done using any of the box methods (white, black or gray) but is best suited for gray-box testing when the tester has some knowledge of the internal code of the individual units, as well as the expected system functionality.

- *System testing* is conducted on a complete, integrated system to evaluate the system's compliance with its specified requirements. System testing is one of the most common black-box testing methods and, as such, does not require knowledge of the inner design of the code or logic. System testing combines all of the integrated components that have successfully passed integration testing with software that has been integrated with hardware and tests them as a single system. The purpose of integration testing is to detect any inconsistencies between the software units that have been integrated (called assemblages) or between any of the assemblages and the hardware, as well as the exchange of data to external applications and systems.

- *Stress testing* is a form of testing that is used to determine the stability of a given system. It involves testing beyond normal operational capacity, often to a breaking point, in order to observe the results. The stress test puts a greater emphasis on robustness, availability and error handling under a heavy load, rather than on what would be considered correct operation under normal circumstances. The goals of such tests may be to ensure the software does not crash in conditions of insufficient computational resources (such as memory or disk space), unusually high concurrency, or denial-of-service attacks.

■ *Acceptance testing* is conducted to determine if the requirements of a specification or contract are met and to validate successful system implementation. Acceptance testing is usually created by business customers (the clients or users, so also commonly referred to as user acceptance testing or UAT) and executed prior to accepting transfer of system ownership from the developer or vendor. Acceptance testing provides confidence that the delivered system meets the business requirements of sponsors, users and other stakeholders. The acceptance test may also act as the final quality gateway through which any quality defects not previously detected may be uncovered. Provided certain additional acceptance criteria are met (e.g., security testing, supportability and maintenance standards, usability standards and standards compliance), system sponsors will normally sign off on a system as satisfying contractual requirements and deliver final payment to the vendor upon successful completion of acceptance testing. Acceptance testing is also done internally when major upgrades, patches and the like are involved. The terms *acceptance testing, system testing* and *integration testing* may be synonymous in some organizations and in some testing situations.

■ *Regression testing* is any type of system testing that seeks to uncover new bugs or errors in an existing functional system that has been changed by implementation of patches, enhancements, or configuration changes. It is common for new issues to be uncovered through the introduction of new systems. The intent of regression testing is to ensure that a planned change in software or hardware did not introduce new faults or defects into the production environment. A common method of regression testing includes repeating previously successful tests and checking to see if program behavior has changed or previously fixed bugs have reemerged after a system change.

Test Controls

System controls are implemented to protect the confidentiality, integrity and availability of data and the overall management of a system across environments during design, development, testing and deployment. Some of the most common types of test controls include version controls (also called revision controls), security audits and change controls.

■ *Version control* (or revision control) tracks and provides control over changes to source code. Software developers and testers sometimes use version control software to maintain documentation and configuration files, as well as source code. As teams design, develop and test software, it is common for multiple versions of the same software to be running in different sites and for the software's developers to be working simultaneously on updates. Often, bugs or features of the software will be present only in certain versions due to the fixing of some problems and the introduction of new ones as the program develops. Therefore, for the purposes of locating and fixing bugs, it is vitally important to be able to retrieve and run different versions of the software to determine in which version(s) a problem occurs.

■ *Security audits* are manual or automatic systematic, measurable technical assessments of a system or application. Manual assessments include interviewing staff, performing security vulnerability scans, reviewing application and operating system access controls and analyzing physical access to the systems. Automated assessments include system-generated audit reports and software that monitors and reports changes to files and settings on a system. Systems that require security audits can include personal computers, servers, network routers and switches.

■ *Change control* is a formal process used to ensure that changes to a product or system are introduced in a controlled and coordinated manner. It reduces the possibility that unnecessary changes will be made to a system without forethought, introducing faults, or undoing changes made by other users. Typical activities that would call for change control are patches to software products, system configuration changes, installation of new operating systems, upgrades to network routing systems and changes to the electrical power systems supporting the infrastructure. Change control is also a means by which the number of changes in an environment at any one time is controlled.

Test Results Reporting

Test results reporting occurs throughout the testing process—not just at the conclusion of a test event. Stakeholders and sponsors may expect monthly, weekly or even daily updates on current testing status, activities, schedules and more. Test reporting can be challenging and should be planned out early in the testing process. Common challenges include tailoring test reports to your audience(s), clarifying confusion about the intent of testing, explaining how testing is actually done and understanding which testing metrics are meaningful and why. At a minimum, test reports should address the mission of the test, system(s) or application(s) covered, organizational risk of deploying the system, testing techniques, test environment, updated testing status and obstacles to testing.[7]

Final Evaluation

For most testing projects, the most important deliverable is the final evaluation report, which contains the findings, conclusions and recommendations of the system test. For successful system tests, the final evaluation should confirm to stakeholders that the system has achieved expected results and should specifically address how those test results may affect the anticipated outcomes or benefits. For example, if the results of a system test show that implementation of the system will likely significantly increase the organization's third-party insurance collections, the cost of conducting the test would be considered a sound investment and the benefits of the test would be clear. In addition, the final evaluation report should address the most common stakeholder questions at the conclusion of a test event, including (but not limited to)

- Does the system meet our quality and performance expectations?
- Is the system ready for users?
- What can we expect when x people simultaneously use the system?
- What is our potential risk if we go live with the system now?

Final evaluations may reveal the need for specific end-user training prior to the go-live event. Lessons learned from each test event should be leveraged by the team to improve the planning, execution and evaluation of future tests. Beyond the go-live date, evaluation continues to play a critical role in a system's life cycle. Post-implementation evaluations are critical for measuring initial and long-term user satisfaction, system usability, business and patient care impacts and benefits and the system's potential for expansion or integration with other organizational systems.

Summary

A successful way to mitigate risk in deploying new or modified systems is through the development of a thorough testing and evaluation strategy. And including the right people in this strategy, at the right time, is also a critical element to the success of this phase and the overall project. Healthcare systems support workflows for a variety of clinical users and clinical specialties and may be deployed across a complex healthcare network, so testing can be complex and time consuming but is, nevertheless, essential to ensuring consistent performance that supports the delivery of safe and efficient patient care.

References

1. DAU (Defense Acquisition University). *Defense Acquisition Guidebook*. Washington, DC: DAU, 2012.
2. Wikipedia. Software testing. August 2019. http://en.wikipedia.org/wiki/Software_testing (accessed September 1, 2019).
3. NIST (National Institute of Standards and Technology). Software Errors Cost U.S. Economy $59.5 Billion Annually. Gaithersburg, MD: NIST, 2002. http://www.abeacha.com/NIST_press_release_bugs_cost.htm (accessed September 1, 2019).

4. Software Fail Watch, 5th Edition. https://www.tricentis.com/wp-content/uploads/2019/01/Software-Fails-Watch-5th-edition.pdf (accessed March 20, 2020).

5. Inflectra. Software testing methodologies – learn the methods and tools. 2020. https://www.inflectra.com/ideas/topic/testing-methodologies.aspx (accessed March 31, 2020).

6. Testing Excellence. Test strategy and test plan. 2018. http://www.testingexcellence.com/test-strategy-and-test-plan/(accessed September 1, 2019).

7. Kelly, M. Dimensions of a good test report. *InformIT,* March 24, 2006. http://www.informit.com/articles/article.aspx?p=457506 (accessed September 1, 2019).

Chapter 8

Privacy and Security

Learning Objectives

At the conclusion of this chapter, the reader will be able to:

- Define and implement organizational policies and procedures to ensure confidentiality, privacy, security, availability and integrity of data
- Assess and mitigate privacy and security vulnerabilities
- Define and implement user access controls according to established policies and procedures
- Assess and implement physical, technical and administrative controls to ensure safeguards are in place to protect assets (e.g., servers secured, unattended computers, two-factor authentication)
- Define organizational roles responsible for managing vulnerabilities (e.g., information security, physical security, compliance)
- Develop and implement data management controls (e.g., data ownership, criticality, security levels, protection controls, retention and destruction requirements, access controls)
- Validate on an ongoing basis the security features of existing systems

Introduction

Concerns about privacy and security of health records are not new to this age of electronic health records (EHRs). In the days of paper records, patients had valid concerns about the privacy of their health information. They expected access to those records would be limited and their contents would remain confidential. What has changed in the era of EHRs is the ease with which health

DOI: 10.4324/9780429442391-11

records could potentially be lost or breached, even from great distances, and the potential scale of these incidents.

Patients have the right to have their health information protected regardless of the form the data is in. Providers are expected to safeguard the patient's health information in order to maintain the patient's privacy rights. The content of a patient's health record is a very valuable asset to the patient and to the provider giving care to the patient. The underlying principle is to do no harm to the patient. Having this health information in a complete and definitive format at the time care is rendered helps the provider make a more informed decision for the patient's plan of care. This formatted health information empowers the patient to be an active member of the care team by having their data readily available to them in many electronic formats and online.

Defining Requirements, Policies and Procedures

Today, numerous laws and regulations exist on international, national and state levels regulating the privacy and security of EHRs. As the use of technologies such as EHRs, personal health records (PHRs), health information exchanges (HIEs) and e-prescribing expands the need for organizations to implement and maintain strong security will continue to be of high importance.

A primary area of focus for many laws and regulations is patient-sensitive health information that is transmitted or maintained in any form or medium. Those rules may impose restrictions on how organizations (including governments in some cases) may use or disclose health information.

In some cases, an individual organization may elect to put in place policies that further restrict access for a variety of reasons, especially when dealing with research that is on the front lines of medical science. For example, the presence in an individual's DNA of a certain genetic marker may not indicate anything today, but as science develops, that same marker could predict a condition that might have negative consequences for the patient.

Health information has been digitized for many decades; however, the Title II Administrative Simplification section of the Health Insurance Portability and Accountability Act (HIPAA) of 1996 established criteria and requirements for a covered entity in the United States to develop and maintain a program to ensure the confidentiality, integrity and availability of this protected health information (PHI). The confidentiality of the data refers to the properties of the information, which render it unavailable such that it cannot be disclosed to unauthorized persons or processes. Integrity is the property that data or information has not been altered or destroyed in an unauthorized manner. Availability means the data is accessible and usable on demand by an authorized person.

This comprehensive HIPAA Administrative Simplification Compliance Program is designed to provide the appropriate policies and procedures to achieve and maintain compliance through internal and external certifications. The

Compliance Program is to be in accordance to the published HIPAA Privacy and Security standards that will position a provider for unannounced inspections by the Office of Civil Rights (OCR), the government entity that will be enforcing compliance of these standards. HIPAA policies and procedures are to address each of the privacy standards and the security standards. Policies define what an organization will do. Procedures define how they will do it. A methodology to achieve and maintain HIPAA compliance can be: project initiation and organization; develop and maintain expertise; provide enterprise awareness and education; establish a baseline assessment of compliance; develop a strategy and compliance plan; remediate gaps in the baseline assessment; implement the program; and have a plan to maintain compliance, effect change control and complete compliance audits.

The HIPAA privacy standards consist of rules for appropriate use and disclosure of patient information; the consent and authorization of these uses; a Notice of Privacy Practices that details how the provider will maintain the privacy of the patient's information; the patient's rights to access, amend, restrict and have an accounting of the flow of their data; training of the provider's workforce members; a patient complaint process; and a process to sanction violators of the policies and procedures plus mitigation so the violation does not happen again. The privacy standards also address any entity the provider contracts with, who is not a provider, but must use the provider's patient information to provide a service. These entities are called business associates and are expected to maintain the confidentiality, integrity and availability of the patient's data in a private and secure manner. This expectation is defined in a business associate agreement with the provider. The Health Information Technology for Economic and Clinical Health (HITECH) Act of 2009 elevated business associates to a level whereby they are held to the same level of accountability as a provider for breaches of privacy and security.

The HIPAA security standards consist of administrative safeguards, physical safeguards and technical safeguards along with organizational requirements. Providers are to have a security program that includes a risk management process, workforce security management, PHI access management and controls, awareness and training, security incident process, contingency plans to protect and ensure uninterrupted access to PHI, facility access controls, workstation use and security, device and media controls, transmission security and business associates agreements. The security standards are classified as either required or addressable. Required standards are to be implemented. Addressable standards are to be documented such that they cannot be reasonably and appropriately implemented and include what can be implemented to meet the intent of the standard. Providers are advised to do an assessment of each standard and document compliance with implementation.

Paramount to having these two programs is to keep them up-to-date, incorporate them into the organizational culture and to do constant surveillance (auditing) to ensure compliance so that the patient has the comfort level that their PHI is secure, handled with integrity and no breaches have occurred.

The HITECH Act established for the healthcare industry a breach notification process similar to the one used in the financial industry. A breach of this type is the unauthorized acquisition, access, use or disclosure of unsecured PHI that compromises the security or privacy of the PHI. Providers are to provide timely and appropriate notice to affected individuals after a breach has been confirmed and it is believed the PHI has been accessed, acquired or disclosed as a result of such breach. To confirm a breach, a breach notification evaluation can be used. Step one of the evaluation is to determine if the incident involved unsecured information. If there was unsecured information, step two is to determine if there has been an impermissible use or disclosure of PHI under the Privacy Rule. Step three is to determine if the incident falls under one of the exceptions of the breach definition. Step four is to assess the probability that the impermissible use of the PHI would cause harm to the patient. All inappropriate uses of PHI are to be presumed to be a breach unless it can be proven that there is a low probability that the PHI has been compromised. Providers are required to notify the patient of the discovery of a breach without unreasonable delay. For breaches that affect less than 500 individuals, providers are required to enter the breach in an online database with the Centers for Medicare & Medicaid Services (CMS). Providers are required to immediately notify the local media and the Secretary of HHS of any breaches affecting 500 or more individuals.

A prominent international law that includes medical information is the General Data Protection Regulation (GDPR). The GDPR.eu website[1] provides an overview of this regulation. It states that the GDRP is a European Union (EU) law that was implemented on May 25, 2018, and requires organizations to safeguard personal data and uphold the privacy rights of anyone in the EU territory. This regulation includes seven protection and accountability principles of data protection that must be implemented. These principles are:

1. Lawfulness, fairness and transparency
2. Purpose limitation
3. Data minimization
4. Accuracy
5. Storage limitation
6. Integrity and confidentiality
7. Accountability

This regulation also includes eight privacy rights of the EU people. These rights are:

1. The right to be informed
2. The right of access

3. The right to rectification
4. The right to erasure
5. The right to restrict processing
6. the right to data portability
7. The right to object
8. Rights in relation to automated decision making and profiling

Some key GDPR legal terms to be familiar with are:

- Personal data, which is any information about an individual who can be directly or indirectly identified. Personal data can include religious beliefs, web cookies and political opinions.
- Data subject, which is the person whose data is being processed.
- Data controller, who is the person who decides why and how personal data will be processed. This can be a business owner or an employee of the business. Data controllers have to be able to demonstrate they are GDPR compliant.
- Data processor, a third party that processes personal data on behalf of the data controller. The data processor cannot legally process personal data unless they meet one of the following criteria:
    1. The data subject has given consent to the processing of his or her personal data for one or more specific purposes
    2. It is necessary to execute or prepare to enter into a contract
    3. To comply with a legal obligation
    4. To save someone's life
    5. To perform a task in the public interest
    6. There is a legitimate interest to process someone's personal data

Organizations who must be GDPR compliant are to implement appropriate technical measures such as two-factor authentication and end-to-end encryption to handle data securely. Organizations are also expected to implement organizational measures such as staff training, developing a data privacy policy and limiting access to personal data.

The fines for not being GDPR compliant are a maximum penalty of €20 million or 4% of global revenue, whichever is higher. Other sanctions can include a ban on data processing or public reprimands.

HIPAA covers US-based healthcare organizations (covered entities) that handle PHI. The GDPR covers the personally identifiable information (PII) of a EU citizen. This mean if a US-based healthcare covered entity uses or stores the PII of a EU citizen this US-based entity must be GDPR compliant regardless of the location of the US-based entity. If there is a breach of this EU citizen's PII, then according to GDPR, the citizen must be informed within 72 hours, where HIPAA has a longer timeframe of notice and a process to evaluate if harm has been done to the patient.

GDPR.eu is co-funded by the Horizon 2020 Framework Programme of the European Union and operated by Proton Technologies AG.

Risk Assessment

Once an organization has developed an awareness and understanding of applicable privacy and security laws and requirements, it should undertake an assessment of the organization's readiness with regard to each of those elements. This assessment should focus on identifying gaps between what is required and what actually exists within the organization's operations. A number of tools may be used in such an assessment.[2,3] Some examples include:

- Review of current policies, procedures, contracts and other documents relevant to privacy and security
- Organizational surveys or questionnaires that measure knowledge of, and compliance with, applicable privacy and security requirements
- Facility walk-throughs to identify areas where physical security limitations need to be addressed
- Technical penetration or intrusion attempts or other tests to assess security vulnerabilities
- Updated legislation, regulations or international agreements that may drive new approaches
- Root cause analysis of any security breach that may have occurred since the last assessment

This information should serve to give the organization a realistic assessment of its risk. We can think of risk as the likelihood of a given incident occurring, as well as the adverse impact of such an incident. We often think of such risks in terms of threats—potential scenarios that would have a negative impact on security or privacy—and threat sources—persons or events with the ability to actualize a threat. Examples of threat sources include humans (e.g., malicious hackers and employee saboteurs), natural disasters (e.g., foods and earthquakes) and environmental events (e.g., power grid failure and a nuclear or chemical accident). Threats and threat sources are dangerous to any organization that has not made itself entirely immune to them. We use the term *vulnerabilities* to describe flaws or weaknesses that allow exploits or events to result in a security breach or other violation of an organization's security policies.

Risk Management Process

A risk management process includes identifying threats and vulnerabilities, assessing risk and then executing steps to reduce the risk to an acceptable level. A threat is the potential for a thing to go wrong which triggers or exploits a specific vulnerability. A vulnerability is a flaw or a weakness in system components that can result in a breach or violation. Risk is factored by setting a numeric value to the probability a threat will exploit vulnerability and how bad (criticality numeric value) will the result be. These values are commonly set to HIGH, MEDIUM and LOW on a scale to come to a risk factor. A risk-mitigation process can be used to reduce the risk factor. The process can include what is to be done to reduce the risk, implement controls to reduce the risk and then document the residual risk.

Vulnerability Remediation

The analysis resulting from a risk assessment should go a long way toward identifying the most significant vulnerabilities an organization faces. Additionally, audit reports, reports of atypical system behaviors, vendor advisories and a system security analysis can be used to identify system vulnerabilities. Once those issues have been identified, the organization should embark on a remediation process to eliminate or mitigate the related risks. During the process of remediation, existing policies and procedures will be reviewed, new policies and procedures will be developed, education and training will take place and controls will be put into place to safeguard critical systems and data. The controls include physical safeguards, administrative safeguards and technical safeguards, which will be discussed below. With these tools at its disposal, an organization can decide to take one of two approaches to reduce risk to an acceptable level:

1. No action. The current risk level is deemed acceptable by the organization.
2. Mitigate. Implement safeguards to reduce risk to an acceptable level, along with policies and procedures in support of those safeguards.

User Access Controls

To maintain data confidentiality, integrity and availability, an organization must control access to systems and data. User access controls prevent access by unauthorized users. User access controls can be broken down into the following categories, sometimes termed the AAA or the triple-A approach:[4]

■ Authentication
■ Access
■ Accounting

Authentication is the process of attempting to prove that users are who they say they are before allowing them to access a system. Three primary methods exist to authenticate users:

1. Something a user knows (e.g., personal identification number (PIN) or password)
2. Something a user has (e.g., smart card or token)
3. Something a user is (e.g., fingerprint, palm print or retina scan)

Once a user has been authorized or authenticated, an appropriate level of access must be set. Access privileges are ideally set to allow the minimum access necessary in order to perform a job. Role-based access is often defined by a user's role within the organization. For example, physicians generally have the ability to place orders and to create and sign documents to which a nurse may not have access. A midlevel provider and medical student may each have subsets of the rights granted to a physician, while a pharmacist may have yet another set of privileges in the system.

All authorized users of PHI are to access information systems with a unique user-id. This unique user-id belongs to one person and allows the system to track this user as they do their work to see what data was accessed, modified or deleted. Along with a user-id is the password. Think of the user-id as the key that goes into a door lock. The password allows the key to be turned to open the door. Passwords should have strong characteristics so they are not easily guessed by an unauthorized user or password tracker algorithms. Some of these characteristics of a strong password may include upper and lower case characters, numerical characters, special characters, minimum length, that it cannot match the user-id, is changed periodically and is not reused. User-ids and password should not be written down, stored online, sent to someone in an unsecured e-mail or text and the password should not be sent in the same correspondence as the user-id. Passwords should not be stored on servers or other devices in clear text form. Security criteria set within electronic policies within systems can ensure the rules for user-ids and passwords are followed and not circumvented.

At one time having a password was the effective way to activate a user-id and was very secure; however, advancement of technology and the ease of a program that can be written to crack a password necessitate the need for additional evidence to be entered by the user to further validate who they are. This additional evidence is referred to as two-factor or multi-factor authentication and is known as strong authentication. This additional evidence can be a randomly generated code sent to a mobile device, a PIN, a smartcard, a digital certificate, or a biometric. The goal is to identify and validate the user entering the authentication credentials is the one authorized to use the system. Accounting is the final piece of the user access puzzle. Audit reports and other controls will provide assurance that users are not overstepping their bounds by accessing information that is not required for care delivery and may be forbidden by many privacy laws (e.g., looking up coworkers, neighbors, or celebrities in the system). Audit reports should be generated on both a scheduled and a random basis to ensure ongoing compliance.

Confidentiality, Integrity and Availability

A primary focus of healthcare information technology (IT) security is the area of confidentiality. Confidentiality is the process of limiting disclosure of a patient's personal information to comply with policies and regulations, and to maintain the trust that patients have placed in healthcare organizations.[5] Two other areas that concern healthcare security professionals are integrity and availability of data. Integrity refers to the accuracy and completeness of data. To preserve the integrity of its health information, an organization must successfully implement policies and procedures to protect the data from unauthorized modification, deletion or destruction and to keep it consistent with its source. Additionally, the organization must provide auditing mechanisms to ensure data has not been altered, deleted or destroyed in an unauthorized manner. Availability calls for information to be protected from any unplanned destruction, whether by accident, vandalism, natural disasters and so on. Availability also makes certain health information is available to patients when they need it. Care must be taken to ensure that records will be available and survive the organization in the event of closure, merger or similar events. This could also apply to other countries and their internal and external ties through treaties and the like.

Organizational Roles

An expert who understands which privacy laws apply to an organization and how they should be properly interpreted plays a crucial role in most healthcare organizations. Laws in many jurisdictions require that each organization appoint an individual, sometimes with the title of chief information security officer, who is tasked with these responsibilities. Among this individual's tasks will be:

- Assessing and maintaining knowledge of rules and regulations
- Developing policies and procedures
- Cultivating organizational and cultural awareness and developing educational plans in support of policies
- Managing appropriate access for external business partners and ensuring documentation exists in support of such access
- Monitoring compliance with policies
- Responding to complaints and other issues that arise
- Conducting or directing others to conduct scheduled and random access audits
- Investigating known security breaches and reporting information to appropriate regulatory or governmental agencies as required by law

The privacy standards require the provider to identify a position who will be responsible for the privacy program. The security standards have the same requirement and this person is responsible to ensure the security standards are consistently met. These individuals are commonly referred to as the privacy officer or the security officer. They can be two distinct people or they can be the same person. This person(s) is to be responsible for the development, maintenance and adherence to all policies and procedures needed for the provider to be HIPAA compliant.

An important process the privacy officer and/or security officer can oversee is the security incident management process. All incidents, threats or violations that affect or may affect the confidentiality, integrity, or availability of confidential information are to be reported and responded to in accordance to policy and procedure. The officers can oversee these processes and take steps to mitigate so the incidents will not be repeated in the future.

Data Management Controls

To ensure the security of protected data, a number of safeguards may be deployed. These safeguards seek to meet certain goals, including controlling electronic access to systems containing sensitive patient information or other private data; controlling physical access to locations or devices that may have ready access to secure data; managing data in transit, including e-mail and file transfer; and encryption of data on laptop computers, flash memory drives, or other devices that might be easily lost or stolen.

Safeguards can be categorized into three main groupings: administrative, technical and physical. Administrative safeguards are administrative actions, policies and procedures that an organization deploys in support of its security aims. Administrative safeguards include such actions as the ongoing education of employees on security requirements and scenarios in which data may or may not be used or disclosed, as well as developing policies and procedures that provide safeguards within the physical and technical realms.

Technical safeguards are electronic means of ensuring that data is not accessible, or that it is encrypted in a way that makes it useless to a third party. Examples of technical safeguards would include the use of network firewalls, secure protocols on any public networks carrying patient data and encryption of storage media on laptop computers and mobile devices.

The last type of measure, physical safeguards, consists of physical measures, policies and procedures that protect electronic information systems from natural and environmental hazards, as well as unauthorized intrusion. Examples would include data centers that are located outside a floodplain and have redundant sources of power, and limited access to server rooms or areas where data may be accessed or damaged. One of the major threats security professionals face today is cybersecurity—or the unauthorized access and malicious attack of healthcare information systems and patient health information data and more recently, ransomware—holding that patient health information "hostage" for payment.[6]

A data classification policy can be designed to support the minimum amount of data needed by a user to do their job. This ensures the information will be protected from unauthorized disclosure, use, modification and deletion. This policy is applicable to data is created, received, stored and/or maintained by the provider. This data is to be consistently protected throughout its life cycle, from origination to its destruction. Data will be protected in a manner commensurate with its sensitivity, regardless of where it resides, what form it takes, what technology was used to handle it and what purpose(s) it serves. Common data classifications are Public, For Internal Use Only, Confidential and Restricted Confidential. A data classification matrix can be developed to document for each classification examples, criteria, handling standards, copying standards, storage standards, destruction standards and workforce classification and access availability.

The volume of data being created, maintained, received, stored and transmitted by healthcare providers is enormous. Data management is necessary to ensure the most useful data is quickly available. Providers are advised to develop a data retention and destruction policy and procedure so non-useful data or data that has reached its end of life can be systematically destroyed. Destruction schedules can be developed to define the data and define the timeframes for destruction based on workflow process needs, regulatory reporting, state regulations, or federal regulations. The data owners (those who generate and maintain the data) can be the party to define the content of the destruction schedules. Review of these schedules should be done on a routine basis to stay abreast of any recent regulatory changes.

Disaster Recovery and Business Continuity Plans

While everyone has responsibility for protecting patient privacy and ensuring healthcare data security, the healthcare IT security professionals must be involved in the development of an organization's disaster recovery and business continuity plans. Contingency plans in this area should include the following:

■ Analysis of applications and data criticality. Applications and data should be prioritized in order of importance to the organization so a logical sequence of data recovery can be planned
■ Data backup plan. Detailed plans must be developed to ensure the existence of a retrievable backup copy of the organization's critical data
■ Disaster recovery plan. Procedures must be documented that define how to restore data after any loss, for any reason
■ Emergency-mode operation plan. Downtime plans should be spelled out that will enable the organization to continue to operate in emergency mode while access to electronic data is not possible
■ Testing and revision. All contingency plans must be routinely tested and revised to fill gaps that are discovered and to address changing organizational needs and infrastructure

Auditing

An essential component of an organization's security plans is the ability to audit all access to protected data. No matter how good an organization's policies and procedures are or how strenuously it works to limit access, individuals may still be able to access records they may not need to access to perform their daily duties. Audit reports enable an organization to identify any breaches or other policy violations, from employee snooping to a large criminal attack.

Validation of consistent compliance with the HIPAA security standards is a structured security audit program and risk-assessment process for any changes made to security features of all systems in the providers' IT environment. These audits can be done internally or externally by a third party. Industry standard is to have an objective third party conduct annual external network penetration testing from outside the provider's network to identify vulnerabilities in the network perimeter that would allow unauthorized individuals to access the provider's core network infrastructure and render the network inoperable. This same testing can include an internal network vulnerability assessment, a wireless network assessment, medical devices assessment, social engineering and a firewall rules review. The findings from the third-party assessment can then be incorporated into the provider's risk-assessment process to document a starting risk, mitigation, controls and residual risk in order to show security features are being maintained at the highest level of integrity.

Ongoing System Evaluation

Ensuring security is an ongoing and critical process. Crucial to maintaining compliance is a continuous evaluation of the security features of existing and new hardware and software. Network diagrams that include the location and configuration of firewalls, servers and routers must be maintained. Documentation of software and hardware, as well as vendor contact information, must be kept up-to-date. As new applications are introduced, technical and user interfaces and other data access points must be evaluated and care must be taken to assess whether an application or interface might introduce new security vulnerabilities. Additionally, existing applications must be reevaluated on an ongoing and regular basis in the face of organizational changes and evolving local, national and international attitudes, laws and regulations.

Summary

Ensuring the privacy and security, while also guaranteeing the confidentiality, integrity and availability of health information, is an ongoing and critical process. The introduction of EHRs has also shifted the landscape of what maintaining and protecting a patient's record looks like. New policies and procedures, new laws and regulations and new personnel and workforce focused on these important tasks have grown significantly over recent years. It is important that organizations focus on privacy and security on a consistent basis. It is not something that should be periodically "checked-in" on. Compliance programs must be in place, audits should be conducted regularly, data management controls and safeguards, administrative, technical and physical, should be in place, risk assessments that identify vulnerabilities should be occurring regularly, with mitigation plans enacted, disaster recovery and business continuity plans should be documented and contingency planning should be a continuous focus. And, although there are organization roles that are primarily responsible for this, health information privacy and security is everyone's responsibility.

References

1. Complete Guide to GDPR Compliance. https://gdpr.eu (accessed September 6, 2019).
2. ONC (Office of the National Coordinator for Health Information Technology). Security Risk Assessment Tool. Washington, DC: ONC. https://www.healthit.gov/providers-professionals/security-risk-assessment-tool (accessed November 10, 2015).
3. HIMSS (Healthcare Information and Management Systems Society). Risk Assessment Toolkit. Chicago: HIMSS. http://www.himss.org/library/healthcare-privacy-security/risk-assessment (accessed November 10, 2015).
4. Newman RC. Computer Security: Protecting Digital Resources. Sudbury, MA: Jones and Bartlett, 2010.
5. HIMSS (Healthcare Information and Management Systems Society). Privacy & Security Toolkit. Chicago: HIMSS, 2013. http://www.himss.org/library/healthcare-privacy-security/toolkit (accessed November 10, 2015).
6. HIMSS (Healthcare Information and Management Systems Society). 2015 HIMSS Cybersecurity Survey. Chicago: HIMSS, 2015. http://www.himss.org/2015-cybersecurity-survey (accessed November 10, 2015).

MANAGEMENT AND LEADERSHIP

Chapter 9

Management and Leadership

Learning Objectives

At the conclusion of this chapter, the reader will be able to:

- Contribute to organizational strategic planning (e.g., measure performance against organizational goals)
- Assess the organizational environment (e.g., corporate culture, values and drivers)
- Forecast technical and information needs of an organization by linking resources to business needs
- Develop and implement an IT strategic plan and departmental objectives that align and support organizational strategies and goals
- Evaluate performance (e.g., SLAs, goal/performance indicators, systems effectiveness)
- Evaluate effectiveness and user satisfaction of systems and services being provided
- Promote stakeholder understanding of information technology opportunities and constraints (e.g., business and IT resources, budget, project prioritization)
- Develop policies and procedures for information and systems management
- Comply with legal and regulatory standards
- Understand and comply with the organization's ethical business principles
- Employ comparative analytics (e.g., indicators, benchmarks)
- Prepare and deliver business communications (e.g., presentations, reports, project plans)
- Facilitate group discussions and meetings (e.g., consensus building, conflict resolution)
- Provide consultative technology services to the organization

DOI: 10.4324/9780429442391-13

- Develop educational strategies for the information and management systems function
- Maintain organizational competencies on current IT technologies and trends
- Apply effective risk management to internal and external processes (e.g., risk assessment, risk mitigation)
- Maintain effective and ethical working relationships with internal and external stakeholders (e.g., clinicians, vendors, partners)
- Present interpretations and recommendations of data analyses to decision makers
- Employ organizational change management techniques in support of solution implementation
- Define roles, responsibilities and job descriptions for healthcare IT functions
- Evaluate staff competency in information and management systems skills
- Manage projects and portfolios of projects
- Manage contractual agreements with vendors and partner (e.g., contract cost, schedule, support, maintenance, performance)
- Manage budget and financial risks

Introduction

Management and leadership skills are critical for the success of healthcare information technology (IT) organizations. Leaders and managers are expected to interact with other management and employees at all levels within an organization. This requires expertise in planning, communicating, reporting, forecasting and understanding all intricacies of healthcare regulation and policy. Leaders in healthcare IT are expected to have ethical working relationships with both internal and external stakeholders. Many organizations have implemented program management offices (PMOs) and this chapter covers managing projects, portfolios and change management. This chapter also reviews facilitating meetings, understanding roles and positions in healthcare IT and developing educational strategies for IT teams. Excellent leadership and management skills are necessary in all aspects of the work we do.

Participation in Organizational Strategic Planning

Leaders are responsible for setting the strategic goals and priorities for the company, division, department and new initiatives. A strategy is a formal or informal plan of action to achieve a goal. Regardless of where an organization is today, its strategies focus on where it would like to be at some point in the future. To outline and explain its strategies, an organization typically will use one or a series of statements that will be published for the benefit of the employees and customers. These statements express the mission, vision, values and goals of the organization.

Mission

The mission is a statement of why the organization exists—its purpose. Mission statements can vary from simple and concise to complex and hard to understand. The best mission statements are those that can be easily understood and remembered by any member of the organization or those that may be customers of your organization. Once read, it is not easily forgotten.

At the organizational level, it is typically the chief executive officer (CEO) and board of directors who set the mission of the company. The mission does not change with any regularity unless the business of the company or direction of the industry is changing as well. Nevertheless, each employee of the company has a responsibility to understand the mission to be sure that as they are evaluating their daily work, they can tie that work to the mission of the company.

Vision

A second expression that a company uses is the vision statement. A vision is the company statement that defines where it wants to go or what it wants to be. The vision is what the company is striving to achieve as it completes the daily work, a futuristic perspective. The CEO and board also typically set the vision. Depending on how far the vision reaches into the future, it may be altered with more regularity than the mission.

Values

The addition of values to corporate ideologies is much more recent than mission and vision. A list of values allows individuals to understand what the company supports and appreciates most. Values are often presented in a list that individuals can compare against their own personal values, as well as the values that are built into the activities they undertake at work. Examples of a healthcare organization's values might include compassion, service and respect. Employees should use the values as guides for their behavior at work and assess whether the values align or conflict with your work assignments. If an initiative lacks alignment or it conflicts with at least one value, it should be called into question. Values also reflect the corporate culture in the organization. Corporate culture is an all-encompassing set of attitudes, goals and beliefs about working for the organization that all employees accept to be true. Healthy corporate culture is usually a set of positive feelings about working for a specific company.

Goals

Goals are the measures to support vision accomplishment. The list of goals must be SMART: specific, measurable, attainable, relevant and time bound. Examples of organizational goals might be breaking even on Medicare reimbursement, leading in clinical quality and employing primary care providers of choice for the community. Clearly articulated goals that support the mission and vision serve as guides against which to measure accomplishments of the organization.

Organizational Environment

Every department of a large organization can benefit from having a formalized plan that demonstrates how the work being performed aligns with the strategic goals and objectives of the organization. The complexity and detail of such a plan will vary by organization, as well as by the size and complexity of a department. For very small information management and systems departments, the question that arises is whether a full-fledged strategic plan is appropriate. A plan with objectives is a good idea regardless of the organization's size.

In many organizations, it will be satisfactory to create a table or spreadsheet that crosswalks the organizational vision and goals down through each of the individual projects or initiatives being worked on within a department or area. Companies often engage leaders in formal governance and leadership committees to promote understanding of the potential projects that may be coming in the next 12–18 months. A detailed plan is then created for that time period. Detailed planning much beyond 18 months out, other than for routine replacement, may be less valuable given the rapid changes in the IT industry.

Maintaining a project crosswalk provides a visual summary of the initiatives being handled by an area of service. This crosswalk can then be used within the department and at administrative review sessions to demonstrate the linkage between vision, goals and projects. Additionally, this same tool can serve as a link to the detailed work plans and project updates that are maintained by staff. In Figure 9.1, you can see how a series of projects are weighted by scoring each

Index	Request		Exceptional care	Effective and efficient use of resources	Strategic growth	Exceptional experience	Nation leading research and education	End user experience	Innovation	Sites impacted	Score	Relative rank
		Weight	29.00%	24.00%	14.00%	9.00%	9.00%	5.00%	5.00%	5.00%		
Index	Request										0–9	
	Example: Enhanced privacy		1	3	3	9	1	1	1	1	2.48	28
1	Home care/hospice		9	3	1	3	1	3	3	9	4.48	15
2	Transplant		9	9	1	3	9	3	3	1	6.34	5
3	Mobile devices		1	3	1	1	1	9	9	9	2.68	26
4	Nurse triage		9	9	1	3	1	9	3	9	6.32	7
5	Surgical clinic outreach		9	3	1	3	1	9	1	1	4.38	16
6	Anesthesia IntraOp U/S/R		9	3	1	1	1	3	1	3	4	18
7	EKG upgrade		3	3	1	1	1	9	1	9	2.86	25
8	Remote hospital growth		9	9	1	9	1	3	1	1	6.06	8
9	Remote clinic growth		9	9	3	9	1	3	1	1	6.34	6
10	Health clinics		9	3	3	9	3	3	1	1	5.08	13
11	HR system		3	9	3	1	9	3	9	9	5.4	12
12	MFM ClinDoc tools		9	9	1	3	1	3	1	1	5.52	11
13	Affiliate epic care link		1	3	3	9	1	3	9	9	3.38	22
14	CPM upgrade		9	9	1	1	1	9	1	9	6.04	9
15	Organizational analytics		9	9	1	1	9	1	9	9	6.76	1

Figure 9.1 Project rankings based on organizational goals and priorities.

against the organization's goals and priorities. The resulting score and relative rank of each project is calculated, can be shared and helps provide objectivity to project priorities.

Forecasting Technical and Informational Needs of an Organization

Leaders in healthcare IT aid and provide direction in support of the goals and initiatives of the company. This requires a careful balance of leadership and support. It is important that all organizational leaders understand that operational goals direct IT and not the reverse. Lack of clarity regarding the relationship between operations and IT can put projects at risk. All projects need operational leadership and, as necessary, IT guidance and support.

Information management and systems leaders need to be keenly aware of organizational goals and be ready to actively recommend appropriate systems and technologies in support of those goals. Organizations that stay focused on goals will not catch the IT leader off guard. When goal deviation is suspected, the IT leader needs to be ready to challenge the request and to get the project back on track. Remaining focused on goals will help the IT leader and the organization to avoid creating the service gap that occurs when requested services surpass what the internal staff can provide.

New project requests are likely to come from a variety of sources. Some of the requests will be more fully developed than others. Requestors will need support in determining their project's scope, definition and objective. Requestors will also need potential relationship support with a vendor that can undertake the request. The IT leader needs to have program evaluation staff that can sit with requestors and help them work through a new project request. Lacking resources and structure, customers may suggest a solution to a problem that has not been well defined. They need to understand new technology, device integration options and infrastructure limitations. They also need to understand how to leverage the existing application portfolio and how to utilize network services. IT can assist with evaluation of new vendors and provide internal and external consulting services.

All leaders need to know how to assess the tactical steps that are in place to support the organizational goals. Focused goals will bring clarity to the strategies that need to be achieved. Be wary if an organization does not have the discipline to understand what is within its ability to accomplish in a defined time period. Leaders have a responsibility to serve as the organization's conscience regarding IT requests and service overextension. Activities must be clearly prioritized so that all leaders are operating from an institutional strategic plan.

Goals, strategies and tactics will inevitably require both redirection and an occasional time-limited expansion of scope. An IT leader must know which personnel resources are available and understand their readiness to manage contingency planning when unexpected resource issues occur. This knowledge will help the organization remain flexible and make more efficient and well-thought-out decisions in matters requiring IT support.

Not only must IT leaders understand and support the organizational goals with their system-level knowledge and expertise, but they must also have a methodology that supports the organization's ability to measure activities against their stated goals and objectives. They must facilitate a process in which all leaders work together to define the organization's measures of progress and, ultimately, success. If agreement cannot be reached on a measure, it will be difficult to know when the related goal has been achieved.

The measures can be used for internal benchmarking, in which the organization defines its current place, defines the objective and then measures activity against both the starting point and the end goal at regular reporting intervals. Local and national benchmarks may be available, but a contract may be required to use them. It can often be costly gain access to private benchmark data.

Benchmarking data are available in many, but not all, aspects of IT management. Be sure that any benchmarks used are comparable to the data your organization is capable of supplying. Careful clarification on the front end may decrease the challenges of apples-to-oranges comparisons, but a few disparate data points may well remain.

Developing the IT Strategic Plan

Among the many responsibilities of IT leaders is developing the IT strategic plan. In a very large organization, the IT strategic plan may serve as a reference tool for prioritizing the work that is to be done throughout the organization. In small or less complex organizations, the IT plan may be more appropriate as a section or addendum to the organizational strategic plan. When developing an IT strategic plan, it is important to include the input of operational leaders and the staff responsible for the actionable components.

Begin the process of developing an IT strategic plan with copies of both the current IT plan and the organizational strategic plan. If the organizational plan has not been developed or refreshed in the last 12 months, then you must start the process by validating the strategies and tactics of the organizational plan first. The IT strategic plan must be perfectly aligned with all the organizational priorities. If there is no previous IT plan to work from, a myriad of free templates and resources can be found on the Internet[1] and used as models for formatting and organization.

Consider taking the following steps to develop your IT plan:

■ Initiate the document by including the mission, vision, goals and strategies of the organization. IT supports the business and therefore must be grounded in that business and its strategies

- Identify the current state of the systems and processes that support the business and assess their effectiveness in meeting their stated functions
- Define the gap that exists between the functions that are or can be provided and those that need to be developed or procured
- Compare the timeline for staff to manage the development and costs associated with external development or purchase
- Identify who will take responsibility for the initiatives to be addressed

The initial stages of the plan need to reinforce the idea that there is no such thing as an IT project. All projects are organizational and strategic in nature, and IT is only one component within the bigger initiative. Once top managers understand and agree to that, they will recognize why every major initiative will need to be sponsored by operational leaders. A well-developed plan will map the organizational strategies and the supporting applications and processes for each strategy. Once fully developed, the map will provide a visual representation of the current systems' status, an indicator of the expected useful lifeline of the systems or the gap that exists between the strategy and the needed technology.

The remainder of the plan can focus on the gaps—the gap analysis. The plan can outline the current state and desired future state. An approach to consider would be to evaluate the strengths, weaknesses, opportunities and threats (SWOT) of the current organization. In cases where it is not likely that the gap can be bridged with a single process or system change, the plan needs to outline the steps that can be laid out to achieve the desired outcome. As many of the steps may each take several years to complete, the plan's details need only focus on the first step or two, and then more high level for the remaining steps. This is practical, as the technologies and organizational priorities may change during the interval.

Finally, the plan needs to outline some of the pure IT initiatives and personnel needs. Examples of this might include advanced technologies like virtual ICUs, system transitions to cloud technologies, radio-frequency identification (RFID), artificial intelligence and advanced device integration. The plan would include regular system upgrades or replacement strategies. Planning to accommodate current and future resourcing needs, as well as the transition and succession plans for staff and leaders is crucial to ensure consistent leadership. All organizations experience turnover. Is there someone who has the appropriate education and skill set to step into an interim role? Does that person have the qualities to take on the role permanently? How about key managers and supervisors? Each leader should have a mentee within the organization who is being groomed and educated to move up when the time is appropriate. A well-prepared organization has the bench strength to maintain leadership stability in the same way it has system redundancy to maintain continuity.

Implementing the IT Strategic Plan

Once developed, the IT strategic plan needs to remain a living object and therefore must be regularly maintained. To achieve this, the document needs to be part of the organizational strategic plan and updated accordingly with any changes to its companion. The key IT objectives must be visible to the entire department, so that they have an opportunity to see and commit to each objective regularly. Annual performance objectives can be tied back to this plan, and regular reports can be produced and used as measures against the IT strategic plan. Finally, treat the plan itself as a project. Maintain a color-coded scorecard of goal progress and achievement for all to see.

Reporting on System Performance, Evaluating Performance and Evaluating Customer Satisfaction

Measures that monitor the effectiveness and progress of departmental activities are necessary for leaders to evaluate overall performance of a work unit. In an operational sector that has both projects and services, two types of measures will be necessary.

Project Tracking

Tracking a project is most effective when using a project plan and a related Gantt chart. A project plan lists tasks with estimated timeframes, dependencies and responsible resources. A Gantt chart, associated with a project plan, includes a series of rows detailing each of the steps and sub steps to be completed within the project. Each row has multiple columns identifying start dates, projected end dates and completion percentage. The project plan and the Gantt chart provide an excellent way of visualizing an entire project in both highly summarized and detailed ways. Commercial project-tracking software products are available, but many organizations effectively manage projects using a simple spreadsheet. An example of measuring a project against goals is included later in this chapter.

In departments where service is a component of the work done, it will be important to have a service-level agreement (SLA) with indicators that are tracked at regular intervals. The expected service level can be internally derived, negotiated with the customers, or driven by externally agreed-upon benchmarks. Service-level parameters can best be measured using a dashboard visualization tool. A dashboard is a series of graphs or tables that indicate the current performance, the historic performance for an appropriate time interval, the expected quality of services, and if appropriate, the acceptable level of variation below and above the stated goal. In addition to the quality-of-service goal, there may be a stretch goal, though it is

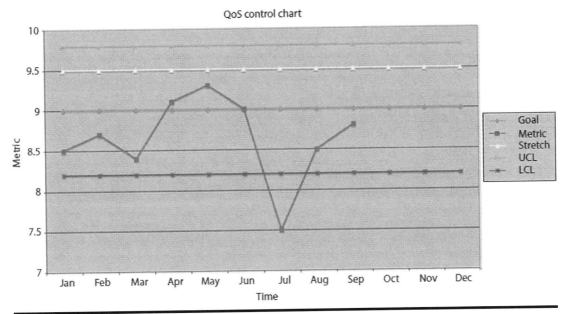

Figure 9.2 Quality-of-service (QoS) control chart. UCL, upper control limit; LCL, lower control limit.

not usually on a control chart. The stretch goal is typically an internally desired target that exceeds any quality-of-service parameters that have been agreed to.

A typical dashboard includes a series of control charts. Control charts are statistical representations of the graphs discussed above. They add lines representing the upper control limit (UCL) and lower control limit (LCL). This considers that there will be natural variation in the results represented around a mean. To the extent that a series of points begins to move in one direction or the other, it will become necessary to review the process looking for special-cause variation. In any business, variation will often increase costs. In healthcare, variation may also signal changes in the quality of patient care and therefore warrants immediate attention and understanding. A sample quality-of-service control chart is presented in Figure 9.2.

Assessment

At times, organizational leaders may find that they have become too detached from the organization and the stakeholders they are serving. IT leaders may be especially prone to this because they often work in a separate location from where care services are provided or because the complexity of their work slowly removes them from the day-to-day environment of care. Regular departmental and system assessments will prevent isolation and enhance communication with stakeholder communities throughout the organization. The assessments need to include the effectiveness of both the systems supported and the services provided.

Measuring system effectiveness needs to start with a baseline analysis. This ties in very nicely with the earlier discussion of understanding service-level benchmarks. It is important to have both an objective and a subjective assessment of the quality metrics. A simple example of this can be seen in an assessment of system availability. Ninety-nine percent uptime for a computer system sounds highly efficient and tracks very nicely along a control chart. Customers, however, report that they struggle with the average of 1.75 hours of system downtime each week. Even though that falls within the 1% deemed acceptable, a customer assessment helps the leader understand the customer's point of view. Furthermore, the environment factors into this assessment. For example, the 24/7 healthcare environment has expectations of 99.999% system availability.

A baseline assessment can be accomplished in several ways. Face-to-face interviews have value for systems that affect only a small number of stakeholders, especially when they work in disparate parts of the company. Unit rounding will be effective when actual observation of the system in use is needed. What better way to demonstrate an interest in stakeholders' work than to be present in their environment? Typically, it is most efficient to meet with a group of users together. This can be done by going to departmental or unit meetings that are already scheduled. Alternatively, you may choose to call a town hall meeting to look at a general situation or a focus group to examine specific situations. Both can be organized as either physical or virtual meetings.

The baseline assessment is designed to gather data regarding the systems that the stakeholders are using and the way they are being used. Take the time to understand the stakeholders' expectations of system availability and performance. Listen to their past internal and external experiences and pay special attention if they note adverse changes in systems performance. Use the assessment time to accept feedback regarding opportunities for system operating improvements. Be clear that not all requests can be accommodated but remain open-minded to what will result if some meaningful feedback is directly addressed.

Once the baseline is determined, commit to a regular process of follow-up analyses. Identify the interval that is most appropriate. If the organization concurs with an initial assessment that the performance of IT systems and services is satisfactory, then an annual follow-up assessment will be enough. A lower than desirable assessment warrants a prompter turnaround and more frequent follow-up. Regular communication or monthly status reports should address commitments to improvement. Effectiveness should be reassessed at regular intervals agreed upon with customers.

The process for the follow-up assessment can be accomplished by telephone or web-based surveys. Providing easily accessible feedback tools within the applications themselves will prompt regular responses. Customers will appreciate the availability of immediately accessible feedback because it will enable them to avoid making calls to the help desk.

Departmental Effectiveness

Departmental effectiveness needs to be differentiated from system effectiveness as you do your assessment. The distinction is necessary because customers and stakeholders have a multitude of different needs. The methodology for retrieving feedback about the two can be essentially the same, but the objectives will be different. In the departmental assessment, the value is in understanding how the personnel respond and relate to others within the organization.

Departmental effectiveness is measured using interpersonal metrics reported by customers. Leaders have an advantage because they have also had the opportunity to receive customer service. A typical first impression of customer service is formed by the response time to inquiries. Keep in mind that customers are providing clinical services and therefore are not typically in one physical location for more than a few moments at a time. Any response time greater than just a couple of minutes is likely to cause dissatisfaction. A popular service management framework to consider is the Information Technology Infrastructure Library (ITIL).[2]

Additional factors to be considered when evaluating customer satisfaction include:

- Does IT staff empathize with the concerns and frustrations of customers?
- Does IT staff communicate regularly with customers when they are working on a problem that takes more than a short time to resolve?
- Does IT staff communicate resolution of system issues back to customers who originally reported the problem?

Managing Customer Relationships with Business Leaders

Customer relationship management (CRM), a widely accepted practice in healthcare, is an organization's approach to interactions with customers, patients, vendors and other business associates.[3] CRM involves using proven methods to attract new customers, retain current customers and reestablish relationships with past customers. It also involves leveraging technology, such as the Internet and social media, and traditional marketing techniques to organize, automate and synchronize business processes. Using CRM, healthcare organizations can achieve increased quality and efficiency, reduced overall costs and greater profitability.

Unlike many industries that are product driven, healthcare organizations are uniquely service driven, ultimately aimed at developing relationships to improve patient loyalty by getting the right information at the right time to everyone involved in the continuum of care. By customizing service offerings to better meet customer expectations, and by continuously training and rewarding employees for delivering exceptional customer service, healthcare organizations can achieve profitable customer relations not only with patients, but also with payers, regulators, vendors and other stakeholders.

To improve customer satisfaction levels, a comprehensive systems approach is recommended.[5] It is critical to set a clear customer experience strategy. Customer service involves more than creating an organizational slogan. To establish a good strategy, it is important to understand the organization's vision and mission; determine the organization's customer service direction, slogan and values; share the customer service strategy by using a comprehensive communications program; emphasize customer service is a key responsibility for each department; and ensure the customer service strategy aligns with the other organizational strategies.

Selecting the right team and developing, motivating and managing staff members are some important areas of consideration. Interpersonal skills and the right attitude are two qualities critical for employees to possess when providing customer service. Emphasizing functional expertise, technical competence and knowledge is less important, and many of these can be taught. Employees working directly with the customer need to understand the organization's culture and learn key communication skills. Four steps needed to build a culture of excellent customer relations are as follows:

1. Provide training in key skills needed to deliver excellent personal service
2. Use ongoing coaching and feedback to reinforce improved customer relations
3. Regularly measure and monitor performance levels
4. Reward performance with both monetary and nonmonetary awards

Effective service delivery creates efficient customer interaction, eliminating the need for third-party intervention to keep customers satisfied. To help ensure a positive customer experience, it is important to identify preferred service delivery processes, review critical success points in those processes and determine service standards and objectives. In addition, it is vital to establish service delivery procedures to maximize material service and create SLAs to improve customer satisfaction.

Regardless of how well trained the staff is or how effective the organization's current service delivery processes are, opportunities for improvement can always be identified. It is important that problems and issues be resolved quickly by building continuous improvement into the service delivery procedures. To properly manage the customer experience, it is necessary to identify where opportunities for improvement are by actively soliciting customer feedback; teaching staff how to handle customer complaints effectively by using the correct blend of empathy, apology and resolution; focusing on the root of the problem and not just the symptoms; and being proactive in seeking to prevent issues instead of reacting to events that have already occurred.

Although senior management support is vital for creating and maintaining a successful CRM program, involving midlevel management in the change process and empowering them to be key change agents is essential. To do this, it is vital to engage the management team early and often, to involve management members in formulating the customer service strategy and to develop managers' coaching skills so that they are able to understand and reinforce key personal service skills. In addition, management should include managers as facilitators during training sessions; reward managers for establishing, monitoring and updating service delivery processes; and motivate managers to be examples to their teams.

Providing Customer Service

Healthcare is primarily a people business—it calls for the organization to be particularly customer focused, or customer centric. HIMSS defines customer centric as "placing the customer as the center or focus of design or service."[6] It is excellence in service that distinguishes the IT department as responsive and knowledgeable, or as customer centric. There are several specific factors and approaches to consider in organizing the customer service functions in the IT department. Leaders in healthcare IT are expected to have ethical working relationships with both internal and external customers. In the healthcare sector, internal customers can be physicians, nurses, human resources representatives and others with a vested interest in the success of the organization. External customers include patients, consultants, vendors and others connected to the institution via services, a contract or an agreement. The frame of reference is important when considering how to categorize a customer. In the example above, the entire hospital would be considered the frame of reference. In a situation where a single department is considered, internal customers might be the a much smaller group, and external customers might be others within the organization.[7]

Delivering outstanding service requires the building of a culture that focuses on customer relations. This can involve changing all aspects of an organization's service delivery. The investment of time and effort can be significant, but the rewards can be enormous, building long-term patient and customer loyalty and helping to ensure business profitability.

Promoting Stakeholder Understanding of IT Opportunities and Constraints

Health information and management systems' leaders have a responsibility to discuss the opportunities and systematic limitations of using information systems to address organizational goals and objectives. Leaders must educate stakeholders by highlighting opportunities to be gained using technology as well as explaining any limitations.

The initiation of a project charter is a critical juncture in IT's support of the organization. Success can be achieved using a well-articulated and accepted process that facilitates understanding and communication between the leader and the stakeholders. A method for initiating a project is via the utilization of an SBARC. SBARC is an acronym for situation, background, assessment, recommendation and communication. This is an extension of the SBAR (minus the communication step) developed at Kaiser Permanente by Michael Leonard.[8] The one- to two-page SBARC proposal helps to frame a situation or request and a method of addressing it. It is an easy way to document a situation and proposed approach to a very wide audience. The simplicity of the tool makes it easy for a knowledgeable team member to complete and provides a concise summary for leaders to assess prior to committing to a full project proposal or a *pro forma* financial plan.

The SBARC process begins a discussion of the key goals and objectives of an initiative and frames some of the potential strategies for resolution. As appropriate, the SBARC may be followed up with a more formal business planning process and *pro forma* financial plan. A disciplined approach to framing and initiating projects ensures that the stakeholder and the project team members are operating from an identical framework. Ways of assessing the process improvement needs might include the utilization of either a Lean (production practice looking at resource consumption) or Kaizen (continuous improvement processes) methodology as a tool for optimizing the performance of a system. Once developed, the framework includes the deliverables of the project, along with the cost and timing, together defined as the scope of the project.

A well-written plan that has been signed off on by all stakeholders will help to eliminate the opportunity for scope creep to infiltrate the project. Scope creep is a common event in the life of a project. New opportunities or events will warrant that new analyses occur. A disciplined analysis following the project planning approach outlined above will weigh the merits of new opportunities in the context of the project. This is referred to as scope or project change control management. If a value-added suggestion is made and approved, then the plan is amended and communication undertaken. Scope creep is the undisciplined addition of new goals, objectives and milestones that may have a negative effect on the cost or timeline of a project. This occurs when inadequate analysis of suggestions occur, and additional work is added to the project. An effective way of avoiding scope creep is to anticipate it and have a method of reviewing recommended changes in scope with the project's leadership team on a regular basis.

At times, a more appropriate method of project planning is the agile methodology. Using this approach, initial objectives are expressed and a series of sprints are defined. At the end of each sprint, the team members review the product and suggest enhancements to be included in the next sprint interval. This method allows for more flexible development cycles.

Developing Policies and Procedures for Information and Systems Management

The implementation of policies and procedures within an organization facilitates the standardization of actions and operations for employees, patients and guests. Often, policies and procedures can be implemented in any portion of the organizational structure, from the entire company to the very smallest operation. Leaders face two questions: Is the policy really needed? If so, at what level of the organization must that policy be implemented? To maintain their accreditation in the United States, a healthcare organization is required to have a defined set of policies on information management and security and privacy policies. IT leaders in other countries will need to understand the accreditation standards that apply to their operations.

Prior to policy implementation, consider for what purpose you are developing a policy, and whether it is necessary to have a policy and procedure to govern that activity or process. If so, do not begin from scratch. Peers, both locally and nationally, have addressed many of the issues you face, and those same peers will have advice and examples to share. Start with a local survey of your peers. This has the advantage of helping you establish local networking connections and begin to create a community standard for the policy in discussion.

If local support is not available, then move to national peer groups, but ask yourself why you may be in front of the curve for your community. You can always look to organizations like HIMSS,[9] International Federation of Health Information Management Associations (IFHIMA),[10] and International Medical Informatics Association (IMIA)[11] or other national professional associations allied to the field. These organizations will all have examples of a variety of policies.

A reason for *not* adopting a policy or procedure is your inability to audit and report on the effectiveness of the policy in question. If you do not have the ability to audit, then you run the risk of a challenge by health system accreditors. Do what is measurable, measure what you do, review what you have measured and act on the results of what you have reviewed.

Be prepared to act on the results of your audit measurements, and make sure that the implications of failing to adhere to a policy are built into the policy itself. The consequences of noncompliance, when embedded within the policies and procedures, will help close the loop for employees. If there needs to be room for exceptions, those exceptions must be outlined as part of the policy as well. Once again, if there are no consequences for deviation from policy, then you must ask yourself whether there is a need for the policy in the first place.

On some occasions, policies and procedures are used as much for education and training as for any other purpose. A good example of this is a password policy. It is inevitable that a challenge will be brought forward regarding the implementation of a password policy. As most, if not all, systems allow the definition of the policy to be incorporated directly into the software, it really is unnecessary to have a separate policy because the system will not allow staff to create a password that does not meet the standard. In this case, a policy explaining the risks of weak password construction, in addition to meaningful education on how to create a strong password that is easy to remember, might be a better overall strategy.

Complying with Legal and Regulatory Standards

The discipline of information and management systems includes a complex web of legal, regulatory, accreditation and other compliance issues. Each country is going to have its own sources of oversight. IT leaders have a responsibility for knowing the sources of those standards in their own country. In the United States, navigation of meaningful use, e-prescribing, conditions of participation and Health Information Portability and Accountability Act (HIPAA) is just the beginning of this complex responsibility. Effective leaders need to either understand the many nuances of these standards or have easy access to individuals who can assist in their understanding. Those individuals include the corporate compliance officer or equivalent, legal counsel and the lead Joint Commission liaison, among others.

Depending on the size of the organization, all the responsibilities may fall on the shoulders of one individual. Most likely though, the responsibilities will be distributed around the organization, with those individuals coming together under the auspices of a corporate compliance committee, a Joint Commission International (JCI)[12] steering committee, or perhaps an audit and education committee. The information that these individuals are responsible for is ever changing. Their knowledge comes from several key documents, most of which are available directly or by purchase over the Internet. In the United States, the information can be obtained from the Centers for Medicare & Medicaid Services (CMS),[13] and internationally, from JCI.[12]

The two most influential sources of standards for healthcare organizations in the United States are CMS and the Joint Commission, formerly known as the Joint Commission on Accreditation of Healthcare Organizations.

CMS can be found at https://www.cms.gov/. CMS is a part of the Department of Health and Human Services (HHS). The key operating document for a hospital that receives any funding from CMS is "Conditions for Coverage and Conditions of Participations." The details of this framework are found at https://www.cms.gov/Regulations-and-Guidance/Legislation/CFCsAndCoPs/. A healthcare organization is held to these conditions in order to receive funds for services. On a day-to-day basis, the *Federal Register* serves as the "the official daily publication for rules, proposed rules and notices of Federal agencies and organizations, as well as executive orders and other presidential documents," and the first and last indications of proposed rule changes.[14]

JCI is located online at http://www.jointcommissioninternational.org/. It serves as the voluntary accreditation body for more than 100 countries throughout the world. Accreditation is accomplished by complying with a comprehensive list of standards published by JCI. Organizations meet the standards through preparation, followed by a scheduled site review by a team of JCI surveyors.

Adhering to Ethical Business Principles

Corporate financial implosions and evidence of legal and ethical impropriety bring the need for organizational and leadership ethics to the forefront. As an organizational leader, it is important to the practice of your profession and your position as a role model to your staff that you adhere to an identifiable code of business or corporate ethics.

In the context of your role, you must understand and adhere to the corporate code of ethics and values as established by the administration or board of directors of the organization where you work. On one end of the spectrum, business ethics are meant to ensure that all members of the organization are complying with local, state and federal laws in the work that they do, and that they as individuals feel both compelled and safe to report any activities that are not within the scope of the law. Both large and small organizations will have a person or department charged with corporate compliance.

Corporate compliance programs are made up of a set of basic elements. Senior management must be aware of and involved in the process of compliance. Policies and procedures must reflect the organization's procedures for achieving compliance. Education about compliance must be given to both management and employees. And, there must be both monitoring programs and disciplinary procedures to act on those who do not adhere to the compliance approaches. Actions need to be in the best interest of the company and absent of any financial gain for individuals or for any member of their immediate family.

At the other end of the spectrum, business ethics extend the concepts of fairness and equity both inside and outside the organization. The organization is a member of the business and local communities, and there is an implied duty to be a contributor to those communities.

Employing Comparative Analysis Strategies

Organizational leaders need to understand more than their own departmental goals, measures and metrics. IT leaders are often part of the operational leadership of the entire organization. They need to understand the organization's overall financial and budgetary reports, its comparative benchmarks and its overall performance.

Budgets

To understand how the organization is doing financially, it is necessary to be able to read and understand a budget spreadsheet. Typically, such reports will be summarized and reviewed by the financial leaders of the company. These reports include the annual budgets by line item and the projected budget and expenditures to date. Variances between budgeted and actual expenditures to date will be reported, and there may also be a column that enables comparison with actual expenses for the most recent historic comparable financial period. This often consists of last year's expenses for the same time period. Many expenses are spread evenly over the year and are easy to predict, measure and compare. Other expenditures have unique timing considerations that, if not understood, can lead to a false understanding of the reports. Revenue and expenses that are recognized on a semiannual or quarterly basis can make year-to-date results appear far from expected, especially if the budget is constructed with an even distribution of those same expenses and revenues. A well-constructed budget report will include notations explaining the timing of events.

Other Financial and Nonfinancial Indicators

Financial and nonfinancial indicators are measured to compare one organization with another, or against national benchmarks. Days in accounts receivable, or A/R days, is an expression of the average amount of time it takes for the organization to receive payment from payers after the bills have been submitted to the guarantor. The discharged not final billed (DNFB) is an indicator of the expected amount of money to be billed to the guarantor, but not yet submitted due to outstanding documentation or procedural issues. Both indicators are important, as they represent money due to the organization but not yet received. Cash available to the organization is referred to as the day's cash on hand and represents the number of days the organization could continue to operate if no further new funds were received by the organization. The larger the number, to a point, the better it is for the organization.

Benchmarks

In addition to the previously discussed benchmarks specifically for information and management systems, there are benchmarks for organizational operations. These too are made up of both internal and external comparisons. The internal benchmarks are usually set by operations or the board of directors and are often reflections of the financial indicators listed above. Typically, the organization will set its goals for the number of days in A/R and days cash on hand. External benchmarks may include additional financial indicators, but are likely to reflect quality, safety, regulatory, or accreditation measures.

Quality Indicators

Quality indicators may be set by state or federal government agencies or payers to the organization. They may serve as goals to be met and aggregate data to establish benchmarks. Each country may have its own voluntary or required quality benchmarking processes. In the United States, the Department of Health and Human Services (HHS), which is a part of CMS, has several quality reporting programs depending on the type of setting. Other indicators are available from external services, such as the University Health System Consortium or Premier®. These entities will take extracts of your organization's data and aggregate them with comparable data from other organizations. This information is then distributed back to the data contributors so that each organization can compare its own results with different slices of the healthcare continuum. The advantage of these external comparison groups is that they enable an organization to compare itself with other organizations of like size, educational service, payer mix, geographic location and so forth. The downside is that some of these programs are subscription services that provide comparisons only to paid subscribers.

Quality Standards and Practices

Oversight for an IT department, especially one that has responsibilities for software development, requires careful attention to quality control standards. The National Academy of Medicine (formerly known as the Institute of Medicine (IOM)) has produced many publications citing issues with patient quality and safety, including *Health IT and Patient Safety: Building Safer Systems for Better Care.*[15] While a U.S. publication, the principles and recommendations set forth have international relevance.

Software as delivered, and its subsequent configuration by IT staff, requires comprehensive and regular review to ensure safe and high-quality performance. Quality assurance begins with the staff that implement and configure the software technically. Performance can be measured against testing results provided by the software vendors themselves and internally developed quality assurance scripts. As an example, external quality and patient safety organizations such as the Leapfrog Group[16] can provide testing to ensure appropriate decision support and alerts for computerized practitioner order entry (CPOE) programs.

Leaders must set clear expectations, or a plan, for the quality standards to be delivered and then measure, report and modify the plan to continually improve on the products delivered. Publishing current performance, as well as goals and objectives, will remind the entire department of the expectations and aspirations for which the group is striving.

Managing Projects, Project Portfolios and Vendors

Another major role of the IT professional is project management. Project management methodology is used in healthcare organizations to successfully implement new and complex IT systems. Project management is the discipline of planning, organizing, securing, managing, leading and controlling resources to achieve specific goals. A project is a temporary endeavor with a defined beginning and end. The temporary nature of projects stands in contrast with organizational operational initiatives, which consist of repetitive, permanent, or semi-permanent functional activities. Hospitals that support both project and functional initiatives are called matrixed organizations. In cases where multiple interdependent projects exist, program management is used to manage all the projects in a portfolio.

Health systems with multiple independent projects and resources that require a formalized framework for tracking, allocating and managing them effectively often adopt project portfolio management (PPM). PPM is the centralized management of processes, methods and technologies used by project managers (PMs) and PMOs to analyze and collectively manage a group of current or proposed projects based on numerous key characteristics. As the PPM landscape has been evolving rapidly, healthcare organizations are looking to manage their project initiatives through a single, enterprise-wide system called enterprise project portfolio management (EPPM).

In contrast to the traditional approach of combining manual processes, desktop project tools and best-of-breed PPM applications for each project portfolio environment, EPPM takes a more integrated and top-down approach to managing all project-intensive work and resources across the enterprise.

Project management has the following phases:

■ Initiating phase. In this phase, project stakeholders are identified, the project charter and the preliminary scope statement are developed and the project charter is approved.
■ Planning phase. This phase involves planning the project scope, quality and risk management and schedule. The project scope is defined through creating the project management plan, developing the scope management plan and creating the work breakdown structure (WBS). Quality and risk management planning involves identifying and analyzing risks and planning the risk responses. The project schedule is developed by defining and sequencing activities, estimating activity resources and duration, determining the project schedule and planning human resources.

- Executing phase. This phase involves directing and managing project execution; acquiring, developing and managing the project team; performing quality assurance; and procuring project resources.
- Monitoring and controlling phase. This phase involves managing the integrated change control process; controlling quality; controlling changes in cost, schedule and scope; measuring performance; and monitoring and controlling risks. An effective change control methodology will address both reactive and requested changes and will include processes for categorizing changes and determining how changes will be requested, reviewed and implemented.
- Closing phase. This phase involves releasing the final deliverables to the customer, handing over project documentation to the organization, terminating supplier contracts, releasing project resources and communicating project closure to all stakeholders. The final step is to undertake a post-implementation review to identify the level of project success and note any lessons learned for future projects.

According to the Project Management Body of Knowledge (PMBOK®) Guide, project management consists of nine knowledge management areas[17]:

1. Project scope management involves ensuring all the required work is performed to complete the project successfully. Scope creep is a key reason why many projects fail. Project scope management is accomplished by defining and controlling what is included in the project and what is not. Project scope management activities include the scope plan, scope definition, WBS, scope control and scope verification.
2. Project time management involves developing and controlling the project schedule. Project time management components include activity definition, activity sequencing, activity resource scheduling, activity duration, schedule development and schedule control.
3. Project cost management involves estimating the project cost and ensuring the project is completed within the approved budget. Accordingly, cost management includes the cost estimate, cost budgeting and cost control.
4. Project human resource management consists of obtaining, developing and managing the team who will perform the project work.
5. Project procurement management encompasses managing the acquisition of products and services from external sources in order to complete the project. Project procurement management includes planning acquisitions, negotiating contracts with sellers, selecting sellers, administering contracts with sellers and closing contracts.
6. Project risk management focuses on the identification of project risks and appropriate responses. Project risk management includes identifying risks, performing a risk analysis, developing a risk response plan and monitoring and controlling risks.

7. Project quality management involves ensuring the project satisfies its objectives and requirements. Project quality management includes performing quality planning, quality assurance and quality control.
8. Project integration management consists of the integration of the various project activities. Project integration management includes developing the project management plan, directing and managing project execution, monitoring and controlling the project work and closing the project.
9. Project communications management ensures project information is generated and distributed promptly. Project communication management activities include planning communication, distributing needed information to project stakeholders in a timely fashion, reporting the project performance and project status and resolving issues among the stakeholders.

The PM is an important stakeholder in bringing projects to successful completion. The PM is responsible for working with project sponsors, the project team and others involved in the project to meet project goals and deliver the project within budget and on schedule. The PM should also control the assigned project resources to best meet project objectives; manage project scope, schedule and cost; report on project progress; and facilitate and resolve issues, conflicts, risks and other obstacles to project success.

Managing Vendor Relationships

Healthcare chief information officers (CIOs) are increasingly turning to vendors for the expertise and support they need to meet the technology requirements of their organizations. This reliance on vendor partnerships enables vendors to play a key role in the success of many healthcare organizations. A well-managed vendor relationship will result in increased customer satisfaction, reduced costs, better quality and better service from the vendor. If problems arise, a well-managed vendor will be quick to remedy the situation. Vendor management is not simply negotiating the lowest price possible. It involves working with vendors on contract performance, schedules and costs, product functionality and support and maintenance agreements in order to mutually benefit both organizations.

The vendor management process begins with selecting the right vendor for the right reasons. This involves analyzing business requirements, performing a vendor search, selecting the winning candidate and successfully negotiating the contract. The contract should be carefully considered to ascertain that restrictions or exclusions, penalties and terms are beneficial to both parties. Once the relationship with the vendor has begun, vendor performance must always be monitored, with attention to the requirements that are most critical to the healthcare organization. Regular communication between the vendor and the healthcare organization will help to avoid misunderstandings and address issues before they become problems.

Three common pitfalls should be avoided in order to achieve successful vendor management.[18] First, it is important not to confuse vendor selection with vendor management. Equal importance needs to be given to managing the vendor relationship during and after the selection and contracting phases. Second, do not select a vendor based on price alone. Instead, give priority to a vendor that understands the value of developing a relationship that is mutually beneficial. Third, do not forget to evaluate how your vendor relationships affect your business. In addition to examining SLAs and contract fulfillment, IT leadership determines whether an engagement has brought value to the organization and whether both parties have received a return on their relationship.

The following 10 vendor management principles will enable healthcare organizations to build effective relationships with their suppliers and service providers[19]:

1. Use project management methodology. Due to the high visibility and accountability of today's complex healthcare projects, attention should be given to the basics of project management, such as creating a well-defined and properly planned project, recruiting effective project sponsorship, clarifying roles and responsibilities, establishing formal change control management and ensuring effective issue management.
2. Understand vendor management is multifaceted. Effective vendor management involves evaluation and selection, contract development, relationship management and delivery management.
3. Be aware of the contract details. This includes understanding what the vendor is responsible for, managing the project and vendor according to the contract and understanding what incentives motivate the vendor.
4. Formal documentation is key. All changes to the project and communications must be in writing and formally controlled.
5. Contract complexity should be consistent with project risk. The procurement process and the contract's level of detail should correspond to the level of project risk.
6. Include all important deliverables in the contract. Important deliverable specifications; the methodology used to create the deliverable; specific resources, roles and responsibilities; planned communications; deliverable acceptance criteria; and project success criteria should be included in the contract.
7. Management commitment is key. Senior management's commitment and flexibility are important to making the vendor-customer partnership work.
8. Focus on benefiting both the customer and the vendor. Both parties to the contract should give high priority to developing mutually beneficial resolutions should issues and tensions arise.
9. Clarify contractual terms and expectations. All terms and processes in the contract should be reviewed, explained and clarified to avoid conflicts and misunderstandings.

10. Ensure vendor and customer roles and responsibilities are clear. All parties' roles and responsibilities should be precisely defined in the contract. Particular attention should be paid to interactions between the procurement department and the project team, the contract administrator and the PM and the vendor's PM, sales team and accounting and legal departments.

Consulting Services

Consulting services are frequently purchased when personnel resources are in short supply or when a specific skill is lacking within the organization. Most frequently, an organization goes to the outside to facilitate a large initiative when internal resources cannot be spared. It is possible to retain professional services on an issue-by-issue basis or to keep a firm on retainer. Additionally, an organization could supply in-house consultation as a means of managing, staffing, or advising on any manner of need.

In-house consultation can be provided by individuals on an as-needed basis, but larger organizations are beginning to implement a PMO.[20] The IT and facility/plant management departments and staff often have the greatest depth of experience in managing large and complex projects at any organization, and the PMO may grow out of one or both of those areas. The PMO has personnel who are trained or certified in project management methodology as sponsored by the globally recognized Project Management Institute, Inc (PMI).[21]

Staff of the PMO are skilled at meeting with operational personnel to understand the detailed requirements of the project at hand and translate those requirements into a plan for execution. They understand the processes of resource gathering, project planning and project scope management, as well as the tools for visualizing the life of the project. They have the skills to manage development of the project's *pro forma* financial statements and the ongoing project budget. As the organization moves from IT projects to strategic operational projects with IT components, the IT project leaders can begin to alter their focus from operational leadership to true project management.

IT leaders may also serve as the voice of internal expertise. As departments throughout the healthcare organization begin to automate, they may need guidance or advice as to how to incorporate technologies into their workflow. The IT leaders or the PMO can provide innovation support to explore existing technologies to implement or watch for these departments. Partnership between the operational and technology experts creates an opportunity for innovation

Preparing and Delivering Business Communications

It is critical for leaders and managers to possess excellent written and verbal communication skills, and to have the ability to organize and manage business meetings. Organized meeting preparation helps the attendees to understand the goals and objectives of the meeting and the importance of the time invested. Well-prepared documents outline the topics and time to be spent on each issue. An example of a comprehensive meeting agenda is presented in Figure 9.3.

Organization name	Name of your committee

Meeting information			
Meeting name:	November ITSC	Meeting date:	11/28/2007
Time:	7:00 am to 9:00 am	Location:	Room 106

Attendees		
Names: ☐ Chairperson ☐ Attendee 1	☐ Attendee 2 ☐	☐ Attendee 3 ☐

November guests:
☐ Guest 1 and reason for attendance
☐ Guest 2 and reason for attendance

Agenda			
Discussion point	Expected outcome	Responsible party	Time (min)
Agenda review	Agree to meeting goals		5
Prior meeting review	Approve prior meeting minutes Review/update action items Review/update issues status		5
Item 1	Discussion v. decision		10
Item 2	Discussion v. decision		10
Item n	Discussion v. decision		30

Committee action items			Completion date		Status
Action item	Comments/Progress made	Responsible party	Original	Revised	
2008 IS budget	• Send 2008 IS budget communication to ITSC committee members		10/31/07		
Data center approval request — November board	• Send data center summary information to ITSC committee members		11/2/07		
Tactical plan for all IS initiatives	• Listing of all current and requested service requests for IS • Tool will become a part of decision-making process • Draft to be presented at October ITSC for approval		12/20/07 Awaiting System Capital Project Approval Process		

Committee action register — pending items			Completion date		Status
Action item	Comments/progress made	Responsible party	Original	Revised	

Figure 9.3   Meeting agenda template. *(Continued)*

Organization name	Name of your committee				
Complete IS 5-year assessment/estimate of infrastructural requirements and associated cost	• Expand 5-year incremental costing grid to include expense/capital impacts related to replacement equipment/upgrades, etc. (known costs of doing business)		TBD		
Develop ITSC dashboard	• Define metrics — situational/operational	Team	TBD		

Open issues (from previous meetings)			
Issue	Action taken or required	Assigned to	Status

New issues raised		
Issue	Action taken or required	Assigned to

Tentative future meeting agendas			
Dicussion point	Planned outcome	Responsible party	Time (min)
Simple sign-on/CCOW/biometric access technology	Establish strategy for technology access • Educate committee on capabilities pros/cons, complexity, and implementation impacts • Decide how to perform exploration — funding • Potential to neutral/external party with industry expertise define scope	Team	

Key decisions made

Meeting minutes		
Discussion point	Discussion Notes	Time (min)
Agenda review	Meeting began at 7:00 am.	
Prior meeting review		
Item 1		
Item 2		
Item n		
Adjourn	Meeting adjourned at 9:00 am.	

Figure 9.3 (*Continued*) **Meeting agenda template.**

A meeting agenda template for all meetings and minutes of the meeting will help meeting facilitators. Use of these tools creates a uniform method of communication that allows the staff to learn how to identify issues, actions and decisions in a consistent way. Variations in templates and formatting add a level of complexity for the meeting attendees and customers.

The agenda template in Figure 9.3 starts with the organization's name and the committee's name. Each header defines the section to follow. "Meeting Information" states the date, time and location of the meeting, while the subsequent section, "Attendees," lays out the expected participants and the roles they will play. The agenda itself lists each of the discussion points, the expected outcomes, the parties responsible to lead the discussion and the time limit for the presentation, discussion and decision, if necessary.

The "Committee Action Items" and "Committee Action Register" sections list the pending actions from the most recent meeting and other prior meetings, respectively. These sections enable all parties to have a comprehensive understanding of the status of all action items that remain open. Lacking those sections, it would be easy for a busy committee to lose track of items that have lower levels of priority than others do. It is acceptable to push back the date of some deliverables, but those changes should be made in a transparent way with the support of the committee.

The remaining sections of the agenda keep a record of actions and issues that are yet to be resolved. "Open Issues" lists items that were not completed by the desired action during the previous scheduled meeting. Any item that has been tabled will be left in the "Open Issues" section. "New Issues" serves as a tracking section for the meeting record keeper and the chair. This location is used to add issues that will need attention or completion in the time between meetings.

Presentation skills help define a leader. Leaders must speak clearly and with authority. First, let the audience know the purpose and the desired outcome of your presentation. Is the purpose to inform or to have an action result from the materials presented? During the presentation, include all the information that attendees need to understand, but highlight the key points rather than every detail. In closing restate, both the purpose and the desired outcome and address any questions or concerns, as this prevents disruption and loss of continuity during the presentation.

Project plans and status reports are important tools for everyone from executive leadership to project managers and staff. Figure 9.4 shows an example of a project status report for an organization's electronic health record (EHR) implementation. Like other communications, status documents need to provide an initial brief summary and follow with necessary supporting documentation. For project communications, the timeline and the completion status are the best first materials for review. In a project status report, a color-coded summary of tasks and status provides valuable visual clues. Use of arrows also provides quick indicators of the general direction of the elements compared to their immediately preceding status. Keep the reports simple by using red, yellow and green to identify tasks that are out of compliance, at risk or on track, respectively. Status reports need only be a single page with a table of color-coded tasks, a summary of the issues, the responsible parties for each task and the estimated date of resolution or completion.

Area	Topic	Apr-05	May-05	Jun-05	Jul-05	Aug-05	Sep-05	Oct-05
Project assessment	Overall status	◎	◓ ↑	◓	◓	◓	◓	◓

Area	Topic	Apr-05	May-05	Jun-05	Jul-05	Aug-05	Sep-05	Oct-05
Project management	Staffing	◎	◎	◎	◓ ↑	◓	◓	◓
	Detailed project plan	◎	◎	◎	◎	◎	◎	◎
	Implementation progress	◎	◓ ↑	◓	◓	◓	◓	◓
	Communication	◎	◓ ↑	◓	◓	◓	◓	◓
	Change management	◎	◓ ↑	◓	◓	◓	◓	◓
Go live	On schedule	◎	◎	◎	◎	◎	◎	◎

Area	Topic	Apr-05	May-05	Jun-05	Jul-05	Aug-05	Sep-05	Oct-05
Cadence	Staffing and			◎	◓ ↑	◒ ↑	◓	◓
	Workflows			◎	◓ ↑	◓	◓	◓
	Reporting needs			◎	◎	◎	◎	◎
	System build				◎	◎	◎	◎
	Testing							
	End-user training							
	Postlive activities							
HIM	Staffing and			◓	◓	◓	◓	◓
	Workflows			◎	◓ ↑	◓	◓	◓
	Reporting needs			◎	◎	◎	◎	◎
	System build				◎	◎	◎	◓↑
	Testing							
	End-user training							
	Postlive activities							

Figure 9.4   Status report for EHR implementation.

This report does not reflect the project budget. The budget status needs to be reported regularly using current period and year-to-date summaries. All variances, greater than a predetermined amount, need to be explained.

Facilitating Group Discussions and Committee Meetings

It is important for a leader to facilitate conversations and it is equally important for a leader to guide a group through difficult discussions. This differs somewhat from a typical business meeting. Knowing the issues, controversies and positions of meeting participants helps to manage the discussion. Construct meeting agendas with consideration for the time it will take to resolve issues and keep controversial decisions at the top of the agenda or as the sole item so there will be adequate time for discussion and resolution. If able, meet with key committee members in advance and begin a process of negotiation and education.

Complex decisions and controversial topics can make meeting management a challenge. Become familiar with *Robert's Rules of Order*[22] and define the expected rules of participation with committee members at the formation of the committee or at the beginning of any particularly challenging meeting in which you might anticipate conflict or debate. Keep a record of all motions and seconds. Record the essence of key discussions, including the names of participants when there is dissension. Ideally, decisions will be arrived at by consensus, but when necessary, keep a detailed record of the vote. As the discussion leader, do not let any committee members dominate the conversation, especially if they do not wait their turn in the queue. Ask speakers to clarify whether they are speaking in favor of or against the motion at hand. Do not hesitate to clarify whether a member is contributing new insights to the discussion or just echoing another's thoughts. In the interest of time, the focus needs to be on the specific discussion and who supports or does not support the topic.

The committee chairperson must not dominate the conversation. The chair carefully guides the conversation through the selection of speakers, asks probing and clarifying questions and contributes or highlights commentary as necessary. Use the straw poll as a tool. Identify those in favor of a motion and those who can live with the motion. If some attendees cannot live with the motion as stated, they should be asked to offer an alternative solution that serves the goals of all parties at the table. This keeps attendees accountable for problem solving.

Steering Committee Meetings

In today's complex healthcare environment, steering committees are essential in providing guidance and practical direction for IT project and operational initiatives. According to the Computer Economics IT Steering Committee Adoption and Best Practices 2017 study, nearly 72% of all IT organizations have steering committees.[23] The use of IT steering committees ranks first as the most mature IT management practice out of 15 practices covered in the study.

A steering committee is defined as an advisory committee, usually made up of high-level stakeholders or experts, which provides guidance on key issues such as company policy and objectives, budgetary control, marketing strategy, resource allocation and decisions involving large expenditures.[24] IT steering committees are a best-practice approach in healthcare organizations for aligning strategic business and IT priorities. Steering committees, which usually include executives and department heads, focus on three main tasks: IT strategic planning, project prioritization and project approval. Clear mandates and a real ability to influence decision making through executive participation increase the value of IT steering committees.

To ensure success in this important area of IT governance, healthcare CIOs should consider adopting four strategies:

1. Create a committee charter that includes the desired outcomes. This should help everyone understand the role and purpose of the group, which includes promoting improved communication and recognizing the partnership required for a successful IT deployment.

2. Establish a scope that reflects a corporate-wide perspective. The broader focus will be helpful when mediating conflicts in priorities or departmental perspectives that may not be in the best interest of the entire organization.
3. Consider indicating the specific level of authority of this group and its role in decision making. For example, the committee may be identified as a coordinating body that will resolve priorities, endorse proposals prior to approvals and monitor progress of major IT initiatives, but will have no role in budget approval or other departmental expenditure decisions.
4. Designate someone other than the CIO to chair the IT steering committee. Assigning a non-IT person, such as the chief operating officer (COO), chief medical information officer (CMIO), or chief finance officer (CFO), to chair the group communicates the message that IT is accepted as a critical resource and recognized as such by the entire organization.

To form an effective IT steering committee and keep it on track, three important steps should be considered[25]:

1. It is important to develop a case by aligning IT priorities with strategic business priorities. Focus on core IT strategic objectives and not IT resource allocation. In addition, stress shared decision making and foster a culture of communication between business units.
2. Develop a steering committee charter. It should outline the key tasks and responsibilities of the committee.
3. Keep the IT steering committee small and schedule regular meetings. Ensuring the membership is consistently informed, engaged as often as needed based on the project scope and timelines and includes executive decision-making authority, is critical to the success of the IT steering committee.

The use of IT steering committees is a proven method of driving better IT and business alignment. It is most effective in the area of IT governance, strategic planning, project prioritization and project approval. By developing an IT steering committee that has clear objectives, strong executive participation and a commitment to meeting regularly, IT leaders can significantly improve the value of IT to the organization.

Managing Risk

A key piece of the IT planning process integrates with the organizational efforts to manage risk. Issues of risk can be addressed along two dimensions. The first is magnitude of risk: If the event does occur, how big of an impact will it have on the organization, process or project? The second dimension is the likelihood of the risk: What is the best estimate of the likelihood that the risk event will in

		Magnitude of risk		
		Low 1	Medium 2	High 3
Likelihood of risk occurring	Low 1	1	2	3
	Medium 2	2	4	6
	High 3	3	6	9

Figure 9.5   Risk matrix.

fact occur? Within each dimension, the risk is low, medium or high and assigned a point value of 1 to 3, respectively.

The tool shown in Figure 9.5 depicts these two dimensions in a matrix. The values of each pair of dimensions are multiplied to generate a numeric score. A score of 1 is the lowest risk, while a score of 9 indicates the greatest risk. Color-coding the scores highlights the degree of risk being borne.

Organizations' risk management strategies will vary depending on their tolerance for risk. Typically, scores of 6 or higher will warrant the creation of a contingency plan. A contingency plan is an alternative path, project or process that would be considered if the primary path is disrupted. A simple example would be a backup plan to print and distribute paper reports if the electronic distribution process is disrupted for longer than a preset amount of time. Within any one very large project, there are likely to be multiple smaller contingency plans to account for any individual event that may occur.

Risk management and business continuity planning are taking on great prominence in healthcare. Leaders have the responsibility to bring to light the full effects of system loss and the costs associated with mitigating those risks. The solutions are often expensive and will create considerable conversation, especially around the likelihood of any event happening.

Once a risk has been identified, a plan for risk mitigation is the next logical step. Risk mitigation helps the organization understand the risk and guides the organization to take steps to prevent a disaster. Risk mitigation should be applied to situations where both internal and external customers are involved. To mitigate internal customer risk, you might use a more collaborative approach, whereas to mitigate risk for an external customer, the process may be a bit more formal. For example, if the quality department identifies a risk, they typically work with the internal departments to prevent problems. If an external entity, a vendor for example, creates risk, then an organization must mitigate risk contractually or halt relations with the vendor.

Financial Risk Management

It is important for healthcare organizations to make sound decisions in order to manage financial and budget risks. Without a solid understanding of financial risks and their impact, they cannot be expected to make the right decisions about their capital and operating investments. The fundamental idea behind managing financial risk in healthcare is to reduce and protect against the inherent unpredictability of future costs.

Enterprise risk management (ERM) is a proven methodology that organizations use to manage overall risk. While ERM has been used to address clinical, human resource and legal risks in the hospital setting, it has not been frequently applied to financial risk management. This could be due to the complex and highly specialized nature of the tax-exempt capital markets, which can be intimidating to many risk management professionals. Despite its complexity, financial risk can be handled in the same four steps as other forms of risk:

1. Identification—Listing financial risks that can occur as a result of either negative factors or favorable events (e.g., when unexpected success leads to exponentially increased demand for services)
2. Quantification—Assessing the likelihood or probability a risk-related event will occur and the magnitude of its impact
3. Risk response—Determination and implementation of a response to the risk, such as acceptance, transference, mitigation or avoidance
4. Monitoring—Continuous review of existing and future risks

Core financial skills are needed to reduce the risks associated with IT investments. Today's IT professionals should be knowledgeable about budgeting and planning; financial purchasing options, such as capitalized and depreciated assets; operating expenses; basic accounting principles and standards; financial models and methods; and compliance regulations. In addition, the IT professional should use a broad range of methods and tools, such as return on investment (ROI) calculations, budget-tracking tools, revenue creation reports, monthly financial reports and variances, technology pilots where available, SLAs to improve vendor performance and soliciting buy-in for IT initiatives from business and clinical unit executives to minimize and reduce IT procurement risks.

Budget Risk Management

Managing budgets is one of the basic disciplines that all managers must master. An organized approach to developing and maintaining the budget will go a long way in helping reduce risks. In addition, to prepare for the possibility that some risks will not be managed successfully, a risk contingency budget should be created. Funds from the risk contingency budget can then be used to prevent a project from going over budget.

For today's IT managers, having solid budgeting and forecasting skills is critical in reducing budget risk. Understanding the annual budget cycle is important, particularly in avoiding the fiscal year-end crises that often occur as organizations attempt to balance their budgets. The business requirements for expenses should be accurately assessed. The budget should be developed in detail. At the line-item level, capital and operating expenditures should be differentiated and long-range capital planning should be identified. Capital expenditures are payments by the organization for fixed assets, such as buildings and equipment. Capital expenses are incurred when a company buys assets that have a useful life of more than one year and are typically depreciated. The long-range capital plan, which covers five years or more, should be the result of an executive review process that determines the proper mix of existing assets and new investments needed to fulfill the healthcare organization's mission, goals and objectives, and should reflect the priorities for the year. Operating expenditures are incurred in the course of ongoing, day-to-day business activities and include payments for rent, utilities, salaries and benefits, training, software maintenance fees and telecommunications. Operating expenses relate to items that have a useful life of one year or less and are not depreciated.

It is important for a consistent model or software system to be used to manage the budget. Budget risk can be addressed by paying attention to contracts and maintenance fee increases and by adjusting and reforecasting the expenditures. Healthcare organizations may be required to make budget reductions; therefore, maintaining multiple budget scenarios is important. These can be reserved for times when revenue is low, when critical enhancements are made or when revenue-generating projects are planned.

The following important steps should be considered when managing budgets[26]:

- Negotiate an effective budget to start with. Spending the necessary time at the beginning of a project will eliminate budget challenges later in the project schedule.
- Plan for unexpected expenses. This will allow for flexibility should unforeseen expenses arise.
- Prepare early for year-end budget activities. Finalizing budgets at the end of the fiscal year is an important and time-consuming activity. It is best to start planning for this early or on an ongoing basis.
- Stay close to budget. Attempt to finish as close to budget expectations as possible and avoid being significantly over or under budget, as this will affect the following year's budget allocations.
- Account for cost allocations. Identify charges or transfers that may occur to or from other departments to your department.
- Understand the key budget numbers. Know all the critical numbers for your department and be aware if any of the numbers are wrong.

Roles and Responsibilities for IT-Related Functions

The increased adoption of technology in healthcare has greatly expanded the role of IT. In addition to traditional IT functions, healthcare IT has created exciting new roles and responsibilities. Healthcare IT is the area of IT involving the design, development, creation, use and maintenance of information systems for the healthcare industry. Healthcare IT includes electronic coding, accounting and billing systems; electronic medical records (EMRs) or EHRs; and clinical or departmental applications, such as lab, radiology, pharmacy and nutrition. It includes support for ancillary systems such as cardiology and radiology. Clinics in the ambulatory space require practice management systems that handle appointment scheduling, billing and patient follow up.

IT-related careers in healthcare can be found in many different types of organizations. These include hospitals, physician clinics, payer organizations, health information exchanges (HIEs), community health centers, long-term care, ambulatory surgery centers and more. Health IT is also prevalent in educational institutions, academic medical centers, government agencies, the military, vendor organizations and consulting companies. Both general IT and healthcare IT roles exist in these organizations. Individuals with a clinical background who are interested in a career in healthcare IT will find excellent opportunities in many of the organizations listed above. To make the transition from clinical practice to IT or from general IT to healthcare IT can be challenging; however, those who do it successfully often thrive in their new careers. The HIMSS Professional Development Staff and associated professional development committees have created a document that contains job descriptions for health information technology professionals. This document can be found on the HIMSS web site in the Resource Center.

Senior Management Roles and Responsibilities

Board of director, executive management and medical executive committee support are essential for the success of IT in a healthcare organization. The CIO is generally the most senior-level IT executive. In many health systems, this role also carries the vice president or senior vice president designation. Additional IT executive leadership roles can include the CMIO, the chief nursing information officer (CNIO), the chief technology officer (CTO), the chief information security officer (CISO), chief health information officer (CHIO) and chief pharmacy information officer (CPIO). Second-level leadership typically entails IT department directors, clinical informaticists and physician and nurse champions. Recently, health systems have developed new roles, such as the chief innovation officer, chief applications officer, chief digital officer, chief experience officer, chief business development officer and chief privacy officer positions, to meet the dynamic and complex technology environment.

General IT Roles and Responsibilities

Healthcare organization IT departments are staffed with internal full-time employees (FTEs) or outsourced staff that support traditional IT-related roles. Job descriptions for these roles are categorized as senior level, midlevel and entry level and typically include titles such as director, manager, architect, analyst, engineer, technician, administrator, programmer, analyst and developer. Common areas that these roles are responsible for are generally divided into three major sections. The infrastructure team is usually responsible for the data center, IT helpdesk, communications, database administration, backups, network support and IT security. The business group manages applications to support human resources, payroll, supply chain, finance, marketing and web development. Clinical applications teams support EHRs and all clinical ancillary applications. Technical integration teams support interfaces between all types of systems.

Healthcare IT Roles and Responsibilities

To meet the evolving technology demands of healthcare organizations, particularly considering the increased usage of EHRs, many clinical, business and project-related roles now require healthcare IT knowledge and a blend of healthcare business, clinical, management and technical experience. Some of the most in-demand clinical and business positions are analyst roles. These include specialty roles covering all categories of applications, administrative services, customer support, workflow analysis and configuration. Other important healthcare IT roles include informatics, clinical engineering, go-live events, implementation consulting, integration, project management, quality assurance, usability and human factors analysis. Trainers are crucial in healthcare for all personnel and all applications. Change management, transformation and IT communications teams are also becoming more common in healthcare institutions.

Staff Competency in Information and Management System Skills

With the myriad of roles in a typical healthcare IT department, it is important to consider professional development, training and competency for the applications supported. Some applications require professional certification in order to perform configuration within. Others require one-time certification. A solid plan for team development can reduce turnover and increase employee satisfaction.

Employee Development

Employee development is a key component in ensuring that healthcare IT staff attain the necessary competency in information and management system tools and skills. Mastering those skills, along with developing the soft skills needed to collaborate and work together as a team, is essential in ensuring the success of the organization. Staff improvement programs provide employees with the proficiencies and qualifications needed for advancement within the organization, and help staff form positive attitudes and interpersonal skills to work effectively.

Employee development can be provided through training and in-service programs, certification classes, community college or university educational courses, conferences and workshops, professional association involvement and self-study through books, industry magazines, videos and online resources. Effective leaders also provide opportunities for employees to mentor others or ask senior colleagues for mentorship. Shadowing an executive for a day can be an enriching experience for an employee. It is common practice to implement goals during the annual review process, adding a "stretch" goal or a goal to take someone out of their comfort zone gives the individual the opportunity to grow and learn.

Organizational Training and In-Service Programs

Training and in-service programs may originate from several sources. Human resources typically have responsibility for organization-wide training requirements (e.g., security and safety regulations, discriminatory practice and quality improvements). Supervisory, management and leadership development may be designed and offered by a leadership department within the organization or through human resources. The department or group in which an employee works provides programs such as in-service or online training. In addition, IT projects for information and management system deployments usually include a training budget for system developers, administrators and end users who will be supporting and using the product.

Job-Related IT Certifications

IT-based certifications have long been a mainstay of IT education and professional credentials. Certifications have two main advantages. First, they provide a framework by which technical staff can learn and gain a level of proficiency in a specific IT-related topic. Second, a certification provides the recipients with a credential showing they have a defined body of knowledge in a specific area. Although a certification by itself will not qualify a person for a new job or promotion, it does demonstrate that the individual has mastered either a basic or advanced level of a specific knowledge area and it is often viewed as a positive contributing factor in the decision of whom to hire. It is recommended that clinicians keep their clinical licensure and certifications active and up-to-date, even if they are no longer in a clinical role. Similarly, IT professionals should also consider keeping their IT certifications active, particularly those certifications that are in high demand in healthcare IT.

The Certified Professional in Healthcare Information and Management Systems (CPHIMS[SM]) certification is an essential credential for all healthcare IT management, management engineering and process improvement professionals, military personnel and consultants. Developed and sponsored through HIMSS, eligible candidates become certified by passing the CPHIMS examination. The

CPHIMS certification demonstrates an international standard of professional knowledge and competence in healthcare information and management systems. Similarly, HIMSS offers the Certified Associate in Healthcare Information and Management Systems (CAHIMS[SM]) certification allowing those who do not qualify for eligibility for the CPHIMS, an opportunity to demonstrate their professional knowledge.

New projects can bring a significant change to organizational workflows and processes. It is important to include change management in healthcare IT processes. The ADKAR™ model for change emphasizes ***awareness*** of a project through communication, addressing the ***desire*** for change, creating ***knowledge*** around the change, understanding the customer's ***ability*** to change and ***reinforcement*** of why the change occurred and importance of keeping the change in place.[4] ADKAR Change Management certification can be attained via a three-day course or a condensed one-day course.

Many of today's highly sought-after healthcare IT certifications can be obtained only by employees of organizations that are engaged in a specific vendor product deployment, such as an EHR or healthcare information systems project. However, healthcare systems also value generally available certifications, particularly if they are in the process of deploying related methodologies throughout their organization. These include certifications such as the Project Management Professional (PMP®), ITIL® and Lean Six Sigma.

Miscellaneous Professional Development

Healthcare IT professionals should consider other professional development and education opportunities. These are particularly useful in helping individuals become well rounded and remain current in the rapidly evolving healthcare environment. Employees are typically responsible for the costs of their professional development, but many companies pay for such education as a benefit of employment. Several of the more common sources of professional development are healthcare IT conferences and workshops; programs sponsored by national and local professional associations, such as HIMSS; university certificate programs and bachelor's, master's and doctorate degrees in healthcare IT, informatics, information management and information systems; and self- or group study using books, industry magazines or journals, videos and such online resources as white papers, webinars, conferences and training.

Performance Evaluation

Performance evaluation is an important tool that healthcare administrators can utilize to monitor and improve employee competencies. Performance evaluation is the ongoing process in which employees' work, outcomes, attitudes and interpersonal skills, professional growth and adherence to organizational values are assessed and feedback is provided. In the evaluation process, the employee's actual performance is compared against the expected performance. In order to be effective and objective, the performance evaluation process must start with specific and measurable performance goals. The performance goals should be defined and communicated to the employee at the start of the year.

A variety of methods can be used in the performance evaluation process, the most common being the rating scale. The scales will specify personal traits and behaviors expected, such as teamwork, communication skills, adherence to values, dependability and initiative. Also specified will be specific job attributes, such as quality and quantity of work.[26] Each trait or behavior is accompanied by a range of numbers and words that the evaluator marks to indicate an employee's level of performance.

Some organizations use the 360-degree method of performance appraisal. In this method, other individuals are asked to rate the employee on specific criteria. Raters may include individuals who work with the employee on teams, subordinates, peers in the same department, employees in other departments and sometimes outside customers and vendors. The employee is also given the opportunity to perform a self-assessment. The results of all these assessments are taken into consideration in the final evaluation that is completed for the employee. In this process, it is important to provide confidentiality to the raters for the evaluations they provided.

During the performance appraisal process, it is important for the manager to provide feedback to employees at regular intervals during the year. Employees should never be surprised during a formal appraisal that they were found to be performing at a less than adequate level in some aspect of their role. Sub-par performance should be dealt with as soon as it is identified. This type of feedback gives the employee an opportunity to improve performance. Alternatively, if an employee is performing at an excellent or exceptional level, the interim positive feedback will help to preserve that positive behavior. Although interim reviews can be done formally or informally, it is advisable to complete a formal, written interim review if an employee's performance requires improvement.

When disciplinary action is needed, it must be taken based on clear facts and with documented justification. If disciplinary action is needed, it should be done progressively over time—starting with verbal discussions, then utilizing written and verbal communication and possibly ending with termination. This approach provides consistent communication to the employee about what needs to be done to resolve the problem. Communication may be oral at first. If the problem persists, documentation should be completed in the form of notes to the employee's personnel record and written warnings with substantive examples of the inadequate performance. At all steps during the process, it is advisable to communicate with and seek the advice from the human resources department.

Developing Educational Strategies for IT Staff

Leaders are hired due to a combination of their experiences and skills. They will likely select individuals to work for them based on similar criteria. The staff will continue to gain experience as they do their jobs, but there is very little opportunity for them to continue their education and expand their knowledge unless someone creates opportunities for them. Education can be provided in many ways and at relatively little overall cost.

At the very least, education needs to be valued. Commit to the time it will take for staff to complete further education and commit to supporting the cost of the education as well. Encourage staff to broaden their skills by taking opportunities to stretch their current skills or cross-train in areas that are beyond their current experiences. When it becomes tempting to reduce costs by eliminating educational support, also consider how much it will cost to recruit new staff and whether the skills sought are those the current staff may be lacking.

Initiate your educational support by creating low-cost educational opportunities for the staff. Ensure that staff members are signed up as members of all the vendor user groups, both locally and nationally. Take advantage of professional societies, interest groups and other local educational opportunities as well. Many of these organizations sponsor local presentations and educational dinner meetings as conveniences to their members. Professional associations, like HIMSS, offer both local and global membership. In many cases, education is free and is often available in multiple media formats so that individuals can attend in person or via webcasting, webinars and other telecasting options. Many vendors will also make free educational opportunities available to the staff.

When funds are available, consider having staff take turns attending vendors' user conferences or professional society conferences. That way, staff members can attend conferences every couple of years. Ask those staff who go to take time to explore specific educational sessions of interest to the whole organization. Upon the conference attendee's return, arrange for a team luncheon at which that person can report on information learned and share any gathered materials. Most societies and large user groups make their conference presentations available online, so it is very easy to share content with staff.

As noted earlier, succession planning is an important part of the overall IT planning process. An investment in education and the thoughtful application of the new skills expands the capabilities of the IT staff and helps to ensure a well-balanced, mature and knowledgeable department.

Current IT Technologies and Trends

The overall education of the IT team members extends beyond the applications they service and the immediate issues and objectives that are at hand. Team members need to stay connected to a variety of disciplines related to their specific sphere of expertise. The greatest opportunity for this added education comes from within the organization itself. Listen to the feedback of colleagues and peers. Be engaged and ask questions to become more knowledgeable. So much of the work we do overlaps with the work of others. Knowledge will expand your effectiveness in the work you do.

Outside of your own colleagues, a valuable educational resource is the media and printed press. *The Guardian, Healthcare IT News, People's Daily* and the *Wall Street Journal* are often the first to pick up on and report trends or activities that have national or international significance in many disciplines. Take the time to review the headlines and articles in order to stay up on current events. Organizational leaders will be regularly asked to comment on materials in those publications.

Many publications now offer really simple syndication (RSS) or other services that will e-mail the headlines or article titles that align with subjects you are interested in. Given the option of being proactive or reactive, a successful leader will choose the former path.

Developing System, Operational and Department Documentation

With the vast amount of expertise required to manage healthcare applications, it is crucial that teams develop detailed documentation to create a knowledge base for auditing and use by teams. The documentation can be system, operational, or departmental in nature. This ensures that teams are organized, and that customers understand the IT process.

System Documentation

System documentation includes the documents that support analysis, decision making, acquisition and implementation processes. It also addresses system features and functional and technical requirements. Systems analysis documentation includes the information gathered in the process of "collecting, organizing, and evaluating data about IT system requirements and the environment in which the system will operate."[27] It also includes documents such as functional requirements, design specifications, requests for information and proposals and related vendor responses. Also considered part of system documentation are procedure manuals, computer programs and machine operating manuals; details of standards compliance; and records of the initial system testing process and results (e.g., data collection and input procedures).

Operational Documentation

Operational documents relate to ongoing systems operations and maintenance. They include information about ongoing testing of systems and results, audit processes and database management, as well as training manuals. Operational documents also encompass implementation time frames, flowcharts and progress reports; data backup and recovery procedures; and system retirement, tuning and logistic support requirements.

Department Documentation

Department policies and procedures (P&Ps) help to guide the processes and actions employees should use to perform their work and are essential for healthcare organizations to achieve various accreditations. A department or organizational policy formalizes what is expected or required of employees, among other things. A procedure document describes how an outcome is to be accomplished. Therefore, policies and procedures serve two purposes: (1) they set performance requirements that can be used to motivate or discipline employees and (2) they serve as ongoing references for employees and orientation documents for new hires.[28] In developing P&Ps, the following steps are useful: (1) identify a need; (2) draft a policy or procedure that addresses the need; (3) get management approval; (4) distribute the approved document to employees and educate them on its contents; (5) revise, replace or withdraw the policy or procedure as needed; and (6) coordinate with human resources, corporate compliance or other areas when applicable.

Department P&Ps will address elements such as security (e.g., access control, entity authentication, audit trails, data encryption, firewall protection and virus checking), privacy protection (definitions of access rights and instructions for handling specific information and patients) and information retention and availability of medical information. In addition, communication of medical information, management of licensed software, handling of service requests, the IT strategic plan and the IT budget should be addressed. It is also important to consider change management, project management and process improvement; development methods and standards; and copyrights and ownership in department P&Ps.

Summary

Today's healthcare IT arena could be considered extreme by some. There is a movement towards innovation and disruptive technologies in our healthcare system that demands excellence in leadership and management. Healthcare organizations strive to lead with new technology and deliver the highest quality care to patients. For an IT leader or manager, this means handling multiple projects and doing more with less. IT leaders must be experienced in strategic planning, complex reporting and dealing with internal and external customer relationships. IT leaders must manage risk, budgets and large teams of professional resources. New roles and responsibilities in healthcare IT are constantly emerging. Today's leaders require a blend of clinical and business awareness. They need experience in project management and change management to be successful. Stakeholder engagement using effective steering committees and monitoring customer satisfaction are critical for success.

References

1. McNickle M. 5 tips for creating a strategic plan for IT. *Healthcare IT News*, March 29, 2012. http://www.healthcareitnews.com/news/5-tips-creating-strategic-plan-it (accessed November 30, 2015).
2. ITIL. https://www.axelos.com/best-practice-solutions/itil/what-is-itil (accessed November 30, 2015).
3. Shaw R. *Computer Aided Marketing & Selling*. London: Butterworth Heinemann, 1991.
4. Hiatt JM. *ADKAR A Model for Change in Business, Government and Our Community*. Loveland, Colorado: Prosci Research, 2006.
5. Nash D, Nash S. Customer Relationship Management: 6 Steps from Customer Service. North Yorkshire, UK: Team Technology. http://www.teamtechnology.co.uk/customerservice2.html (accessed April 22, 2016).
6. HIMSS (Healthcare Information and Management Systems Society). *HIMSS Dictionary of Healthcare Information Technology Terms, Acronyms and Organizations*. 3rd ed. Chicago: HIMSS, 2013, p. 35.
7. Shaw PL, Carter D. *Quality and Performance Improvement in Healthcare*. Chicago: American Health Information Management Association, 2015.
8. Institute for Healthcare Improvement. SBAR Toolkit. Cambridge, MA: Institute for Healthcare Improvement. http://www.ihi.org/resources/Pages/Tools/SBARToolkit.aspx (accessed November 30, 2015).
9. HIMSS (Healthcare Information and Management Systems Society). Healthcare Cybersecurity Community. Chicago: HIMSS. https://www.himss.org/membership-participation/cybersecurity (accessed November 30, 2015).
10. IFHIMA (International Federation of Health Information Management Associations). http://www.ifhima.org/ (accessed November 30, 2015).
11. IMIA (International Medical Informatics Association). http://www.imia-medinfo.org/new2/ (accessed November 30, 2015).
12. Joint Commission International. http://www.jointcommissioninternational.org/ (accessed November 30, 2015).
13. CMS (Centers for Medicare & Medicaid Services). Conditions for Coverage (CfCs) & Conditions of Participations (CoPs). Baltimore: CMS. http://www.cms.gov/Regulations-and-Guidance/Legislation/CFCsAndCoPs/index.html?redirect=/CFCsAndCoPs (accessed November 30, 2015).
14. Federal Register. https://www.federalregister.gov/policy/about-us (accessed November 30, 2015).

15. Institute of Medicine. *Health IT and Patient Safety: Building Safer Systems for Better Care.* Washington, DC: National Academies Press, 2011.

16. The Leapfrog Group. http://www.leapfroggroup.org/ (accessed November 30, 2015).

17. PMBOK. *A Guide to the Project Management Body of Knowledge.* 4th ed. Newton Square, PA: Project Management Institute, 2008, pp. 13, 43.

18. Perelman D. Six steps to successful vendor management. *eWeek*, May 17, 2007. http://www.eweek.com/c/a/IT-Infrastructure/Six-Steps-to-Successful-Vendor-Management (accessed April 22, 2016).

19. Horine G. *Absolute Beginner's Guide to Project Management.* 2nd ed. Indianapolis: Que Publishing, 2009.

20. Price MP. *Business Driven PMO Setup.* Plantation, FL: J. Ross Publishing, 2009.

21. Project Management Institute. https://www.pmi.org/ (accessed November 30, 2015).

22. Robert's Rules of Order. http://www.robertsrules.org/ (accessed November 30, 2015).

23. Computer Economics. IT Steering Committees Are Vital for IT Governance. 2017. https://www.computereconomics.com/article.cfm?id=2458 (accessed April 1, 2020).

24. Business Dictionary. Steering committee. http://www.businessdictionary.com/definition/steering-committee.html (accessed April 22, 2016).

25. Info-Tech Research Group. Establish an effective IT steering committee. London: Info-Tech Research Group. https://www.infotech.com/research/ss/establish-an-effective-it-steering-committee (accessed April 22, 2016).

26. Owen J. *The Leadership Skills Handbook.* 2nd ed. San Francisco: Jossey-Bass, 2012.

27. Santiago A. How to break into a career in healthcare IT. 2014. http://healthcareers.about.com/od/administrativeandsupport/p/HealthITjobs.htm (accessed April 22, 2016).

28. ONC (Office of the National Coordinator for Health Information Technology). Get the Facts About Health IT Workforce Development Program. Washington, DC: ONC. https://www.healthit.gov/sites/default/files/get_the_facts_workforce_development.pdf (accessed April 22, 2016).

Chapter 10

Questions

Chapter 1: Healthcare Environment

Question 1
What are the "four pillars" of the healthcare environment?
 A. Ownership, classification, cost and tax status
 B. Quality, care setting, physicians, and access
 C. Cost, access, value and quality
 D. Quality, cost, ownership and location

Question 2
Hospitals may be classified many different ways. Which of the following statements is true regarding hospital classification?
 A. Private hospitals are always for-profit organizations
 B. Urban, rural and children's hospitals are classified by their geographic locations
 C. Rural hospitals are most frequently classified as teaching hospitals
 D. Hospitals may be classified in more than one way; for example, an urban hospital might also be classified as a government-owned hospital or as a general hospital

Question 3
An ambulatory surgery center would be best classified as
 A. A teaching hospital
 B. An outpatient care setting
 C. A general hospital
 D. A rehabilitation hospital

DOI: 10.4324/9780429442391-14

Question 4

From the perspective of the healthcare delivery organization, payments generally come from three types of entities:

A. Employers, employees and government entities

B. Government-financed and managed programs, insurance programs managed by private entities and patients' personal funds

C. National health systems, national insurance systems and multipayer systems

D. Uninsured, underinsured and insured

Question 5

In considering the purpose for interrelationships among healthcare organizations, identify the purpose below that is correct:

A. Enable access to comprehensive care services from only one healthcare organization

B. Ensure effective transfers of care facilitated by the provision of essential health information

C. Facilitate obtaining appropriate rewards for care referrals

D. Facilitate marketing of healthcare services regardless of patients' consent

Question 6

Ensuring the general portability of healthcare is facilitated by

A. Health information exchanges (HIEs) such as Canada's Health Infoway and the U.S. HIE programs, including the Nationwide Health Information Network (NHIN)

B. The Organisation for Economic Cooperation and Development (OECD)

C. Insurance programs administered by private entities

D. The secondary use of healthcare information

Question 7

An example of the secondary use of a patient's health information would be when the information is shared

A. To support transfer of the patient's care between two providers

B. Through an authorized health information exchange to support the portability of care

C. In support of a diagnostic test required to further the treatment of a patient

D. With public health officials for statistical reporting or in support of clinical research

Question 8

In the financial reimbursement area, the interrelationships between healthcare organizations

A. Are unrelated to the efficiency of healthcare claims processing

B. May assure government payers that quality healthcare services have been delivered

C. Do not support private insurance organizations in their assessment of the quality of delivered healthcare services

D. Are designed to maximize reimbursement for covered healthcare services

Question 9

Key information technology and information management professionals in healthcare organizations include the

- A. Chief information officer (CIO), chief executive officer (CEO) and chief medical information officer (CMIO)
- B. Chief information officer (CIO), chief security officer (CSO) and chief medical information officer (CMIO)
- C. Chief information officer (CIO), chief financial officer (CFO) and chief technology officer (CTO)
- D. Chief information officer (CIO), chief executive officer (CEO) and chief nursing informatics officer (CNIO)

Question 10

Nongovernment professional associations may perform regulatory roles for their profession. Which of the following is *not* a typical role for a professional association?

- A. Determining qualifications for a profession by defining professional examination criteria
- B. Making laws and regulations regarding reimbursements for their profession
- C. Issuing a code of conduct to guide professional behavior
- D. Implementing disciplinary procedures for those in their profession

Question 11

There has been a shift in care settings to what type of facility?

- A. Academic centers
- B. Outpatient centers
- C. Urban centers
- D. Private facilities

Chapter 2: Technology Environment

Question 1

Patients have an expectation that healthcare providers will keep health information entrusted to them

- A. Private, secure and freely digitally available
- B. Available Monday through Friday
- C. On paper
- D. Available for research

Question 2

Data warehouses include

- A. Data from one hospital only
- B. Information from the patient
- C. Data from many different HIT applications
- D. Financial data only

Question 3

Interface engines support
- A. Interoperability and data integration
- B. Manual connections to financial systems
- C. Cloud storage of patient information
- D. Encryption of patient-identifiable data

Question 4

Telehealth can be used to
- A. Constrain patients to specific providers
- B. Provide a wide variety of care to patients who are at home
- C. Prohibit transfers of patients
- D. Mandate admissions to academic medical centers

Question 5

mHealth applications can address
- A. Contactless access to healthcare services from the patient's home
- B. Global health initiatives
- C. Issues concerning supply chain inventory
- D. Trends in consumer consumption of healthcare products and services

Question 6

What makes healthcare data integration unique to other industries?
- A. Myriad un-adopted standards across health systems
- B. IoT and home devices that are not healthcare grade
- C. Healthcare data is a lot easier to share as it follows clearly defined interoperable standards
- D. Securing patient information like SSNs

Question 7

What are the main goals of an Enterprise Analytics department within a hospital?
- A. Provide retrospective and prospective insights of both operational and clinical activities within a given healthcare system
- B. Generate data-driven predictive models based on outcomes (clinical/operational/financial)
- C. Provide leadership insights into areas where efficiencies can be made
- D. All of the above

Chapter 3: Clinical Informatics

Question 1

According to the American Medical Informatics Association (AMIA), clinical informaticists use their knowledge to do which of the following:

A. Characterize, evaluate and refine clinical processes

B. Lead or participate in the procurement, customization, development, implementation, management, evaluation and continuous improvement of clinical information systems

C. Develop, implement and refine clinical decision support systems

D. All of the above

Question 2

One aspect of the Domains of Clinical Informatics is:

A. Securing executive support for smaller projects

B. Housing services

C. Information and communication technology

D. Transportation services

Question 3

Which of the following is current measurement goals of eCQMs for both Medicare and Medicaid?

A. Patient safety

B. Population/public health

C. Clinical process/effectiveness

D. All of the above

Question 4

The medical specialty of otolaryngology covers the areas of

A. Sinus issues

B. Swallowing difficulty

C. Both A and B

D. None of the above

Question 5

Of the following, which is NOT an eligible hospital (EH) or critical access hospital (CAH) objective/measure?

A. Electronic prescribing

B. Health information exchange

C. Providing up-to-date hardware for clinicians

D. Protecting health information

Question 6

A branch of artificial intelligence (AI) that helps computers understand, interpret and manipulate human language is called

A. Logical Observation Identifiers Names and Codes

B. Natural Language Processing

C. Unified Medical Language Systems

D. Health Level 7

Question 7

What is a noted disadvantage of clinical decision support (CDS)?

A. Data integrity

B. Lack of maintenance and governance

C. Clinical burnout and documentation burden

D. All of the above

Question 8

Which of the following is NOT one of the Five Rights of CDS?

A. Right person

B. Right facility

C. Right time

D. Right format

Chapter 4: Analysis

Question 1

Which of the following is not an objective of the systems analysis phase?

A. Gather, analyze and validate technical, functional and nonfunctional requirements

B. Determining feasibility, objectives and scope

C. Evaluate the alternatives and prioritize the requirements

D. Create software, hardware and network requirements documentation

Question 2

When defining problems and opportunities, major areas of change can occur in the following areas:

A. Analytical, supervisory, financial and administrative

B. Clinical, administrative, financial and infrastructure

C. Supervisory, administrative, financial and clinical

D. Infrastructure, analytical, administrative and financial

Question 3

The value of performing a cost–benefit analysis is to determine

   A. How long a project will take to be implemented

   B. The overall total expenses of the project

   C. How long it will take to achieve the payback period of the investment

   D. The number of personnel resources that will be needed throughout the lifecycle of the project

Question 4

When presenting your analysis to your executive leadership, key elements may include

   A. Possible changes in the project implementation that can be driven by changes in technology standards

   B. Requirements that may change, affecting the strategic capability of the proposal

   C. Sensitivity to challenges or changes in the internal environment that may rely on the establishment of a support team within the organization

   D. Expectations that the implementation of analysis and subsequent proposals will rely on the presence of standard operational processes in the internal environment

Question 5

Of the following tools, which is not a common tool used for conducting a needs analysis

   A. Observation

   B. Documentation review

   C. Interviews

   D. Gap analysis

Question 6

What are the typical priorities taken into consideration when assessing a project?

   A. Patient safety and security, profitability, ease of processes, standardization

   B. Patient safety and security, timeliness, ease of processes, standardization

   C. Patient safety and security, profitability, ease of processes, timeliness

   D. Timeliness, profitability, ease of processes, standardization

Question 7

What process results in documentation of what the system actually does?

   A. Functional needs assessment

   B. Gap analysis

   C. Requirement analysis

   D. Business process improvement

Question 8

DMAIC stands for

A. Define, measure, assess, improve, control
B. Document, measure, analyze, improve, control
C. Define, measure, analyze, improve, control
D. Define, measure, analyze, improve, contract

Question 9

When managing projects and resources, it is important to have a work plan that

A. Is aimed at establishing a generic implementation setup for a project
B. Includes equipment costs
C. Plans the intended workflow processes by managing personnel
D. Analyzes processes and evaluates outcomes

Question 10

Once an organization has made a decision to buy vs. build, the RFI, RFP and RFQ processes help secure the information necessary to move an organization to a decision. As part of the RFP, the following information is collected:

A. Functional specifications, operational requirements, technical requirements, licensing and contractual information
B. Market information, functional specifications, operational requirements, technical requirements
C. Company background, market information, technical requirements, licensing and contractual information
D. Company background, functional specifications, operational requirements, technical requirements

Question 11

The following document protects organizations from having their confidential information being shared without their express written consent:

A. Patient consent
B. Master client agreement
C. Non-disclosure agreement
D. Licensing agreement

Chapter 5: Design

Question 1

Identify two key aspects of system design.

A. Innovation and standardization
B. Efficiency and cost
C. Compatibility and interoperability
D. Agility and availability

Question 2
The following roles are typically represented in a system design team except:
A. Solution architect
B. Board member
C. Information security officer
D. Project manager

Question 3
Which of the following must be considered during system design?
A. System monitoring
B. Disaster recovery
C. Usability
D. All of the above

Question 4
Detailed technical specifications address all of the following except:
A. Availability
B. Programming language
C. Security and data encryption
D. Government regulations

Question 5
Which of the following is not a phase of the Usability Maturity Model (UMM)?
A. Unrecognized – lack of awareness of usability
B. Implemented – recognized value of usability and small teams using
C. Strategic – business benefit well understood, mandated, budgeted and results used strategically in the organization
D. Optimized – continuous improvement applied

Question 6
Unclear or poorly written technical requirements can lead to any of the following except:
A. Positive vendor relationships
B. Vendors submitting high bids
C. Inability of the vendor to deliver
D. Litigation

Question 7
Which of the following is not included in the Data Management International (DAMA®) framework?
A. Data value analysis
B. Data governance
C. Data security management
D. Data quality management

Question 8
Which of the following are included in the Technology Adoption Curve?
  A. Innovators, technology enthusiasts
  B. Early adopters, visionaries
  C. Late majority conservatives
  D. All of the above

Chapter 6: Selection, Implementation, Support and Maintenance

Question 1
Functional requirements could include the following:
  A. Printers
  B. Workflow redesign
  C. Backup and recovery plans
  D. System documentation

Question 2
Which is a characteristic of a request for proposal?
  A. A collection of documents with high-level requirements
  B. A collection of documents with detailed requirements
  C. May or may not include costing information
  D. An informal request for information

Question 3
Implementation execution includes the following:
  A. Definition of the team's roles and responsibilities
  B. Decision on implementation strategy
  C. Planning for how to manage organizational changes
  D. System configuration or build

Question 4
The implementation strategy in which all functionality is implemented in one location followed by everywhere else is called
  A. Phased by location
  B. Big bang
  C. Pilot
  D. Phased by functionality

Question 5
End-user training should be completed at what point in the implementation?
  A. During the activation
  B. Right before the activation
  C. As early as possible
  D. Right after planning

Question 6
Planning for activation should include which of the following?
A. Completing a root cause analysis
B. Scheduling post-live support staff
C. Defining the testing plan
D. Configuration management

Question 7
After the system is live, which of these should be measured and evaluated?
A. System usability
B. Duration of the implementation
C. Quantity of printers
D. Number of vendors responding to the request for proposal (RFP)

Question 8
The business continuity plan includes
A. The release management plan
B. The disaster recovery plan
C. The risk management plan
D. The configuration management plan

Chapter 7: Testing and Evaluation

Question 1
The fundamental purpose of information systems testing is
A. To give leadership the information necessary to perform a build versus buy analysis
B. To give end users an opportunity to provide inputs regarding system development and functionality
C. To manage risks of developing, producing, operating and sustaining systems
D. To justify the expense of the proposed system to the board of directors

Question 2
Testing methodologies are
A. The formal, high-level description of how a system will be tested
B. The formal or informal set of conditions or variables under which a tester can identify issues and determine if the application or software system is working correctly
C. Hypothetical situations to help the tester consider a complex problem or system
D. The strategies and approaches used to test a particular product to ensure it is fit for purpose

Question 3

Test tools include manual and automated tools. Which of the following is a manual test tool?

   A. Automation software

   B. Black-box test

   C. Antivirus program

   D. Test script

Question 4

Testing performed to validate successful system implementation is called

   A. Acceptance testing

   B. Integration testing

   C. System testing

   D. Stress testing

Question 5

The goal of _____ testing is to ensure the software does not crash in conditions of insufficient computational resources (such as memory or disk space), unusually high concurrency or denial-of-service attacks

   A. Integration testing

   B. System testing

   C. Stress testing

   D. Regression testing

Question 6

System controls are implemented to protect the confidentiality, integrity and _____ of data during testing.

   A. Usability

   B. Availability

   C. Format

   D. Security

Question 7

Version control

   A. Is a measurable technical assessment of a system or application

   B. Is a formal process used to ensure that changes to a product or system are introduced in a controlled and coordinated manner

   C. Tracks and provides control over changes to source code

   D. Involves combining individual software modules, applications or units, and testing them as a group to identify any issues in how the integrated components interface and interact with each other

Question 8
Test reporting occurs throughout the testing process and, at a minimum, should address
  A. The test team members and their experience levels
  B. The estimated cost of the test
  C. The expected outcomes of the test
  D. The mission of the test

Chapter 8: Privacy and Security

Question 1
Access privileges for each role should be set
  A. To provide the maximum access necessary
  B. To provide the minimum access necessary
  C. Based on the user's request
  D. Based on the user's physical location

Question 2
Locked doors, property control tags on devices and employee identification badges are all examples of what?
  A. Technical safeguards
  B. Physical safeguards
  C. Audit controls
  D. Access management

Question 3
The underlying principle for safeguarding a patient's health information is
  A. Timely access to the information by a clinician
  B. Make informed decisions on a plan of care
  C. To do no harm to the patient
  D. Empower the patient to be an active member of the care team

Question 4
HIPAA requires a covered entity to maintain a program to ensure the
  A. Privacy, security and standards compliance for PHI
  B. Confidentiality, integrity and availability of PHI
  C. Expertise, awareness and compliance of HIPAA
  D. Restrictions, uses and disclosures of PHI

Question 5
The inappropriate use of PHI is presumed to be a breach unless
  A. It can be proven there is a low probability the PHI was compromised
  B. It can be proven that there was no harm to the patient
  C. It can be proven that the data was secured
  D. It can be proven that an exception to the breach rules applies

Question 6
GDPR (General Data Protection Regulation) applies to
  A. The protected health information of a European Union citizen
  B. The protected health information of an American living in a European Union country
  C. The personally identifiable information of a European Union citizen
  D. The personally identifiable information of an American living in a European Union country

Question 7
The best approach to reduce risk to an acceptable level is to
  A. Mitigate by implementing safeguards to reduce risk to an acceptable level
  B. Transfer risk to a third party
  C. Take no action and accept the risk
  D. Ignore the risk

Question 8
Audits of a covered entity's security plan can include
  A. External penetration testing and internal vulnerability testing
  B. Firewall rules and data schematics
  C. Secret patient and social engineering
  D. Rogue access points and medical device assessments

Chapter 9: Management and Leadership

Question 1
A project manager has been assigned to manage the implementation of a new clinical system. The project manager is responsible for
  A. Appointing the project steering committee from hospital management
  B. Delivering project objectives within budget and on schedule
  C. Delegating project scope decisions to the appropriate team members
  D. Reporting change requests to the CIO for approval or rejection

Question 2

When undertaking a new project assignment, the *best* order of approach is

A. Initiate, plan, control, execute and close

B. Plan, initiate, execute, control and close

C. Control, plan, initiate, execute and close

D. Initiate, plan, execute, control and close

Question 3

An advisory committee made up of high-level stakeholders or experts who provide guidance on key issues such as company policy and objectives, budgetary control, marketing strategy, resource allocation and decisions involving large expenditures is called

A. An IT steering committee

B. A system development life cycle committee

C. A vendor selection committee

D. A policies and standards committee

Question 4

An important step to *avoid* when managing budgets is to

A. Negotiate a good budget at the close of the budget cycle

B. Stay close to budget

C. Beware of cost allocations

D. Use proven budget tools and techniques

Question 5

The widely accepted practice in healthcare for managing an organization's interactions with customers, patients, vendors and other business associates is

A. Enterprise risk management

B. Project portfolio management

C. Customer relationship management

D. Project quality management

Question 6

Documentation which includes the documents that support analysis, decision-making, acquisition and implementation processes is called

A. Operational documentation

B. System documentation

C. Department documentation

D. Development documentation

Question 7

A common model for change management is

A. ITIL

B. CPHIMS

C. ADKAR

D. SBARC

Question 8

In risk management, assessing the likelihood or probability a risk-related event will occur and the magnitude of its impact is called

A. Identification

B. Risk response

C. Quantification

D. Monitoring

Chapter 11

Answer Key

Chapter 1: Healthcare Environment

Question 1
What are the "four pillars" of the healthcare environment?
Correct answer: C. Cost, access, value and quality

Question 2
Hospitals may be classified many different ways. Which of the following statements is true regarding hospital classification?
Correct answer: D. Hospitals may be classified in more than one way; for example, an urban hospital might also be classified as a government-owned hospital or as a general hospital

Question 3
An ambulatory surgery center would be best classified as
Correct answer: B. An outpatient care setting

Question 4
From the perspective of the healthcare delivery organization, payments generally come from three types of entities:
Correct answer: B. Government-financed and managed programs, insurance programs managed by private entities and patients' personal funds

Question 5
In considering the purpose for interrelationships among healthcare organizations, identify the purpose below that is correct:
Correct answer: B. Ensure effective transfers of care facilitated by the provision of essential health information

DOI: 10.4324/9780429442391-15

Question 6

Ensuring the general portability of healthcare is facilitated by
Correct answer: A. Health information exchanges (HIEs) such as Canada's Health Infoway and the U.S. HIE programs, including the Nationwide Health Information Network (NHIN)

Question 7

An example of the secondary use of a patient's health information would be when the information is shared
Correct answer: D. With public health officials for statistical reporting or in support of clinical research

Question 8

In the financial reimbursement area, the interrelationships between healthcare organizations
Correct answer: B. May assure government payers that quality healthcare services have been delivered

Question 9

Key information technology and information management professionals in healthcare organizations include the
Correct answer: B. Chief information officer (CIO), chief security officer (CSO) and chief medical information officer (CMIO)

Question 10

Nongovernment professional associations may perform regulatory roles for their profession. Which of the following is *not* a typical role for a professional association?
Correct answer: B. Making laws and regulations regarding reimbursements for their profession

Question 11

There has been a shift in care settings to what type of facility?
Correct answer: B. Outpatient centers

Chapter 2: Technology Environment

Question 1

Patients have an expectation that healthcare providers will keep health information entrusted to them
Correct answer: A. Private and secure

Question 2

Data warehouses include
Correct answer: C. Data from many different EHRs

Question 3
Interface engines support
Correct answer: A. Interoperability and data integration

Question 4
Telehealth can be used to
Correct answer: B. Provide specialist care to patients in rural areas

Question 5
mHealth applications can address
Correct answer: B. A way to utilize mobile technology to achieve improved health goals

Question 6
What makes healthcare data integration unique to other industries?
Correct answer: A. Myriad un-adopted or poorly implemented standards across health systems.

Question 7
What are the main goals of an Enterprise Analytics department within a hospital?
Correct answer: D. All of the above

Chapter 3: Clinical Informatics

Question 1
According to the American Medical Informatics Association (AMIA), clinical informaticists use their knowledge to do which of the following:
Correct answer: D. All of the above

Question 2
One aspect of the Domains of Clinical Informatics is:
Correct answer: C. Information and communication technology

Question 3
Which of the following is current measurement goals of eCQMs for both Medicare and Medicaid?
Correct answer: D. All of the above

Question 4
The medical specialty of otolaryngology covers the areas of
Correct answer: C. Both A and B

Question 5
Of the following, which is NOT an eligible hospital (EH) or critical access hospital (CAH) objective/measure:
Correct answer: C. Providing up-to-date hardware for clinicians

Question 6
A branch of artificial intelligence (AI) that helps computers understand, interpret and manipulate human language is called:
Correct answer: B. Natural Language Processing

Question 7
What is a noted disadvantage of clinical decision support (CDS)?
Correct answer: D. All of the above

Question 8
Which of the following is NOT one of the Five Rights of CDS?
Correct answer: B. Right facility

Chapter 4: Analysis

Question 1
Which of the following is not an objective of the systems analysis phase?
Correct answer: B. Determining feasibility, objectives and scope

Question 2
When defining problems and opportunities, major areas of change can occur in the following areas:
Correct answer: B. Clinical, administrative, financial and infrastructure

Question 3
The value of performing a cost–benefit analysis is to determine
Correct answer: C. How long it will take to achieve the payback period of the investment

Question 4
When presenting your analysis to your executive leadership, key elements may include:
Correct answer: A. Possible changes in the project implementation that can be driven by changes in technology standards

Question 5
Of the following tools, which is not a common tool used for conducting a needs analysis
Correct answer: D. Gap analysis

Question 6
What are the typical priorities taken into consideration when assessing a project?
Correct answer: A. Patient safety and security, profitability, ease of processes, standardization

Question 7
What process results in documentation of what the system actually does?
Correct answer: C. Requirement analysis

Question 8
DMAIC stands for
Correct answer: C. Define, measure, analyze, improve and control

Question 9
When managing projects and resources, it is important to have a work plan that
Correct answer: D. Analyzes processes and evaluates outcomes

Question 10
Once an organization has made a decision to buy vs. build, the RFI, RFP and RFQ processes help secure the information necessary to move an organization to a decision. As part of the RFP, the following information is collected
Correct answer: A. Functional specifications, operational requirements, technical requirements, licensing and contractual information

Question 11
The following document protects organizations from having their confidential information being shared without their express written consent
Correct answer: C. Non-disclosure agreement

Chapter 5: Design

Question 1
Identify two key aspects of system design
Correct answer: A. Compatibility and interoperability

Question 2
The following roles are typically represented in a system design team except
Correct answer: B. Board member

Question 3
Which of the following must be considered during system design?
Correct answer: D. All of the above

Question 4
Detailed technical specifications address all of the following except
Correct answer: B. Programming language

Question 5
Which of the following is not a phase of the Usability Maturity Model (UMM)?
Correct answer: D. Optimized – continuous improvement applied

Question 6
Unclear or poorly written technical requirements can lead to any of the following except
Correct answer: A. Positive vendor relationships

Question 7

Which of the following is not included in the Data Management International (DAMA®) framework?

Correct Answer: A. Data value analysis

Question 8

Which of the following are included in the Technology Adoption Curve?

Correct answer: D. All of the above

Chapter 6: Selection, Implementation, Support and Maintenance

Question 1

Functional requirements could include the following:

Correct answer: B. Workflow redesign (All others are nonfunctional requirements.)

Question 2

Which is a characteristic of a request for proposal?

Correct answer: B. A collection of documents with detailed requirements (All others are characteristics of an RFI.)

Question 3

Implementation execution includes the following:

Correct answer: D. System configuration or build (All others are part of implementation planning.)

Question 4

The implementation strategy in which all functionality is implemented in one location followed by everywhere else is called

Correct answer: C. Pilot

Question 5

End-user training should be completed at what point in the implementation?

Correct answer: B. Right before the activation

Question 6

Planning for activation should include which of the following?

Correct answer: B. Scheduling the post-live support staff

Question 7

After the system is live, which of these should be measured and evaluated?

Correct answer: A. System usability

Question 8

The business continuity plan includes

Correct answer: B. The disaster recovery plan

Chapter 7: Testing and Evaluation

Question 1
The fundamental purpose of information systems testing is
Correct answer: C. To manage risks of developing, producing, operating and sustaining systems

Question 2
Testing methodologies are
Correct answer: D. The strategies and approaches used to test a particular product to ensure it is fit for purpose

Question 3
Test tools include manual and automated tools. Which of the following is a manual test tool?
Correct answer: D. Test script

Question 4
Testing performed to validate successful system implementation is called
Correct answer: A. Acceptance testing

Question 5
The goal of _____ testing is to ensure the software does not crash in conditions of insufficient computational resources (such as memory or disk space), unusually high concurrency or denial-of-service attacks
Correct answer: C. Stress testing

Question 6
System controls are implemented to protect the confidentiality, integrity and _____ of data during testing.
Correct answer: B. Availability

Question 7
Version control
Correct answer: C. Tracks and provides control over changes to source code

Question 8
Test reporting occurs throughout the testing process and, at a minimum, should address
Correct answer: D. The mission of the test

Chapter 8: Privacy and Security

Question 1
Access privileges for each role should be set
Correct answer: B. To provide the minimum access necessary

Question 2
Locked doors, property control tags on devices and employee identification badges are all examples of what?
Correct Answer: B. Physical safeguards

Question 3
The underlying principle for safeguarding a patient's health information is
Correct Answer: C. To do no harm to the patient

Question 4
HIPAA requires a covered entity to maintain a program to ensure the
Correct answer: B. Confidentiality, integrity and availability of PHI

Question 5
The inappropriate use of PHI is presumed to be a breach unless
Correct answer: A. It can be proven there is a low probability the PHI was compromised

Question 6
GDPR (General Data Protection Regulation) applies to
Correct answer: C. The personally identifiable information of a European Union citizen

Question 7
The best approach to reduce risk to an acceptable level is to
Correct answer: A. Mitigate by implementing safeguards to reduce risk to an acceptable level

Question 8
Audits of a covered entity's security plan can include
Correct answer: A. External penetration testing and internal vulnerability testing

Chapter 9: Management and Leadership

Question 1
A project manager has been assigned to manage the implementation of a new clinical system. The project manager is responsible for
Correct answer: B. Delivering project objectives within budget and on schedule

Question 2
When undertaking a new project assignment, the *best* order of approach is:
Correct answer: D. Initiate, plan, execute, control and close

Question 3
An advisory committee made up of high-level stakeholders or experts who provide guidance on key issues such as company policy and objectives,

budgetary control, marketing strategy, resource allocation and decisions involving large expenditures is called
Correct answer: A. An IT steering committee

Question 4
An important step to *avoid* when managing budgets is to
Correct answer: A. Negotiate a good budget at the close of the budget cycle

Question 5
The widely accepted practice in healthcare for managing an organization's interactions with customers, patients, vendors and other business associates is
Correct answer: C. Customer relationship management

Question 6
Documentation which includes the documents that support analysis, decision making, acquisition and implementation processes is called:
Correct answer: B. System documentation

Question 7
A common model for change management is:
Correct answer: C. ADKAR

Question 8
In risk management, assessing the likelihood or probability a risk-related event will occur and the magnitude of its impact is called
Correct answer: C. Quantification

Index

Note: Locators in *italics* represent figures and **bold** indicate tables in the text.